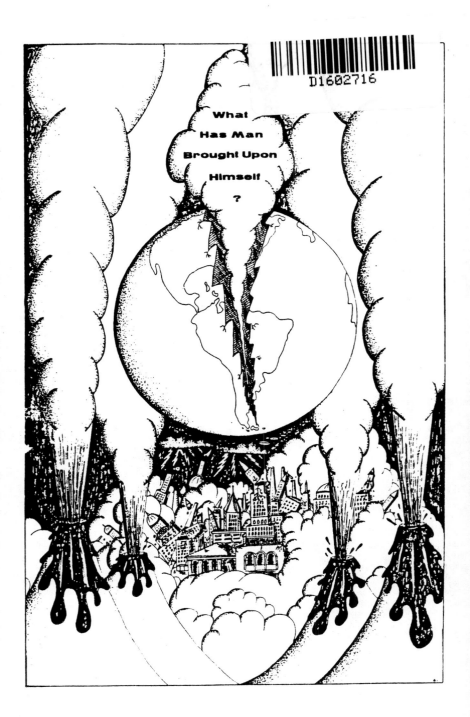

ROLLING THUNDER

THE COMING EARTH CHANGES

IN SEVEN PARTS

By J.R. Jochmans

Foreword by Skip Whitson

Sun Books
Sun Publishing Company
Santa Fe, N.M.

```
First  Printing.....Oct  1980
Second Printing....Mar  1981
Third  Printing.....Jul  1981
Fourth Printing....Nov  1981
Fifth  Printing.....Jul  1982
Sixth  Printing.....Jul  1983
Seventh Printing...Feb  1984
Eight  Printing.....Oct  1984
Ninth  Printing.....Aug  1986
Tenth  Printing.....Jan  1987
Eleventh Printing..May  1987
Twelvth  Printing..May  1988
```

Typesetting: Frank Vales

Paste-Up: Dave Lewis

Artwork by Gustave Dore, Maaret DeGroff,
Jyl Batterman, George Lavoie, Tony Shearer,
and others.

Cover Photo: 18 May 1980 Eruption of Mount St. Helens
Credit: Wide World Photos, Inc.

Sun Books
Sun Publishing Company
P.O. Box 5588, Santa Fe, N.M. 87502-5588
U.S.A.

ISBN: 0-89540-058-8

4

*Dedicated to those
with the courage to change
their Consciousness
and who thus have the power
to change the course
of the Future*

*A special thanks to all those
who helped the author
through 14 years of research
and 2 years of writing--
to all those who helped
in so many ways.*

TABLE OF CONTENTS

Foreword 10
Introduction: Prophecy--A Reflection of Times Ahead....13
Prologue 18

THE FIRST THUNDER
1. "Seasons of Change" -- Coming Famine, Depression, and Earth Movements.. 21
2. A Coming Blow to Israel by the Arabs......................22
3. The Vision of a Founding Father............................ 24
4. Modern Prophecies of Destruction of New York City... 25
5. St. Malachy's Prophecy is Nearing its End................26
6. Political and Religious Changes in the Soviet Union... 29
7. A Prophecy of Present Peace -- And Coming Conflict..30
8. The "Sleeping Prophet" and the Shaking Earth.......... 32
9. The Prophecy of Kate-Zahl.................................37

THE SECOND THUNDER
10. Nostradamus on Inflation and Economic Trouble in America... 41
11. Portents of Future War...................................... 45
12. A Giant Earthquake to Shake Greece and Turkey.......48
13. Gemini Oracles -- Forecasts of the Lusson Sisters....50
14. The Antichrist is Alive and Coming to Power 52
15. John's Dream of the New Jerusalem and New Earth .58
16. A Prophecy in a Tube of Lead.............................58
17. A Powerful Dictator to Dominate the Middle East......60
18. Two Nuclear Accidents Portended for Europe?.........62

THE THIRD THUNDER
19. A Twelfth Century Prophecy About America 66
20. Visions of California -- The New Atlantis 67
21. The "Source" Speaks of Things to Come.................75
22. The Monarchy of Morocco About to be Overthrown ..77
23. Imperial Rome and Modern America -- Is History Repeating Itself? 78
24. The Coming Avatars -- Messengers of Hope............ 80
25. The Sixth Trumpet -- A Prophecy of War From the East..88
26. "Decades of Cataclysm" -- Earth Disasters for the 1980's and 1990's.................................. 89

THE FOURTH THUNDER
27. Dark Days for the Papacy Ahead.......................... 93
28. A Vision of World-Death and World-Rebirth........... 102
29. Sabato -- The Prophet Extraordinaire..................... 107
30. Will You be Ready for the Great Blizzard of 1981? .. 108
31. The Story of the Old Indian..................................... 110
32. Pyramid Prophecy -- Man's Spiritual Progression
    to the 83rd Century 116
33. Prophecies of Erratic Weather and Coming Famine. 120
34. Signs of the New Age of the Spirit 124
35. A Daring Kidnapping by Arab Terrorists................ 126

THE FIFTH THUNDER
36. A Sixteenth Century Account of World War III 128
37. What the Heavens Predict.................................... 134
38. A "Watergate" in the Supreme Court 137
39. The Three Days of Unknown Death 139
40. Daniel's Prophecy of a Middle East War 141
41. Earthquake and Fire -- The Fate of New York City .. 142
42. The Coming False Religion and Mass Persecutions. 145
43. 2000 Plus -- The Psychics Look at the New Age 151
44. The Future According to Ross Peterşon 152

THE SIXTH THUNDER
45. Will the Presidential Death Cycle be Broken? 155
46. Four Nostradamus Prophecies on Coming
    Revolution and War in Russia............................ 156
47. The Four Horsemen of the Apocalypse --
    A Modern Interpretation 158
48. When Britannia Will Sink Beneath the Waves 159
49. A Dream of the Twenty-Second Century 163
50. "Prophetecy" and its Outline of Things to Come 164
51. Visions of Enoch the Prophet -- The Final
    Transcendence of Man 167
52. Two Mormon Prophecies About the
    Future of America 168
53. Is an Attack Coming From Outer Space?.............. 169

THE SEVENTH THUNDER

54. The Philosophers and the Future..........173
55. The Amazing Dream of a Seventeen-Year Old Boy...177
56. Forecasts by a Polish Monk 181
57. The Sibyls Speak of Things to Come 184
58. Armageddon -- The Present Age's Retribution........185
59. Is a Meteor or Comet Going to Strike the Earth? 195
60. Star-Children of the Aquarian Age 199
61. The Day All the Machines Will Stop 203
62. Nostradamus on the New Age and Beyond 206

Epilogue 211
Last Words............211
Bibliography............215
Index............229
Author's Biography............237
Other Books............238

Foreword

In all my years of publishing, I have never encountered a work as truly "Earth shaking" or important as this one. If even a fraction of the events spoken of in ROLLING THUNDER: The Coming Earth Changes come to pass, we are in for very difficult times to say the least. However, this book is not just another work on "doom and gloom" prophecies, for it offers a highly important message of hope. Many people when they read about predicted disasters to come, react by saying, "So what? If it's supposed to happen, it'll happen. There's nothing I can do about it." But this is not true, for as the author of ROLLING THUNDER observes, we have a **choice** as to how we want the future to be--we have the power to **create** the future we actively work for. Others may say, "I don't want to know about such things. If you think about coming disasters, then you're going to cause them to happen." Jochmans reveals instead that prophecies of disaster serve a difinite purpose--to get people to **change** their consciousness and thus **avert** the events. Only if you believe that a future catastrophe will inevitably occur, are you "adding energy" to that event. Yet if you alter your thinking patterns in a more positive way, you can in effect change the entire course of things to come.

This is not to say that **all** future happenings are free and open, the author adds, for some events are "fixed" in time, and are necessary, to aid in altering the overall direction of history at that point, toward a more positive goal. But even here, a transformation of consciousness can determine how gradual or how drastic the coming necessary alterations will be.

Still other people, upon reading the prophecies, may over-react, and begin spending large amounts of their money on stockpiling food, gasoline, weapons, books, etc., to get them thru the hard times forecast ahead. To a limited degree, saving such items may be a wise thing to do for the immediate future, but for the long run it is not the whole answer. The change of consciousness we must go thru to avoid or at least lessen the degree of coming upheavals involves giving up attachments to material goods, which is the number one obsession of our age. There must come an **inner change** as well, or the things you stockpile will be taken away, so that the lesson of **spiritual dependence first** may be learned. That, Jochmans has found from the prophecies, is what the coming changes are all about.

Just before this book went to press, the author spoke to me about another aspect that is very important to an understanding of events to come, on the individual level. A number of the prophecies (particularly those of the Bible, the American Indians, and several modern psychic readings) say that, just before the disasters are to strike, there will be a great "separation" among the world's peoples. For reasons they will not be able to explain, many will suddenly change or even lose their jobs, families, and homes, and will find themselves moving or drifting toward specific places. What will be happening is that **like will be attracting like**--those of a positive consciousness, who have learned to live in true harmony with others and with the Earth's environment, will be gathered in "safe" areas; while those of a negative consciousness, who remain out of balance with their fellow man and nature, are going to be amassed together in areas of "danger." Where people exist who are at peace, the earth will be at peace with them, and will supply them with their needs. But where men are grouped together who have actively harmed each other and the environment, the earth will respond in kind toward them. The degree to which coming disasters will take place, Jochmans believes, will depend on how many people there will be of a positive and negative consciousness: If ninety percent of the world's inhabitants transform their minds and daily lives for the better, then only ten percent of the earth will be affected by upheavals; but if a mere ten percent of the people choose to be of a positive mind, then ninety percent of the planet will suffer disastrous consequences. Again, it will be our choices that will determine the course of the future.

Not all the prophecies in **ROLLING THUNDER** tell of future upheavals, for many speak of a "New Age" to eventually dawn, one in which the dreams of peace, world brotherhood, and spiritual harmony are to become realities. These are the prophecies, Jochmans writes, we should be imitating and exemplifying today, for by doing so we are causing them to be **self-fulfilling**. What's more, if everyone began living the New Age **now**, the prophecies dealing with coming disaster would never have to happen, because these disasters are meant only to awaken us and make us change our ways where we have not done so ourselves.

Finally, it is the author's hope, and my own, that the next twenty years will prove the greater part of **ROLLING THUNDER** to be fiction. If the prophecies of "doom and gloom" come about as predicted, then this book's purpose--to get people to change their consciousness to a more positive mode of being--will have failed. If the prophecies **don't** materialize, or at least don't happen to the severity forecast, then we feel an important good will have been done, for it will mean that the prophetic warnings were heeded, and the direction of the future significantly altered. When the New Age finally comes, Jochmans makes his own prediction that our children, who will become the historians of the future, will look back to our times, and, depending on how the actual course of history followed or varied from the prophetic outline as given in this book, will we in the present be judged by our choices.

If you find the message of this book important and feel you are able to render **useful** service in helping to spread the word (such as contacting a radio or TV talk show host or a bookstore that should have this title) you are invited to write the publisher with your ideas or suggestions.

Skip Whitson, Publisher   9 Sep 1980
Sun Publishing Company

Introduction

PROPHECY--A REFLECTION OF TIMES AHEAD

The ability to prophesy the future is a controversial subject--whether it has occurred in our age or in ages past. It is one thing to make an educated guess at what the world will be like tomorrow, or next year, or in a century. But when we speak of the future as foreseen by prophecy--those full-blown visions of events to come which disturb nightly dreams, or during the day take hold of the conscious mind like a flash from some other dimension, or unfold in the midst of astrological symbols that reflect the influences of the heavens -- then we have entered a very different realm of thinking. Prophecy is an experience beyond man's logic, or his complete control. It appears to come from a source outside himself, born not as a conscious preconception, but as a *revelation*, a detached reality. We have the tendency to see ourselves trapped in time. The past is done with, stretching behind us and unchangeable; the present is that elusive and ephemeral passing of our awareness from moment to moment; and the future lies ahead, a great and empty unknown which, we would like to believe, is totally free and open to any possible creation of our choosing in the here and now. What a shock it is, then, when suddenly, in a dream or vision or horoscope, someone is shown an event which we think should not yet exist, yet nevertheless comes true later on. It is as if these prophecies are telling us something, teaching us that our perceptions are, in fact, faulty:

There *are* certain aspects of the future which *do* already exist, certain events that will transpire, as if they are part of some larger framework. We know from experience, of course, that this framework is not rigid. We still make choices from minute to minute, and "reap what we sow" as future consequences, based on those choices. But it is as if at certain moments in the course of time, the field of possibilities narrows perceptibly toward a specific event or events. These events may appear to be no different from any other, as if made by random choice--but it is prophecy that reveals otherwise.

The study of prophecy thus can never give us a complete or total picture of the future. What prophecy does offer us are details about specific events, and these in turn can be used as guidelines by which directions of the future can be determined. Another important aspect is that every special future event is surrounded by its own "cloud" of prophecy, and its emanations are often received by more than one prophet. Because each human mind has its own unique mental perceptions, what one prophet may receive about an event may be slightly different from another prophet, who foresees the same event. It is like a group of people who witness an accident--each person will describe what took place as he saw it, noting details and forgetting or not noticing others, which will be picked up and remembered by other witnesses. Sometimes, of course, the details will not match. But by checking all the descriptions, a reporter can get a relatively clear consensus of what happened--a much better picture, containing more particulars, than if the accident had been seen by only one person. The same applies for prophets. We can gain a fuller revelation about the same event, because each will supply details not forecast by all the others.

The purpose of this book is to present an overview of prophecies yet to be fulfilled, made by the seers and psychics of today and yesterday. Many of the names of those who have written the prophecies will probably be familiar to most readers.

14

**There is Jeane Dixon, for example, the seeress of Washington, D.C., who has to her credit several accurate, well-publicized predictions on the assassinations of the Kennedy brothers, the launch of Sputnik, the overthrow of Krushchev, the Apollo 13 near-disaster, and the Watergate scandal. Her prophetic accuracy has been as high as 82% to 84%.

**Criswell, another contemporary prophet, is a resident of California and has had his own syndicated column. He is well known for many of his outlandish predictions--many of which have come true. He also forecast the death of John Kennedy, and the assassination of Martin Luther King. His accuracy has been measured at 86% to 88%.

**Of all the seers of modern times, Edgar Cayce, who lived from 1877 to 1945, is one of the most popular and widely read. He accurately foresaw in 1919 the second rise of Germany two decades later; in 1925 the market crash of 1929; in 1939 our entry into war in 1941, identifying '42 and '43 as particularly sad years, with victory in '45. His degree of accuracy has been calculated at an impressive 93% to 95%.

**One of the most prolific of prophets, whose detailed forecasts touched on almost every conceivable subject, was the Frenchman, Michele de Notre Dame, better known as Nostradamus. He lived from 1503 to 1566. In the year 1558, he published a book, *Les Vrayes Centuries* or *The True Centuries*, which contained well over a thousand poems and writings, each with a forecast on events to come. His record so far includes: the executions of Charles I and Louis XVI; the fire and plague of London, which he correctly dated for 1666; the beginning of the French Revolution, which he pinpointed for the year 1792; the advent of Napoleon and Hitler (with both *names* appearing in the verses); the crucial events of World War I and II; and descriptions of 20th century aerial combat and the bombing of cities. His accuracy has been variously estimated between 80% and 95%.

**The two major Bible prophets, the early Christian apostle John and the 6th century B.C. Hebrew seer Daniel, wrote incredible apocalyptic messages that offer a vivid, sweeping panorama of man's spiritual and secular

15

history over the past 2,000 to 2,500 years. Daniel, for example, received visions of the fall of Babylon, and the rise on the world scene of the empires of Persia, Greece and Rome. He also accurately foretold of the rebuilding of Jerusalem and the birth of Christ. The apostle John, writing at the height of Roman power, foresaw Rome's coming decline and ruin, and forecast the Papacy and the Reformation beyond. Many of the events John and Daniel predicted, however, have yet to take place. The ancient foreshadows have so far been accurate to the limit to which such accuracy can be calculated--95% to 98%.

As you read through the prophecies written by these and other famous seers and prognosticators, you will begin to recognize a certain degree of repetition. Though the prophets often employed different language, different symbols, or were of different faiths and philosophies, they nevertheless appeared to be looking forward to basically the same future events. What is more, when examining the total picture the prophets present, it tells us in no uncertain terms that we are heading into a time of tremendous upheaval--what some seers have described as the "end of the world." But the seers and psychics through the ages have also looked forward to today, not only as a time of destruction, but as one of regeneration too. The world as we know it is to come to an end, quickly and suddenly. Yet along with this foreboding is the promise of a new and far better world to be rebuilt beyond. We are heading for deep water, the prophets agree--not to be drowned, but to be cleansed. Mankind, it appears, is about to be stripped of all his material possessions and all his religious pretensions. These are the stumbling blocks that for too long have hindered man's continued development. And now we have arrived at the point where these will be taken away, and mankind, as a child left desolate without his toys and fantasies, shall learn to awaken to a higher, newer maturity and consciousness, to become more fully aware of his inner potentials.

This is what prophecy is really all about--to serve a definite purpose: to warn, and also to instruct, for with foreknowledge comes forebearance. By knowing where

16

we are going, we can gain a better picture of our own individual purpose and destiny--and brace ourselves for the rough path ahead, by keeping our sites on the smoother road beyond. With special times have come special gifts, and those who have been gifted with flashes of foresight have presented us with their warnings and hopes, their portents and promises. The prophecies are like rolling thunder sounding on the horizon: They are the sign that the storm is coming, and soon not only the skies but the earth itself will shudder with sudden tragic violence. Yet the turmoil and storm will pass, and a new morning, a new beginning, will dawn.

Ultimately, it is up to us to decide whether or not to heed the message of this rolling thunder, and act upon the warnings we have been given. The future is coming, steadily and unavoidable. Our choice is where we want to fit into it--and change it if we can....

September, 1980

17

Prologue

I saw a mighty angel come down from heaven, clothed in a cloud, with a rainbow around his head, his face shining like the sun, and his feet glowing like pillars of fire.

In his hand was an opened little book.

And the angel placed his right foot in the sea, and his left foot on the land, and he cried with a loud voice that sounded like a lion's roar. With that cry, he announced the Seven Thunders.

And the Seven Thunders spoke, each in their turn, prophesying the future.

And when the Seven Thunders had each told their story of things to come, I was about to write them down, when a voice from Heaven spoke and said, "No, do not write what the Thunders have foretold--for they are sealed, hidden for the end of the age." And at that very same instance, my memory was erased of the words they had said, and could not write them down.

Then the angel who stood in the sea and on the land raised his hands to heaven, and declared that Time was now at an end. And with these words, Time seemed to advance far forward, and the end of the age was suddenly here.

And the voice from heaven said, "You have heard the voice of the angel--know that the mystery of the future, as has been declared to the prophets and seers of old, is also nearing its end."

And the voice continued, "Now is the time to take the opened little book from the angel, wherein are the prophecies of the Seven Thunders."

So I stood before the angel, and asked him to give me the little book. And the angel said, "Here it is. But I warn you: You may think that it is sweet as honey to taste, yet you will soon find that it is bitter to digest."

Puzzled, I took the opened little book out of the angel's hand. I read its contents eagerly--and soon discovered the meaning of the angel's words. I had thought that knowing the future would be a pleasant experience, for we tend to think of the future as we would like it to be. But the prophecies in the little book showed me Truth instead--the bad as well as the good to come--and their stark words were indeed heavy and sobering to contemplate. With Truth comes the responsibility of knowing.

Then the angel spoke again to me, "Now you have read what the Seven Thunders have prophesied. It is the end of the age. Go, and spread the word abroad. Tell the story to all peoples--to all nations, races, and religions--and to all men high and low.

"The mystery is now finished."

Revelations, Chapter 10, paraphrased

All Things Must Pass

THE FIRST THUNDER

1. "SEASONS OF CHANGE"--COMING FAMINE, DEPRESSION AND EARTH MOVEMENTS
A Virginia group, Associations of the Light Morning, has been a channel for startling prophecies of events to come, in recent years. The messages were first received by a student of altered states of conciousness in March, 1973. Later, a circle of seven sensitives gathered to study and psychically seek further information regarding the initial readings. The result is a view of the future with striking clarity.

The readings first say we are entering a time of climatic disorders when heat and drought will effect some places, and freezing and too much moisture will plague others. This will have increasingly graver repercussions in agricultural production, leading to severe food shortages. The first shortage periods--which we have experienced since these prophecies were given--will be of very short durations, but these will be preludes to a long shortage to last seven years. It will occur both in this country and abroad. In fact, the drying up of our surpluses, which will no longer be shipped overseas, will precipitate the food shortages world-wide.

Accompanying the food shortages, the economy will collapse, leading to a national financial depression. Understandably, there are going to be more chaotic conditions, especially in the large cities. The readings speak of long lines in front of stores, and of many people having to live off government supplements, which will not be enough to survive on. Crime rates will soar. Desperate urbanites, thinking they will find food and valuables outside the cities, will band together and drive into rural areas nearby to steal and plunder. Completing the picture of bad times ahead, the Association readings couple the coming food shortages and financial collapse with a third disaster--changes in the earth's surface. In the scenario of events to come that was given, tremors and earthquakes will first occur in South America and Mexico, with major eruptions of Vesuvius and Etna in Italy. These will be portents for a major quake to hit California. Three months later, a similar destructive movement will shake New York City and the East coast. These two catastrophes will generate a market crash from which the economy will not recover for some time. Creating more confusion will be quakes in the Midwest, which will occur next, during which the Great Lakes will empty into the Mississippi valley, forming a string of new lakes south of the present bodies.

The earth alterations to cripple America will only be part of a series to effect the globe as a whole. Japan will disappear, sections of the coast of China will likewise be submerged, as will portions of Arabia, India, Nova Scotia, and a large part of Scandinavia. These alterations will culminate in 1998, when the globe will undergo a pole shift, and change in polarity. The shift will be very abrupt, taking place in a single 24-hour period, followed by three days of earth-shaking readjustments, which will change the face of the surface drastically. But then will come a quieting and settling, and mankind will have a chance to rebuild again.

2. A COMING BLOW TO ISRAEL BY THE ARABS

The recently signed treaty between Israel and Egypt has ended over thirty years of hostilities between the two nations, and it promises to be a keystone of lasting peace. But Israel's troubles are not over, for she still remains in a semi-state of war with her neighbors to the east, in particular Syria and Iraq, who have announced their joining together as a single military power to combat the Jewish state. Four centuries ago, the prophet Nostradamus--himself of Jewish blood--bemoaned the fact that the return of his people to the Promised Land will someday be marred by frustration and defeat. Nostradamus prophesied:

La Synagogue sterile san nul fruit
Sera recue entre les infideles:
De Babylon la fille du poursuit
Misere et triste lui tranchera les ailes. VIII, 96.

The Synagogue (the Jerusalem Temple) sterile, without bearing fruit,
Will be received into the hands of the infidels (the Moslems),
From Babylon she will be pursued,
Miserable and sad because her wings of flight shall be clipped.

Here is a verse that describes a situation that is the reverse of what existed in the sixteenth century. In Nostradamus' day, Palestine, in particular the site of the Jerusalem Temple, was under Mohammedan domination. Nostradamus predicted, however, that a day would come when Palestine would be free of Moslem influence, for the second line forecasts that the Holy Land will be "received" *back* "into the hands of the infidels"--the infidels, to sixteenth century Christendom, were the Moslems. It was not until 1917 that the Arabs lost Palestine to the British, and in 1948 and 1967, the Jews once again gained full possession of their land and Holy City. But Nostradamus looked beyond the present, and his prediction is indeed foreboding: The Israelis are fated to eventually lose an important battle to their Arab neighbors. This will occur at the time the "Synagogue" or Temple is "sterile, without bearing fruit"--that is, it still remains unrestored, as it is today. Part of the cause for Israel's defeat, as the prophet foresaw in the last line, will be that she will be "miserable and sad because her wings of flight shall be clipped"--the Israeli air force, which played such important roles in past conflicts, will this time be destroyed. And the third line describes the antagonists, and the direction the attackers will come. As in centuries past, it will be from "Babylon", the old empire now occupied by Syria and Iraq, that Israel will be driven back in defeat. The first two lines suggest that, as a result, the Israelis will lose their coveted control over the city of Jerusalem.

3. THE VISION OF A FOUNDING FATHER

One of the most wide-ranging prophecies on the destiny of America was given to George Washington, during the bitter winter of 1777, at Valley Forge. One afternoon, while alone and in deep contemplation in his headquarters, a strange being appeared before him. A series of scenes were then presented to the awe-struck General, of future events of the then infant nation of the United States. In the first scene, Washington beheld a cloud gather in Europe and envelop the rebelling colonies, and he heard the groans and cries of their peoples. But the murky folds then retreated, and immediately after the General beheld towns and cities spring up one after another, across the continent from the Atlantic to the Pacific. The scene forecast the end of the American Revolution, and the westward expansion that followed.

In the second scene, which Washington was told would take place about a century after the first, a dark shadowy angel approached the land and looked southward. Suddenly, the inhabitants began fighting each other, lines of combat were drawn, and internal conflict, with brother battling brother, was waged. But a bright angel then entered the picture, wearing a crown with the word "Union" upon it, and the people cast down their weapons, joining once again in comradship. Here was a forecast of the Civil War.

The third scene--predicted to occur two hundred years in Washington's future, or some time after 1977--opened with another dark, ominous being sounding three blasts on a wartrumpet. The being then took water and sprinkled it on the continents of Europe, Africa and Asia. From these regions thick, black clouds issued forth and, joining as one, moved toward America. Throughout this mass the General saw terrific explosions of gleaming red light.

outlining in each flash great numbers of armed men, moving with the cloud. The billows struck the nation's coast, and immediately the towns and cities Washington had seen grow in the first scene, were burning with intense fires. He heard the sound of great rolling thunder, canon-like blasts, as the invading forces and inhabitants locked in bitter struggle. But the bright angel who had interrupted the second scene now reappeared, and sounding his trumpet with one hand and waving a sword in the other, helped the stricken American people to overcome the invading armies. The clouds of war finally dispersed, and the nation's cities began to rebuild.

At this point the vision ended. Washington is reported to have told only a few choosen officers of his encounter and the predictions. Later, one of these, Anthony Sherman, related the story to a newspaper man, Wesley Bradshaw, in 1859—two years before the second vision began to be fulfilled. The third scene, of course, has yet to take place, but it is scheduled for our very near future.

4. MODERN PROPHECIES OF THE DESTRUCTION OF NEW YORK CITY

A number of contemporary prophets of the world have made forecasts in recent years in which they agree that something is brewing in the rock strata underneath the great island metropolis of the east coast.

California's Criswell predicts a sinking of New York for the 1980's. Earth tremors will reshape the coastline, Long Island to be submerged first, and soon after Manhattan will become the "Venice of America"--a city of canals. So great will the sinking be that New Yorkers will be forced to abandon their city for higher and drier land farther inland.

The Irish clairvoyant, Jim Gavin, received the same psychic picture of a great submergence to overwhelm New York. He described Staten Island to sink like a raft being pulled underwater, and foresaw lower Manhattan tipping into the bay, the waters reaching as far as 59th Street.

The truth is, geologically speaking, New York is not on very stable ground. According to William Herbert Hobbs of the U.S. Geological Survey, because of the distribution of various faults underlying New York, Manhattan would, in the event of an earthquake, break up into three chunks, destroying all major landmarks--as well as seriously affecting its millions of inhabitants.

If a disastrous earthquake were to strike New York, it will certainly not be confined to the city alone. It is disturbing to note, as experts have, that the fault lines under New York City are part of a larger earth fracture which begins in Maine and runs beneath the Boston and Philadelphia regions as well. Edgar Cayce, in 1932, was asked in trance what major earth movements to expect in America in the future, and he pinpointed the west, central and eastern portions. But the *greatest* of these, he warned, would be along the Atlantic coast. Later, in another reading, in 1941, he specified that the New York and Connecticut areas are to be totally reshaped, with New York City to completely disappear.

In much the same manner, British psychic John Pendragon predicted that all the Atlantic coast from Boston to Baltimore will be completely wiped out. The center of the destruction, he envisioned, will be New York, but serious reverberations will be felt within a radius of five hundred miles of the city, Pittsburgh and Philadelphia to be included. Nothing will be left of these cities, Pendragon wrote, except the sunken sites where cities once stood.

5. ST. MALACHY'S PROPHECY IS NEARING ITS END

With the deaths recently of two Popes, Vatican scholars are once more examining the mysterious "Papal Prophecies," written over 800 years ago. The author of this work was Saint Malachy, of Ireland. In 1139 he traveled to Rome and left there a list of one hundred and thirteen Latin titles, one title for every pope who would reign from Malachy's day forward. The titles were meant to forecast the popes' names, birthplaces, church offices held, crests or major pontificate events.

So far, the Malachian titles boast a 75% accuracy. As examples, for Pope John XXIII (1958-1963) the Irish saint offered the motto *Pastor et Nauta,* or "Shepherd and Sailor." John, before succeeding to the Papacy, had

26

been Patriarch of the old maritime city of Venice. The term *nauta* had also been used in motto #47, for Pope Gregory XII (1406-1415), who was born in Venice. John's successor, Pope Paul VI, was given the name *Flos Florum* or "Flower of Flowers." In medieval Church symbology, the "flower of flowers" was the lily--and Paul's papal crest was dominated by three lilies. The late John Paul I had the next title on Malachy's list, and it saw several interesting fulfillments. The motto is *De Medietate Lunae*, "From the Half (or Crescent) Moon." Some interpreters note that the Pope's secular name was Albino Luciani, which in Latin means, "pale white light"--the moon. Still others see a more tragic interpretation. The Pope reigned for only 34 days, about the length of one lunar cycle. In fact, the day of the full moon, September 16, fell exactly in the middle of his pontificate, meaning that he assumed the Chair of St. Peter during a half moon, and died during a half moon.

Attention is now focused on the next Malachian title, *De Labore Solis*, and how it applies to the new pontiff, John Paul II. The title means, "From the Laboring Sun," the "Eclipsing Sun," or "Rising Sun." If we interpret it with the later meaning, then the title has already seen a significant fulfillment. The "rising sun" denotes the east-- and the new Pope is the first pontiff ever to come from eastern Europe, from Poland. One other fulfilled application of *De Labore Solis* to Pope John Paul II was recently noted by astrologer Doris Kaye. She interprets the motto to read, "To Enter From the Eclipsing Sun." The Pope was born on May 18, 1920--on the same day that a total eclipse of the sun occured. However, John Paul's reign could see other possibilites yet to take place. In the next few years there will be a number of significant eclipses of the sun around the world, which may coincide with major events during the new pontificate. Perhaps, as some commentators have suggested, this Pope's work will somehow be connected with Sunday, the Catholic Sabbath.

The alarming fact about the *De Labore Solis* title is that, following it, there are only two more titles left on Malachy's list. The next motto, for the next Pope, is *Gloria Olivae*, the "Glorious Olive." Possibly he will be associated with the Benedictine Order--also known as the Olivetan. Or perhaps, the device may mean that an olive branch will appear in his papal insignia. Many interpreters pray the symbol may have a broader application, heralding a time of peace. Only time, of course, will tell.

Finally, we come to the last title on Malachy's list, *Petrus Romanus*, or "Peter the Roman." For him the Irish prophet gave not only his name, but dedicated an entire paragraph:

In persecutione extreme sanctae Romanae Ecclesiae sedebit Petrus Romanus pascet oves multis tribulationibus; quibus transactus, civitas septicollis diruetur, et Judex tremendus jubicabit populum.

In extreme persecution of the Roman Church shall sit (in the Chair of the first Peter) Peter the Roman, who will feed his flock amid many tribulations; which things being done, the City of the Seven Hills (Rome) will be removed, and the Great Judge will judge the people.

Commentators are divided as to what these last words mean. Some see it as a dire prediction for the end of the world; others believe it refers to a coming spiritual renewal in the Church, which will be marked by a change in the form of Church leadership. Whatever the exact interpretation, one cannot ignore the references to "extreme persecution," "tribulation," and the fact that the entire city of Rome is to be "removed." These words portend troublous times--and in the days in which we live, what effects Rome, the Church, the Papacy and over seven million Roman Catholics will surely have a decided impact on the rest of the world as well. Important to note, too, is that this prophecy is given for the reign of only two Popes down the line: If one figures the average length of rule for the pontiffs in the last 800 years, and apply that average to the newly elected Pope and his two successors, then the last Pope, "Peter the Roman," during whose reign great transformations are forecast, will come to office before the end of the present century.

6. POLITICAL AND RELIGIOUS CHANGES IN THE SOVIET UNION FORECAST

Several modern day prophets have foreseen drastic changes to soon take place behind the Iron Curtain. Psychic-medium Ethel Johnson Meyers prophesys the Soviet Union is destined to become more capitalistic-- while America becomes more socialistic--and eventually the two powers will become close allies against the rising threat of China. Betty Ritter, whose prophetic accuracy tested by parapsychologist Hans Holzer reached 90%, also predicts that Russia will ally with the United States some day, but not until after the Red power is no longer Red. She sees that in the near future the Russian people are going to rebel against the Communist regime, and that it will be toppled by a major revolution.

A similar psychic picture was also described by Criswell of California. He has predicted that the present Soviet government will remain in power for only a little while longer, and then a new leader will suddenly rise who will bring about great alterations. He will govern for five years, during which time Russia will more fully accept the system of free enterprise, and Communism will remain in name only.

In the early 1970's, the Central Premonitions Registry in New York recorded two premonitions sent in by participants, dealing with Russia. One forecast that the great Asian nation will one day be ruled by a trio of managers who will be pro-production and anti-military. The other predicted that changes would come in the Soviet government as the result of the assassination of a major political figure.

Several other prophets have also spoken of religious changes to come about in Russia's future. The "sleeping prophet" Edgar Cayce, prophesying at the height of Stalin's iron-fisted rule, referred to Russia in terms of a bid for freedom to come, as well as her spiritual transformation. He predicted that through Russia would come the hope of the world. It would not be made apparent through the present ideology of Communism, however. No, Cayce stressed, Russia will see freedom and each Russian citizen will some day live for his fellow man in the truly religious sense. That principle is germinating slowly amidst persecution in Russia, and, as Cayce foresaw, will triumph in the near future.

A very similar prophecy was given in 1917 to the three children of Fatima, Portugal, during the visitations of a spiritual being who identified herself as the Virgin Mary. The spirit told the children that the Great War that was then in progress would end, but another, more terrible war would be fought if men continued in their present ways. To prevent this from happening, the spirit Mary asked that Russia be consecrated through continual prayer to the "Immaculate Heart." If this were not done, not only would there be another war, but soon after Russia would begin spreading her errors around the globe, bringing great persecution to the Church. What is remarkable is that this prediction was made several months *before* the Bolshevik Revolution took place in Russia. The spirit Mary's last words, however, was a prediction that even if these events transpired, spiritual forces will eventually triumph anyway, and Russia will some day give up her beliefs, to be consecrated and converted to a new religious order.

7. A PROPHECY OF PRESENT PEACE--AND COMING CONFLICT

One thing modern prophets try to do when spying out the future is to determine where we are now, in relation to what the immediate consequences of the present will bring. But our modern age has not been the special subject of only today's living seers. Four hundred years ago, the French prophet Nostradamus wrote a prophetic quatrain or four-lined poem that describes our times perfectly--and added a warning of what is just around the corner for us. The poem reads:

Les fleaux passes diminue le monde,
Longtemps la paix terres inhabitees:
Sur marchera par ciel, terre, mer et onde,
Puis de nouveau les guerres suscitees. I, 63.

Diseases extinguished, the world shrinks,
For a long time peace, and lands increased by population,
One will travel safely by air, land, through sea and wave,
Then war will be stirred up again.

The key to this verse is the mention in line 3 of safe travel "by air." In the sixteenth century, when Nostradamus wrote his prophecies, such a feat was deemed impossible. Today, however, it is a commonplace occurrence--and for that reason, the time period for this prediction is limited to our present age.

In line 1, the phrase "Les fleaux passes" can be strictly translated "the scourges past." "Scourges" in a general sense can refer to war; more specifically it means "pestilence" or disease. Interestingly enough, both interpretations apply to the present: The "scourges" of global conflict--World War I and II--are indeed behind us, and we are enjoying a relative quite in the world--"for a long time peace" (line 2)--that has lasted for over three decades. During this same period, history has seen a unique development in man's fight for life--the successful eradication of many of the "killer diseases" so prevalent in the past: smallpox, polio, etc. Nostradamus, who as a physician spent many long years combating the plagues that ravaged his native France in the sixteenth century, would not have failed to take special note of this future time, when "pestilences" would be "extinguished." The effect of reducing the mortality rate by reducing the natural causes of death has in turn had a dramatic effect upon the world in a special way: "Lands greatly populated"--the population explosion. Again, at no other time in the history of the world than in the present decades following World War II has mankind witnessed such a multiplication of his species.

Two other elements peculiar to our age are found in lines 1 and 2: The "World shrinks," and safe travel is accomplished by a variety of means. Through advances in communication the world community has found itself in much closer contact than ever before, and the closeness has been enhanced by the new abilities of covering great traveling distances in much reduced time than ever realized before. Besides the mention of travel "by air" the prophet also alluded to yet another form of transportation unique to our century: British commentator Stewart Robb notes that the mention of travel through "sea and wave" is not redundant. A ship traverses the "wave" or surface of water, but only a modern submarine can literally penetrate "through the sea" or beneath the water.

The last line of the verse contains an ominous message, for it predicts in no uncertain terms that our age of relative "peace" will soon come to an end, and "war will be stirred up again." We have been living with the threat of war, to be sure, during these quiet years, but major conflict has so far been miraculously avoided. Nostradamus, however, prophesies that the threats will eventually be realized, and another "scourge" like those which are in the past--that is, another World War--will shortly be upon us.

8. THE "SLEEPING PROPHET" AND THE SHAKING EARTH

When Edgar Cayce died in 1945, he left behind a legacy to the world of over 14,000 readings he had made while in self-induced trance states, beginning in 1901. These readings, faithfully preserved in transcript form by the Association of Research and Enlightenment at Virginia Beach, Virginia, include many prophecies about the future before us--a future, Cayce foresaw, that will be characterized by drastic changes in the earth.

Cayce's outline of things to come is linked to a specific period of 40 years he forecast when we will see the great earth upheavals to occur. This period began in 1958, and will end in 1998, with the first part witnessing only small disturbances, but these will gradually build up in intensity, until the last years erupt with the real block-buster earthquakes. In one reading, in fact, he pinpointed: "This is understood for the period: the *greater changes* shall be for the *latter portion*." In other words, it is the last half of the 40-year period, from 1978 to 1998--the time we have entered now--that the real disasters will strike. What is alarming is that several modern geologists and seismologists have confirmed that since 1958, the number of earthquakes, tremors, volcanic eruptions and other tectonic activity has been steadily increasing around the world, and warn that we should brace ourselves for a series of "superquakes" toward which conditions seem to be building up.

Equally alarming is that many of the signs which the "sleeping prophet" Cayce gave for the approach of the global catastrophes, have already taken place. In 1934, Cayce spoke in trance, saying that the "early portion" (between 1958 and 1978) "will see a change in the physical aspect of the west coast of America." The violent Alaskan earthquake of 1964, and in the California quake of 1971, geologists noted that a sizeable portion of the coast had indeed been measurably displaced, in some places several feet. Two years earlier, in 1932, Cayce also forecast that when 1) "there is the first breaking up of some conditions in the South Pacific," 2) risings and sinkings in the Mediterranean, and 3) greater activity by Mount Etna, in Sicily, "then we may know *it has begun*"--the period of world upheavals. On January 2, 1976, Etna erupted violently, Greece was struck by a quake, and a shock that registered 6.8 on the Richter scale shook New Hebrides, in the South Pacific. As if to draw further attention to the portents, the very same day also saw a 4.2 tremor in Los Angeles. More recently, on August 4 and 6, 1979, Etna blew up again, with even greater gusto, and a quake shook San Francisco, with a Richter reading of 5.7. Cayce's prophecy has thus been fulfilled to a remarkable degree--the question is, what comes next?

The continental United States, the "sleeping seer" foresaw, is going to be severely affected by earth movements in several places. In a reading in 1941, he specified the West coast, the East coast, and the Central states, to be the hardest hit. Concerning the West coast, Cayce gave a number of details. He said that first, there will be major eruptions in Mount Vesuvius in Italy and/or

33

Mount Pelee in the Caribbean isle of Martinique. Vesuvius last let off steam in 1944, while Pelee has not stirred since 1903. But when these two--one or the other, or both--sound off, Cayce warned, "Then within three months following, the southern coast of California, and the areas between Salt Lake and the southern portion of Nevada, may expect an inundation by earthquakes." One mystery here is that Cayce was not clear if he used the word "inundation" simply as a figure of speech to describe the earthquakes, or whether he was depicting an "inundation" of water--tidal waves of truly gigantic proportions to be caused by the earthquakes. Either way, a superquake that will shake so large an area is bound to cause tremendous damage. In another reading, given in 1934, Cayce put the effects in rather starker terms: "The earth will be broken up in the western portion of America." Going further, in another reading given only a month later, Cayce told a woman client that Santa Barbara is destined to follow the fate of the lost Pacific continent of Mu--that is, it will sink into the ocean. If Santa Barbara goes, this means that other Californian cities will be affected also. In 1941, Cayce named both Los Angeles and San Francisco to be destroyed in the general convulsion.

The California superquake, however, is going to be only the first of a series of similar catastrophes for this nation. In 1941, a businessman asked Cayce while the seer was in his hypnotic trance if he should move out of New York City, because of the threat of wartime bombing. The seer told him in clear language that the east coast of New York, including New York City, "will in the main disappear"-- though this was to occur "in the next generation." The southern part of Carolina and Georgia will also vanish into the Atlantic, but this, he said, "will be much sooner." When the businessman asked if Los Angeles was safe, Cayce answered that that city--and San Francisco--would be destroyed *before* New York City. Organizing this information into the sequence Cayce predicted, we find that 1) the California superquake will happen first, 2) Carolina and Georgia will suffer from flooding, and 3) then will come the New York disaster. Paul James, a Cayce scholar, firmly believes that Cayce's concept of a "generation" is a period of forty years. By placing the New York cataclysm in the "next generation" beyond 1941, Cayce may have meant a time immediately after 1981. James suggests that if this is true, then the California upheaval--which Cayce stipulated is to take place before New York is destroyed--may happen in the early to mid-1980's.

Whenever it takes place, the destruction of New York City, according to the slumbering seer, will prove to be even more catastrophic than California. In 1932, when asked about coming earth disturbances for this country, Cayce remarked that the *greater* change" will be on "the North Atlantic seaboard"--and instructed his listeners to "watch New York, Connecticut and the like."

While both the West and East have something to worry about, so does the Midwest. In the same reading about New York City disappearing, Cayce forewarned that someday the Great Lakes will begin draining into the Mississippi to the Gulf of Mexico, rather than through the St. Lawrence seaway to the Atlantic. The indications are that this will not be a gradual occurrence: The Mississippi valley is an unstable region geologically, subject to very violent shocks in the past. The great 1811 quake, centered near New Madrid, Missouri, was strong enough to topple chimneys in Charleston, South Carolina, and cause the mighty Mississippi to flow *backward* in places, for several days. Cayce's prophecy suggests another big quake is coming to this area, only one that will have more tragic consequences. A large lateral movement of the earth in the northern Mississippi valley, generated on a north-south line, could cause the waters of Lake Michigan to momentarily retreat northward, building up into a massive wall of water. Once the energy began to dissipate, the wall would turn into a gigantic tsunami, or inland tidal wave. The wave would rush back southward, and keep going--first smashing into Chicago, then continuing on through Illinois, obliterating St. Louis and swelling the Mississippi river ten thousand fold, finally washing New Orleans into the Gulf. Either as the result of general subsidence in the Mississippi valley, or more likely

35

because of a new channel dug out by the tidal wave on its path to the sea, the Great Lakes will have a lower outlet to empty by, than the St. Lawrence--just as Cayce predicted.

On the positive side, Cayce did list the places which would remain relatively safe--though the number is not very many. These will be parts of Ohio, Indiana, Illinois (presumably the western portion), southern and eastern Canada, and the area around Virginia Beach, Virginia, where Cayce wisely chose to live. Most of the West and Midwest, however are to be "disturbed." To what extent was revealed to Cayce in a dream he had in 1935, in which he saw himself reborn in the year 2100, in Nebraska. At the time, "the sea apparently covered *all the western portion* of the country, as the city where I lived"--in Nebraska--"was *on the coast*." A major sinking of the West and Midwest of the United States would mean the loss of such major grain and livestock producing areas as Kansas, western Nebraska, Colorado and Wyoming. In a later reading, Cayce noted that, as a result of the coming geologic and subsequent climatic shifts, Montana and the Dakotas would eventually become the new "breadbaskets of the world," with Livingston, Montana a major shipping port.

America's coming upheavals, as Cayce foresaw them, are going to be only a part of transformations to occur all over the globe. Among the major events in the next twenty years, the sleeping prophet envisioned:

1. New lands will begin rising in both the Atlantic and Pacific, off the American coasts--remnants of lost continents from former ages.

2. Dry land will also appear in the Caribbean, and off the island of Bimini, in the Bahamas.

3. The entire continent of South America will be shaken from end to the other. So violent will the earth movement be, that the submarine bed beneath the Drake Passage, situated between Tierra del Fuego and the Palmer Peninsula of Antarctica, will rise dramatically, displacing a tremendous volume of ocean, and creating a "strait of rushing waters."

4. The "greater portion" of Japan will "go into the sea"--the sliding islands presumably filling the adjacent

Japan and Kurii Trenches, which straddle the east coasts.
5. Northern Europe will be "changed in a twinkling of an eye." In a second reading, given in August of 1941, Cayce stipulated that those places that were then the battlefields of the war, were destined to become "ocean, seas, and bays." At that time, the conflict involved Britain, northern Germany, and parts of the Russian Ukraine.
6. "Open waters will appear in the northern portions of Greenland." This will be a sign of changes of an even more radical nature, leading to the final and ultimate event, to occur at the very end of Cayce's period of geologic changes, in 1998. According to the prophet, there will be "upheavals in the Arctic and Antarctic" coupled with the "eruption of volcanoes in the Torrid" or Equatorial regions. Immediately following, the Earth will shift its poles--causing tropical moss and fern to begin growing in what are today "frigid" and "semi-frigid" locations.

The one bright spot in Cayce's outline of things to come is that the Earth shift will bring an end to further geologic transformations. Beyond the year 1998, the world will settle down to a peaceful co-existence with its human survivors, who will rebuild a better life. Meanwhile, we in the here and now must still face the great alterations Cayce forecast in the next two decades. In one reading, a client asked when the earth disasters would occur--their exact dates. The unconscious seer answered by saying that special people would be spiritually chosen to make the warnings at the proper times: "As to the seasons, as to the places, alone it is given to those who have named the Name--and who bear the mark of those of His calling and His election in their bodies. To them it shall be given." These individuals, with their unique ability to sense the approaching disasters, may already be among us.

9. THE PROPHECY OF KATE-ZAHL

In the first century of the Christian era, the great prophet of the ancient Toltecs of Central Mexico, Kate-Zahl, warned his people of what was to befall their rich and sacred city of Tula. He foresaw that it would first suffer from a severe earthquake, then be conquered by the

Tony Shearer

Sacrificers of men--the Aztecs. But Tula would still remain inhabited. Then, however, would come Men of the East-- white-skinned, bearded, wearing suits of shining metal, and carrying "thunder-rods" which killed at a distance. These, of course, were the Spaniards. Kate-Zahl fore-warned that these Easterners would come under the guise of peace, but that his people were not to trust them. He told them to flee into the forests, to hide their sacred books from the coming pillage and slaughter. The prophet then bemoaned the fact that the Toltecs would be scat-tered, Tula destroyed and reduced to rubble, and then burned, to be forgotten to the memory of men for many cycles of time. In the meantime, the Easterners, in their love for weapons, would produce deadlier and deadlier in-struments of destruction, ending in their final annihila-tion. As a sign that catastrophe is imminent, the ruins of ancient Tula were to be rediscovered, uncovered and studied. Modern scholars believe the legendary Tula may be the ancient site of Teotihuacan, ruins not fully un-earthed until just twenty years ago. After the coming Holocaust, however, Kate-Zahl saw the Toltecs, together with spirit-bound brethren the world over, rebuild Tula, and return to it the hidden books of ancient sacred wis-dom. The prophet saw in a vision:

"The heavens parted and a rising golden sun shown down on another Tula. Plainly I could see the valley, but the city was one I knew not. I was lifted beyond the cold earth. No longer I saw the Age of Destruction. Gone was the horrible Age of Warfare. I was looking beyond the Age of Carnage. Walk with me through this Age of the Future. Tula shines in all its glory, but the metals are types we know not. Loving hands have rebuilt the park-ways, have paved the streets, have rebuilt the temples. There is a great building where the books are kept for the scholars, and many are those who came to read them. Tula is a great center of culture. Shining again is my Father's temple. You will see again the same inscriptions which today your eyes are seeing, but now all people can read. Come to the metropolis of the future. Here are buildings unlike those we fashion, yet they have breathless beauty. Here people dress in materials we know not, travel in manners beyond our knowledge, but more important than all this difference are the faces of the people. Gone is the shadow of fear and suffering, for man no longer sacrifices, and he has outgrown the wars of his childhood. Now he walks full statured toward his destiny--in the Golden Age of Learning."

Then, in order that his words might bring hope to those future generations who were to suffer tribulations, he spoke, "Carry this vision on through the ages, and remember Kate-Zahl the Prophet."

THE SECOND THUNDER

10. *NOSTRADAMUS ON INFLATION AND
ECONOMIC TROUBLE IN AMERICA*
Inflation is the number one issue today, and the question uppermost in everyone's mind is, where is it leading us, if we can't stop it? Older citizens among us still have memories of the Depression, and some fear we are heading for a repetition of history. French seer Nostradamus had some alarming words for our present age, which he wrote in the year 1558:

Les simulacres d'or et d'argent enfles,
Qu' apres le rapt au lac furent gettes,
Au decouvert estaincts tous et troubles,
Au marbre script prescript intergetes. VIII, 28.

The counterfeit of gold and silver inflated,
The robbery finished, they will all be thrown out and burned,
Discovered to be worth little and troubled,
Scripts and bonds frozen, laws interjected.

This is a difficult verse to interpret, but its connotations are clear enough to be understood. In line 1, "Les simulacres d'or et d'argent" is a curious phrase, which can mean "similitude," "copy" or "counterfeit of gold and silver." In Nostradamus' day, gold and silver coinage was the prevalent means of monetary exchange. Today, however, paper money, and coinage of base metals, are the standards of currency, these *representing* ("copy" or "counterfeit") a backing of gold and silver, or some form of economic credit. Ever since the introduction of such a system in the nineteenth century, however, troubles have arisen time and time again as to the degree of backing each currency should possess, and the rates of exchange between international moneys. Nostradamus predicted a coming crisis that will be far worse than even the financial disaster that brought ruin and failures in the 1930's. A strict translation of line 2 can read, "After the milk has been skimmed, all thrown into the fire"--the first phrase suggests that speculators will reap large profits on the world money markets, "off the top," like cream off of milk, and this--done at the expense of faltering world economies--will eventually lead to the second situation, money being so worthless that it will be used for burning.

The third line suggests the state many currencies find themselves in at present: "Discovered to be dulled and troubled" (strict translation). The money is *dulled*--that is, its shiny gold and silver backings are depleted or nonexistent, and this creates the *troubled* state of affairs: Like troubled water, they rise and drop and fluctuate, their values now placed at the mercy of day-to-day international rates of exchange. The last line hints at two acts of desperation: "Scripts written in marble, prescripts (laws) interjected" (strict translation). The first part suggests that bonds, certificates, etc. are to be made fast and permanent--"frozen" in monetary terminology; the second portion reflects moves made by the world legal systems to attempt to save the situation by placing new restrictions into effect, or upholding existing monetary regulations in the courts. The verse leaves the crisis unresolved, which implies that no direct solution may be found. The result will undoubtedly lead to a breakdown in international trade and cooperation.

The collapse of international economies will have no small effect on the American economy, and Nostradamus offers us a glimpse of what will happen to us, in a second verse:

Mis tresor temple citadins Hesperiques,
Dans icelui retire en secret lieu:
Le temple ouvrir les liens fameliques,
Repris, ravis, proie horrible au milieu. X, 81.

The treasures kept within a temple by the citizens of
Hesperia,
Therein withdrawn to a secret place (the vaults),
The starving will break the bonds to open the temple,
Reopened, ravaged, a horrible chaos in their midst.

The key to this quatrain is decoding the name "Hesperia." In classical Greek mythology, Hesperia was the
land of perpetual sunshine and plenty, located on the
other side of "Oceanus," or the Atlantic. What the French
seer was alluding to, in effect, is modern America. In line
1, the place where the "Hesperian" or American "citizens"
will place their "treasures" or wealth is described as a
"temple." Some commentators believ' Fort Knox may be
indicated: It contains the largest stockpile of gold in the
world. Other possibilities include the New York Stock
Exchange building, and the U.S. Treasury in Washington,
D.C., both of which are of a classical architecture with
colonnade fronts reminiscent of the temples of Greece and
Rome. It is equally possible, howeve.', that "temple" may
simply stand for banking firms in general--one recalls the
Bible story of Christ and the money-changers in the Temple of Jerusalem.
    The scene pictured in the verse is a very ominous one
indeed. More than just a run on the banks, it is a warning
of panic and riots, of mob action breaking through "bonds"
("cords, chains, locks") to "reopen" and "ravage" the
insides of the place or places where their wealth is kept.
The fact that the destroying crowd of "Hesperian"-Ameri-
cans is "starving" suggests this event will happen during a
time of economic crisis, when food will be scarce or paper
money will be useless to buy food. This is not a situation
which so seriously arose during the last Depression. But
as the prophet predicts, it is a situation that may yet be
for our very near future.
    It is more than just coincidence that Nostradamus'
prophecy of economic crisis for America is finding confir-

mation in the visions of many modern psychics, seers and astrologers. Paul Shockley, of *Cosmic Awareness Communications*, has warned that the United States is heading toward financial ruin, which he believes is being deliberately planned by certain banking interests in this country and abroad. This, of course, is an echo of Nostradamus' prophecy of those who are "skimming the milk" at the expense of others. Shockley foresees that on or soon after the fiftieth anniversary of the Great Crash of 1929 (or October 29, 1979), the stock market will again begin to plummet, and we can expect a depression for the next seven years, leading in the direction of a possible dictatorship by 1984 (shades of George Orwell).

Louise Morse of Kansas City, Missouri has been a most prolific psychic reader and spiritual counselor, as well as the author of several books. Beginning in 1975, she has repeatedly foreseen that the American economy has been steadily declining since 1970--but it will be in the Autumn of 1979 that we will fully come to realize how bad things have become, and will remain that way for *seven years*. She foresees the dollar will become valueless, and the coming years will be marked by hardship, frustration and hunger for many.

It's interesting to note to what degree these predictions have already seen a partial fulfillment: *The Consumer Economic Index Forecast Update* of January, 1980, in an article entitled "October Massacre," observed that between October 5 and 25, 1979, long-term corporate bonds fell 9%, Treasury bonds fell 8.9%, and the Dow Jones Industrials fell 10.1%--a total loss of $145 billion in investments, which is the *worst drop since 1929.* Many economists are pointing to these October events as the *beginning point* of the present severe recession.

Michael Blake Read is a resident of Toronto, Ontario, and he has been the channel through whom a group of ethereal entities speak, called the "Evergreens." In a trance session recorded on February 3, 1978, the Evergreens revealed that 1980 will see a slow but steady decline in international trade and economies, with 1982 through 1983 being very "turbulent" in open markets. Many of the details given are most unpleasant indeed:

44

From now to 1985, all food goods and fuels will either be scarce or very expensive; individual cars will disappear, replaced by mass transit vehicles; a head of cabbage will cost over $3.00; many people will suffer from malnutrition and other deficiency diseases; the breaking in of stores will occur often, even though they will be heavily guarded; and vigilante groups will mushroom here and there, formed to protect neighborhoods from marauding bands of looters. Economic relief is not promised until the late 1980's.

Finally, L.J. Jensen, an astrologer who in 1935 was living in the midst of the Depression, looked ahead in his charts to see when such conditions could arise again. He noted: "When the major slow moving planets, Saturn, Jupiter and Uranus, are 90 or 180 degrees apart in the zodiac, they are found to coincide with economic depression." And the date these conditions will happen again? According to Jensen, starting in 1980, and lasting for more than half a decade.

11. PORTENTS OF FUTURE WAR

Many prophets have warned that China and not Russia will be our real enemy to fear in the future, and foresee that the Oriental giant's millions will some day be locked in a bitter conflict with the United States.

Jeane Dixon, in the late 1960's, predicted that the United States and Russia will one day be at war against China, parts of Africa and the Far East. She warned that China will use germ warfare, and that the Davis Straits-- between Greenland and Baffin Island in northern Canada-- will become a "life-line between two nations." The time for this next war, she foresaw, will be in the 1980's.

Edgar Cayce, over 35 years ago, saw strife to come over "social ills," the disparity between the developed and underdeveloped nations. He forewarned to keep a careful watch on Libya, Egypt, Ankara (Turkey), Syria, the Persian Gulf, and the seas off southeast Asia and to the north of Australia--in other words, the Middle East and Far East. Cayce also pinpointed the Davis Straits as a vital area. It is interesting to note that the Davis Straits would gain military importance, as a communication link between the United States and the Soviet Union over the

North Pole, only if other communication links between the two super-powers--through Europe and through Siberia-Alaska--were for some reason disrupted or broken by a belligerent third power.

Criswell, the Californian seer, received a psychic vision of Russians, Chinese and Koreans fighting in Alaska in the 1980's. He also forecast that about the same time a "foreign power" will attempt to bomb the United States with nuclear missiles. Many will be driven off course, but several will explode over the state of Vermont. California, Criswell further warned, will one day become the arsenal state for the nation against an attack from Asia, and the U.S. will also have to defend its Mexican border and Gulf coast in Alabama and Florida against Central and South America.

John Pendragon, the well-known British psychic, who died in 1970, predicted that the world's future "hot" area will be located in the Far East, in a region with the China Sea as the center--from Peking in the north to Australia in the south. Some time between 1980 and 1985, Pendragon foresaw, the United States will be involved in a war with China, as the Asian giant invades Thailand, Malaya, Indonesia, New Guinea and the Australian continent. Japan and India, the British seer predicted, will be our allies, while Russia will try to remain neutral--until she is attacked through Mongolia. There will also be fighting in the Middle East, between Egypt and Iran.

In the early part of this century, the Countess Francesca de Billiante entertained many European members of state with her gifts of psychic perception. She prophesied: "I see yellow warriors and red warriors (Orientals and Arabs) marching against the rest of the world. Europe will be completely covered with a yellow fog that will kill the cattle in the fields. Those nations which began the war, however, will perish by terrible fire. May the Lord grant my grand-children the grace of perseverance in these times." By placing the events two generations away, the Countess indicated the decade of either the 1970's or 1980's.

Many present day psychics utilize astrology as a means of inspiring visions of the future. D. Modin, in his book *Prophecy 1973-2000*, indicated that, in the United States' astrological chart, Mars the harbinger of war is approaching the midheaven, and will be complete in 1983. Before this, in 1982, America's Sun will be in Aquarius in the eleventh house, with Mars in Libra, Neptune in Virgo in the seventh house—which is an omen for internal as well as external turmoil. Putting his planetary forecasts together with his psychic visions, Modin predicts a major conflict involving the United States, Russia, and China, by the early 1980's.

Irene Hughes, the Chicago seeress, also sees America, Russia, and China at war in the very near future, with a great deal of the fighting to take place in the Middle East. She sees that the war will begin when a "three-pronged flame" will touch America, Russia and India. Conflict will reach Australia, Alaska and Greenland. Ms. Hughes also predicts that trouble with the Orient will erupt again later in the future, in February of 1993.

In 1971, parapsychologist Hans Holzer compiled a "survey of the future" from a number of psychics and seers in America and Britain, who he has been studying and testing for accuracy. When asked about the possibilities of a future war, there was a striking correlation among all the answers. Their visions taken as a whole, they predict that:

1. The United States will be in a war with China.
2. Russia will be our ally.
3. The conflict will take place sometime in the decade of the 1980's.
4. Nuclear weapons and germ weapons will be used, though only to a limited degree. New York, Chicago and the West coast are possible targets for destruction.
5. China will dominate the entire Orient, and important battles will take place in the Middle East.
6. Europe will also be affected by war, several nations joining in alliance with the United States and Russia.
7. Alaska and Greenland will become strategic areas during the conflict.
8. China will eventually lose the war, but only after the

United States and her allies will have suffered great loss.

Are these remarkable similarities only coincidental--or are the prophets trying to tell us something?

12. A GIANT EARTHQUAKE TO SHAKE GREECE AND TURKEY

The eastern Mediterranean has long been known as an area that is geologically unstable, subject to repeated quakes. But there is one upcoming earth tremor which the French seer Nostradamus prophesied, which may happen in the 1980's, and will generate tidal waves the likes of which have never been seen. Three of Nostradamus' prophetic quatrains describe the event:

Mars, Mercury and silver (the Moon) joined together,
In Southern lands (Africa and southern Asia) extreme drought,
Beneath Asia the earth will tremble,
Affecting Corinth (Greece) and Ephesus (Turkey), in perplexity. III, 3.

For several nights the earth will shake,
In the spring, two shocks in succession,
When Corinth (Greece) and Ephesus (Turkey) will swim in two seas,
When war will be stirred up between two valiant in combat. II,52.

At the place where Jason had his ship built (northeast Greece),
There will be a flood very high and very sudden,
It will seem that there is no place to land,
The waves to climb Fiesole, and Olympus. VIII, 16.

In the first two verses, the focus of attention is in southeastern Europe. Corinth was located in eastern Greece and Ephesus in Turkey opposite the island of Samos in the Aegean. The first verse gives some indication as to the scope of the area to be affected: The earthquake's epicen-

48

ter will be "in the depths of Asia"--in central Asia--yet Corinth and Ephesus, several thousand miles away, will be in "perplexity" over its effects. This suggests an earth movement of major proportions.

The second verse offers hints as to the strength, duration and time of the Graeco-Turkish disaster: In the third line of the verse, Corinth and Ephesus are more than just "in perplexity," they are depicted to be completely inundated--"Corinth, Ephesus will swim in the two seas," the two seas being the Ionian and Aegean. According to the first line, the quake will take place for "several nights." This might indicate not one large tremor lasting for days, but rather a series of tremors and aftershocks, each striking approximately every twenty-four hours, and during the hours of the night. Line 2 predicts that there will be "two" major "shocks" of the same magnitude, one to follow soon after the other.

The first line of the first verse offers a time element: "Mars, Mercury and silver (in medieval alchemy, symbol of the moon) joined together." Unfortunately, the meeting of these three orbs in the heavens is a fairly frequent occurrence. However, their being joined in the *spring* season, as implied in the second verse, narrows the possibilities considerably. The next two dates when such a conjunction will take place is in April-May, 1983 when the three will be in the spring sign of Aries, and in early June, 1985, meeting in Gemini.

In the third verse, we catch a glimpse of other effects of the Asian superquake: Three place names are given here, all involved with a flood described in the second line as "very great and very sudden." "The place where Jason had his ship built," is Iolcus, on the southern shore of Magnesia in northeastern Greece--not far from ancient Corinth. About 60 miles to the northwest is famed Mount Olympus, towering 9,570 feet, upon the slopes of which--according to the last line--the flood waters will climb. This by itself is indicative of a tidal wave of no minor proportions. But the infusion into the last line of the word "Fiesole" shows that the wave and its effects are not to be confined to Greece alone. Fiesole is located in central Italy, and rises 950 feet above sea level. That the flood

49

waters will also reach here classifies this tidal wave to be the greatest record-breaker yet. One point to note is that--for the tidal waves to strike Magnesia, Olympus and Fiesole--the shock wave that will generate them will have to be traveling from east to west. In other words, the shock will originate east of Italy and Greece--from the direction of central Asia.

13. GEMINI ORACLES--THE FORECASTS OF THE LUSSON SISTERS

It has often been said--and there is new scientific evidence to support this--that twins share a special mind link, allowing them to increase their field of perception and sensitivity, by knowing what each other is feeling or thinking. It is rare, however, when a set of twins are endowed with the gift of foresight--and by "putting their heads together" as only they can do, that foresight ability is multiplied to new dimensions. This is the story behind the remarkable prophecies of the "Lusson" sisters, "M" and "D." As would be expected, their double mind forecasts have so far been impressive: In 1968, they predicted the Yom Kippur war of 1973 and the resulting oil embargo; in the same year, they foresaw a mounting energy crisis for the nation, beginning in 1973 and lasting for over a decade; and in 1973, predicted Nixon's resignation as a result of Watergate.

Looking toward the future, the Lusson sisters see the next twenty-five years as an era of tremendous change, during which mankind is to be educated, cleansed and awakened for the advent of a coming better world age. It is a time, the twins caution, when the earth plane must heal itself, and they liken their prophecies to the actions taken by a sick body to care for its malady. The time frame for this "curing" process is divided up into seven Cycles of seven years each. Three of the Cycles are already past: The year 1958 began a Cycle of an awareness for personal freedom--the youth movement, equal rights, demonstrations, experiments with drugs; 1965 saw a new Cycle, one of social turmoil; and 1972 started the growing realization that the age of material extravagance is over, and we are running out of resources.

50

With 1979, we entered the Fourth Cycle--and the Lusson sisters forecast that these next seven years are not going to be pleasant. This will be a time of famine and economic depression--long bread lines, millions of the labor force will be jobless, and the Stock Market may be forced to close down forever by 1982. Amid these chaotic conditions, the American government, blamed for its ineptitude and powerlessness, will be faced with a great uprising, a revolution by the common working masses. Adding to the confusion, the period will also see the first major earth changes: Soon after 1980, South America and North Africa will be rocked by giant quakes; Japan, Australia and Philippines will suffer tidal waves of unprecedented destruction; and Mexico, southern California and western Canada will witness complete geographical alterations. The sisters point out, the lesson we will have to learn in these years ahead is survival, and sharing and compassion for others.

Beyond, in the Cycle following, beginning in 1986, we face a time when our survival instincts will face even greater challenges. The sisters predict the Cycle will see a potential world holocaust, in which many nations will wage battle for world leadership. At the same time, however, the earth will experience a second series of land and sea upheavals, on a greater scale than those of the previous Cycle: Portugal and Spain will be destroyed by a gigantic wall of water; the British Isles will shrink in size due to sudden submergences; Japan and most of the Pacific islands will be made uninhabitable; South America will change shape, joined by a land bridge to Antartica; the Australian continent will be joined to Asia in a similar manner; Africa will appear more oval-shaped; and eventually the Arctic will become a semi-tropical region. For America, the twins see the nation split in two by a great strait of water extending from the Great Lakes down what is now the Mississippi to the Gulf of Mexico; the East coast completely transformed, with New York City disappearing beneath the Atlantic; a wider mouth for the Chesapeake Bay; a view of the ocean from the mountains of Georgia, with Florida left as an island; and a land bridge connecting the Bahamas with other Caribbean islands, including the Virgin Islands.

Some of these earth cataclysms, the sisters warn, will be caused by man-made activity--that is, nuclear explosions.

With the dawning of the Sixth Cycle, in 1993, we next face a time of regulation, and a period of further "cleansing" and transformation of a different form, whereby mankind will learn the true nature of worship of the Divine and the Oneness of all Life. There will be great changes in government--the United States will have a more socialistic political system--and also in religion. In the Roman Catholic Church for example, the Pope will no longer be the head, but a new "spiritual leader" will take his place.

Finally, in 2000, comes the Seventh Cycle, and it will bring forth a new enlightened Avatar or world teacher. The twins prophesy he will unite the spiritual consciousness and blossoming universality of man, establishing and helping in the rebuilding of a new earth. As the Aquarian Age progresses, on into the 21st century and beyond, mankind will undergo physical, mental and spiritual metamorphoses, and evolve into a new race of beings the sisters call the "Almen"--a higher form of man who will truly be attuned, with himself, with all other men, with the environment in which he lives, and with the Divine.

14. THE ANTICHRIST IS ALIVE AND COMING TO POWER

Among all the major religions of the world, there is anticipation for the coming of a Savior or Avatar who will lead troubled mankind into the New Age, which many prophecies pinpoint will begin in the 21st century. The Buddhists await Maitreya, the Hindus Kalki, the Moslems Muntazar, the Jews the Messiah, and Christians the Christ. But before that time--between the present and the year 2000--another man will arise on the world scene who will claim to be a Savior figure, but will be everything to the contrary. He will take control of the Roman Church, introduce radical changes, absorb all other Christian factions into the fold, then attempt to force the other world religions to join as well. Those whose religious concepts revolve around Form rather than Spirit will accept this "Savior" as the Awaited One, and be convinced by the counterfeit signs and miracles he will perform. But those who have a truly Spirit-centered faith will recognize that this "Messiah" is without inner Light, and will resist his power and influence. These true Children of the New Age are destined to feel the sting of persecution at his hand.

Among the psychics who have predicted the coming of this Antichrist is prophetess Jeane Dixon. In the early morning hours of February 5, 1962, Mrs. Dixon rose from her bed and, gazing out her bedroom window, was surprised to see not the familiar city streets of Washington, D.C. below, but a desolate waste, a desert stretching into the distance where it met on the horizon with a bright, blue sky dominated by a golden sun. Suddenly, stepping down out of the solar disc to the earth were two figures which Mrs. Dixon immediately recognized as Queen Nefertiti and her Pharoah husband, Ikhnaton. The Queen held in her arms a baby clothed in soiled rags in sharp contrast to the bejeweled attire of the royal couple. Nefertiti placed the child on the ground as if presenting it as an offering. The Queen and Pharoah then disappeared into the past whence they had come, and Mrs. Dixon's attention was now drawn to the baby left on the desert sands. As she watched, she saw him grow to manhood, and above him appeared a cross which expanded, and seemed to encompass the earth. As the vision began to vanish, Mrs. Dixon witnessed the man raise his hands, and kneeling around him in worship were the peoples of every race and religion.

Mrs. Dixon interpreted the vision to mean that some where in the desert lands of the Middle East on the morning of February 5, 1962 a child was born in humble surroundings who is a descendant of the ancient royal house of Egypt. She felt that we will not hear of this child until the early 1980's, and in the succeeding decade to the end of the century, the Middle Eastern man will unite all the religions into one faith.

Ten years later, in a second special vision, Mrs. Dixon was told that the power she had seen eminating from the Middle East child will not be from God, even though he will present himself to the world as being from God. Mrs. Dixon also revealed that this man will attempt to imitate the life of the first Christ in every respect. His birth was heralded by astrological signs--February 4 and 5, 1962 saw an extraordinary configuration of five planets and a total solar eclipse in Aquarius. Soon after his birth, Mrs. Dixon saw, he was taken from his birthplace to Egypt, as had been the infant Jesus. At the age of 11, or some time in either 1973 or 1974, the Washington seeress further noted, something "tremendously important" happened in the youth's life, which made him aware of his life's destiny. This mirrored Jesus' revelation of his work in the Temple of Jerusalem, when he was 12 years old. By the end of 1980, we may receive the first news of his miraculous works, and at the age of 19, in 1981, he will gather his first circle of supporters. But it will not be until 1991 or 1992, when he is 29 or 30 years old, that he will present himself to the whole world as being full of strength and wisdom, and the solver of the world's problems. According to Mrs. Dixon, at that time he will begin frequent visits to North America, where his supporters will gain control of the communications media, and use it to proclaim him as the Savior, the long-awaited "Man of Peace." Soon after, the seeress predicts, his domination will extend to the whole world. By the power of political and military force backing him, he will declare all warfare and strife throughout the earth banned. Going a step further, he will establish a new religion, which Mrs. Dixon foresees will be anti-human, atheistic, and opposed to the existence of all other forms of religion. Finally, in Jerusalem, he shall declare himself to be God, and demand the world recognize him as such. But Mrs. Dixon predicts his worship and tyranny will be brief, plunging the world into universal confusion and turmoil, and culminating in sudden destruction and war. Finally, in 1999, the seeress envisions, in the midst of a world conflict the image of the Cross will be seen in the eastern skies, the Antichrist and his kingdom will be utterly ruined, and mankind will then enjoy a real Peace.

It is interesting that the city of Jerusalem also figures into many Bible prophecies concerning the Antichrist, for it is here, within the "secret chambers" of the Holy of Holies, in the Temple that is predicted to be rebuilt by the Jews in the very near future, that he will usurp the place of God and set up his own throne instead. Jesus of Nazareth, when asked by his disciples 2,000 years ago what would be the signs of the end of the age, gave this response: "Take heed that no man deceive you. For many shall come in my name, saying I am the Christ, do not believe it. For there shall arise false Christs, who will show marvelous signs and wonders, and will deceive many. If they say to you, Behold, *he is in the desert*, do not go; behold, *he is in the secret chambers*, do not believe it." Matthew 24: 4, 5, 24, 26.

Many other prophets, in both the Old and New Testaments, also warned of a coming universal religious power, headed by a man who will force others to worship him as God. The prophet Daniel called him the "king of fierce countenance;" the apostle Paul, "the man of sin," and "son of perdition;" and John, in the Revelation, identified him as, "the beast." When we compare the words of the seers--given in Daniel Chapter 7, Second Thessalonians Chapter 2, and Revelations Chapter 13--we find remarkable agreement concerning the Antichrist's characteristics. They agree that he will oppose the God-Spirit, and exalt himself as the object of worship; lead a persecution against those who are Spirit-centered; enforce his power through political leaders; represent the forces of Darkness through his actions; have complete world dominion; and will be destroyed by the intervention of the God-Spirit at the end of the Present Age. Concerning the time length of the false Messiah's bloody reign, it is symbolized by the Bible prophets as a "time, times and dividing of times," "forty-two months," or "1,260 days," all of which are about three and a half years. This, however, will be preceded by another three and a half period (making a total of seven years), when the false Savior will be rising to power. There are also several other time periods mentioned. In a study of Bible chronology entitled *The First Seven Thousand Years* (Exposition Press, 1970), British scholar C.G. Ozanne has made calculations of the Antichrist's rise and rule, based primarily on the prophetic periods given in the Book of Daniel. Ozanne foresees the following dates to be significant:

1982--Babylon, the power of the Middle East, will be unrestrained. This will be the termination date of the "seven times" or 2,500 years of Daniel 4:25, counted from the fall of Babylon in 539 B.C.

1989--The beginning of the Seven-Year period of Tribulation when the Antichrist makes his first appearance, in Daniel 7:25.

1992--The middle of the Tribulation, the end of the first three and one half years, the beginning of when the "sanctuary" or the earth will be "trampled" underfoot by false religious powers, for 2,300 days, Daniel 8:14; also the beginning of the second three and one half years, of persecution, Daniel 7:25.

1996--The end of the Tribulation of Seven Years, the end of the three and one half years of persecution, and the end of 6,000 years of World History from 4004 B.C. (Genisis Chapter 1; Second Peter 3:8), and the beginning of the Seventh Millenium, the Millenium of Peace (Revelation 20:2-3).

1999--The end of the 2,300 days of the "trampling of the sanctuary," the end of the reign of the Antichrist, and the "sanctuary" or the earth is "cleansed" and renewed.

Notice how Ozanne's dates parallel closely with those given by Jeane Dixon. What is more, they both prophesy a terminal date of 1999 for not only the Antichrist, but the Present Age--a date which closely conforms to that predicted by Edgar Cayce, Criswell, Nostradamus, astrologers, pyramid prophecy, and many other prophetic sources....

15. JOHN'S DREAM OF THE NEW JERUSALEM AND NEW EARTH

One of the greatest messages of hope in the Bible is found in its very last pages, toward the end of the Book of Revelation. Here, the apostle John described for us the visions given him of a yet future, far off time when the world shall be no more, and all its people will have evolved to become immortal spirits, dwelling in the presence of the Divine. Revelation 21: 1, 4, 10, 11, 23, 24 and 22: 5--

And I saw a new heaven and a new earth; for the first heaven and the first earth had passed away.

And God shall wipe away all tears from his children's eyes; and there shall be no more death, neither sorrow nor crying, neither shall there be any more pain: For these former things are passed away.

And he carried me away in the spirit to a great and high mountain, and showed me a great city, the holy Jerusalem, descending out of heaven from God.

Having the glory of God, her light was like a stone most precious, even like a jasper stone, clear as crystal.

And the city had no need of the sun, neither of the moon, to shine in it, for the glory of God lighted it: And the kings of the earth bring their glory and honor into it.

And there shall be no night there, and they need no candle, neither the light of the sun--for the Lord God gives them light. And they shall reign forever and ever....

16. A PROPHECY IN A TUBE OF LEAD

In the spring of 1944, after a bombing raid on Berlin, a parishoner named Nicol Rycempel discovered in the smouldering ruins of the Church of St. Paul a mysterious tube made of lead, which appeared to have been sealed in a wall of the church long ago. Opening the tube, he discovered a manuscript written by an unknown Benedictine monk in the early nineteenth century, listing yearly one-line prophecies beginning in the year 1900 and ending in 2000. Copies of the prophecies were made, and had a wide, immediate reading among the German populous, because the manuscript noted for the year 1945 the "Death of the crooked Lion"--which was interpreted to mean Adolf Hitler. The prophecies had such a disturbing appeal that government police were ordered to round up and destroy all copies and the original. The original, fortunately, was safely hidden away, and when Adolf Hitler did die in 1945, and the Nazi era came to a close, the prophecies enjoyed an even further distribution.

The one-line prophecies are for the most part cryptic in language, but nevertheless have seen interesting fulfillments in recent years. For 1974, for example, the prophecy read, "Road to the stars," which some commentators saw as the significant space achievements made in that year; for 1975, "Storm of the crosses" designated a particularly bad year for schism and discontent in the Roman Church; and 1978 saw "Terrestrial dizziness" in the form of a number of world-wide earthquakes and tremors. For the year 1979, the prophecy, "Death of Judah" might indicate that the Mideast peace treaty may not have been to Israel's advantage.

For 1980 to 2000, the old manuscript appears to portend catastrophes of war, religious tyranny and earth upheavals. Here is the reading:

1980 Rome without a Peter
1981 Triumph of Work
1982 The New Man
1983 Hosanna by the People
1984 Ravings in Space
1985 The Voice of Antichrist
1986 Fire from the Orient
1987 Glade of Crosses
1988 Madness on Earth
1989 Expectation by men
1990 A sigh in the sky
1991 Light in the darkness
1992 Fall of the stars
1993 Death of Man
1994 Roar of a wild beast
1995 Sob of the mother
1996 Flood on earth
1997 Death of the Moon

1998 Glory in the Skies
1999 The new Peter
2000 Triumph of the olive

The meaning of these mysterious prophecies will become clearer, no doubt, as the designated years pass us by.

17. A POWERFUL DICTATOR TO DOMINATE THE MIDDLE EAST

From the perspective of international politics, what happens or can happen in the Middle East is anyone's guess, so radically different and so swiftly can events change from year to year, even month to month. Who would have thought only a short while ago, for example, that Israel and Egypt--the bitterest of enemies for over three decades--would sign a treaty of peace, and become the strongest of allies, opposed by the rest of the Arab nations. Nostradamus, writing in the sixteenth century, has foreseen yet another sudden development, which has the potential of being fulfilled in the very near future. Two of his precognitive verses describe the advent of a very powerful leader in the Middle East, who will unify the Arabs into a single, powerful confederacy:

Il entrera vilain, mechant, infame,
Tyrannisant la Mesopotamie:
Tous amis fait d'adulterine dame,
Terre horrible noir de physionomie. VIII, 70.

Le Prince Arabe Mars, Sol, Venus, Lion,
Regne d'Eglise par mer succombera:
Devers la Perse bien pres d'un million,
Bisance, Egypte ver. serp. invadera. V, 25.

To power will come one ugly, wicked and infamous,
Who will tyrannize over all Mesopotamia (Syria and Iraq),
He will make friends by seducing them,
Lands made horribly black by destruction.

The Prince of the Arabs, when Mars, the Sun and Venus
are in Leo,
The rule of the Church will suffer at sea,
Toward Iran very nearly a million men will march,
The true serpent will also invade Turkey and Egypt.

The interpretation of these poems is that an Arab
leader will arise who will consolidate political power by
force, originating in the Tigris-Euphrates river valley of
ancient Mesopotamia--now modern Iraq and Syria. With
an army of nearly a 1,000,000 this leader will overwhelm
Iran, Turkey and Egypt. The Arabs of the new
confederacy will also strike against the Roman Church
through an undisclosed act at sea.

Taking a closer look, in the first verse the third line is
strictly translated, "All friends of the adulterous lady,"
which may refer to an actual woman accomplice, or may
simply symbolize the "seducing" political schemes of the
Middle Eastern tyrant. The last line reads, "The land
dreadful and black in aspect"--and probably refers to the
marks of coming war upon the Middle East terrain.

In the second verse, in line one, a configuration is given
as a time element: "Mars, the Sun, Venus (in) Leo." This
alignment will next take place on August 21, 1987. It
should be noted that the events predicted will not
necessarily happen exactly on this date; rather,
Nostradamus used astrological configurations to pinpoint
the general period when the events will materialize. We
can only say that the prediction has a good chance of being
fulfilled some time within the decade of the 1980's.

**In lines 2 through 4, the military actions of the "Arab
Prince" of line one are delineated. The fact that military
movements will be directed simultaneously toward Iran
(east), Egypt (south), the Mediterranean (west), and
Turkey (north), points back to a single origin for the
invading forces--dead center from all these--Syria and
Iraq. This is, of course, the homeland of the cruel dictator
of the first verse, thus linking these two prophecies
together.**

61

The one enigmatic description is in line 4--"ver. serp." Most interpreters see this as an abbreviation for "vera serpens," or "true serpent." One interesting variation, however, is "serpent de verre"--"serpent of glass." The exact interpretation, of course, must await fulfillment.

18. *TWO NUCLEAR ACCIDENTS PREDICTED FOR EUROPE?*

The near major disaster at the Three Mile Island nuclear plant in Pennsylvania not long ago aroused concern the world over about the threat of worse radiation accidents occurring, and what effects they might have on a large population. In 1971, French clairvoyant Mario de Sabato forewarned that Britain is going to suffer just such a fate--"a research accident, probably nuclear," he envisioned, that will have "catastrophic results." This prophecy has confirmation in another, made by the celebrated "Brahan Seer," Coinneah Odhar Fiossaiche, in the seventeenth century. The Brahan Seer made several remarkable predictions about his native Scotland, all of which have come true with a prophetic accuracy of 95% to 97%. All, that is, except one prediction, yet to be fulfilled. In his usual cryptic way, he described how something which will look like "a dun hornless cow" will appear "in Minch" and will "bellow" so loudly that it will knock down "the six chimneys of Gairloch House," a local estate. What is amazing is that when the Seer spoke his prophecy, Gairloch House had no chimneys, but a recent restoration and expansion--made by an architect who knew nothing about the prophecy--included the addition of six chimneys. When these chimneys fall, the Seer warned, the whole area will witness "a horrid black rain" that will exterminate life. Scotland, he said further, will be so desolated that "the crow of the cock shall not be heard," and for a time, the survivors--only a handful--shall live in Ireland, having escaped by boat. Some interpreters see the "dun hornless cow" as a nuclear submarine that will accidently explode off the coast, contaminating northern Britain and the Scottish nation with deadly fallout. But this is only a guess--we will have to await the event to understand the exact meaning.

Another set of prophecies, which predict what appears to be a "China syndrome" situation to occur in southeastern Europe, comes to us from the French seer, Nostradamus. Two of his sixteenth century verses read:

Dans les cyclades, en perinthe et larisse,
Dedans Sparte tout le Peloponnesse:
Si grande famine, peste par faux connisse,
Neuf mois tiendra et tout le chersonese. V, 90.

L'horrible peste Perynte et Nicopolle,
Le Chersonese tiendra et Marceloyne:
La Thessalie vastera l'Amphipolle,
Mal inconnu, et le refus d'Anthonie. IX, 91.

In the Cyclades (islands s.e. of Greece), in Perinthus (e. Thrace) and Larissa (n. Greece),
In Sparta and the entire Peloponnesus (s. Greece),
Will be a very great famine, through disease caused by artificial dust,
It will last for nine months, throughout the Grecian peninsula. V, 90.

The horrible plague on Perinthus, and Nicopolis (w. Greece),
In the Peloponnesus Peninsula and Macedon (north of Greece) will it fall upon,
It will also devastate Thessaly and Amphipolis (n. Greece),
It will be an unknown evil, and for a leader named Anthony, a refusal to help. IX, 91.

The key is in the first verse, line three, where Nostradamus foresees that the terrible disease to strike Greece and the Balkans (Macedonia) will be caused by "Faux connisse." "Connisse" is from the Greek "konis" or "dust, particles, ash." But it is called "faux" or "false," a "false dust"--meaning that it is not of natural origin, but rather is *man-made*. The disease this dust will create is called in the second verse "an *unknown* evil"--in other words, it will produce an unnatural plague, one which even Nostradamus, as a physician, could not identify. In the sixteenth century, the idea that a disease severe enough to last nine months and cover an area the size of Greece and the Balkans could be caused by a man-made "dust" would have been considered nonsense. Today, however, being in the Nuclear Age, we recognize this strange dust and its effects as characteristic of radioactive fallout.

In the last line of the second verse, Nostradamus refers to a "leader named Anthony" who will be caught in the disaster, and to whom no one will give aid. In a third verse, the French prophet described "Anthony's" plight further:

Le grand Antoine du nom de fait sordide
De Phtiriase a son dernier ronge:
Un qui de plomb voudra etre cupide,
Passant le port d'elu sera plonge. IV, 88.

Anthony of great name, because of filthiness (infection, contamination),
His body covered by pediculosis (skin lesions, skin discoloring and itching),
He will be one who had desired lead,
Passing the port, the elected one will drown him.

The disease "phtiriase" or pediculosis is usually found with lice, but not always. Nostradamus used the term here because it was probably the closest he could come to, in describing "Anthony's" condition of being covered head to foot by ulcerous, bleeding, and itching sores. What is significant is that this would also be the appearance of a man who had suffered from a *severe exposure to radiation*. The third line contains the key: "He will be one who had desired *lead*." The metal lead is one element which radiation cannot penetrate and, used as a thick shielding, would offer the only source of protection. The last line of the verse suggests that "Anthony" will flee stricken Greece by sea, and seek to enter the port of some neighboring nation unaffected by the disaster. But the

64

people will fear his contaminated condition, and he will be refused permission to land. Then, by orders of an elected official, Anthony's ship will be sunk, so that he and everyone else aboard will not infect anyone else--and will not suffer from a lingering, painful death.

So far to date, there are no nuclear power plants in Greece, but recent news reports suggest that, upon Greece's entrance into the European Common Market, it will have easier access to the technology and financial capital for building the plants. By the mid-1980's, it is estimated Greece could have a number of nuclear power plants ready for full operation. But before the Greek government decides to give the "go ahead" on such a project, perhaps they should look at the potential dangers again--dangers as described by a prophet four hundred years ago.

THE THIRD THUNDER

19. A TWELFTH CENTURY PROPHECY ABOUT AMERICA

Perhaps the earliest vision ever made concerning the future of the United States was made by Saint Hildegarde, three centuries before the New World was discovered. She predicted that one day there would come forth "a great nation across the ocean that will be inhabited by peoples of different tribes and descent"--a good description of the American "melting pot" of immigrants from many foreign countries. For this future nation, however, the Saint sounded several warnings, all of which would come about near or at the time of the appearance of a "great comet." Some translaters believe what she had in mind was Halley's comet, scheduled to light up our heavens in 1986-7. Just before the comet comes, Saint Hildegarde forecast, "many nations" including America "will be scourged by want and famine." When the comet does finally pass over, it will herald two great calamities: First, "the great nation will be devastated by earthquakes, storms, and great waves of water, causing much want and plagues. The ocean will also flood many other countries, so that all coastal cities will live in fear, with many destroyed." The second calamity will be terrible war: In a great battle involving almost all the world's peoples, "the great nation will lose its colonies in the East," as a result of the malevolent activities of two Oriental leaders, alluded to only as "the Tiger and the Lion." While the United States has no colonies, it does have trust territories and military bases throughout the Pacific.

One curious event that will take place during this war, according to Saint Hildegarde, certainly was not understood in her day--but has grave implications in our times today. During the future fighting, "A powerful wind will rise in the North carrying heavy fog and the densest dust, and it will fill their throats and eyes so that they will cease their butchery and be stricken with a great fear." In modern terms, we might identify the "fog and dust" as some form of chemical or bacteriological weapon. If the Saint is right, then some enemy power will some day disperse this weapon in the Arctic, and let the prevailing winds carry the poison southward across the North American continent.

Fortunately, however, Saint Hildegard looked beyond, and also forecast that after the great comet, and after earth upheavals and wars are finished, the globe will eventually enter a peaceful age. It will be a time when citizens of the "great nation" will carry no weapons, and the only use men will have for iron will be to make plowshares for cultivating a land brought back to abundance and tranquility. Other comets shall streak past in the skies, but no more will they ever be an omen of disaster and terrible wars--for these things shall pass away from memory.

20. VISIONS OF CALIFORNIA--THE NEW ATLANTIS

Geologists for a long time have known that southern California is a "high risk" earthquake zone, with that portion of the state criss-crossed by several major earth fractures, the most notable being the San Andreas, which runs roughly from the north of San Francisco to the Gulf of California. There is no longer the question in the experts' minds *if* a disasterous quake is coming--the real questions are *when* and of what *intensity*. The potential for a major catastrophe looms very large, and it is no

68

great wonder that it has been the favorite subject of many a psychic and seer--as well as every day men and women who have recieved precognitive dreams and visions. What is remarkable is that many of the prophecies--made by people with no training or background in geology--conform precisely with what the experts know could really happen.

In 1969, the Future Foundation of Steinauer, Nebraska published a small book entitled *1970-1980 Prophecies of Cyrus*, containing "channeled" material on future events. The channel forecast that San Francisco will one day completely disappear into the Pacific, with nothing left "sticking out of the water." The California coast will be broken back toward the mountains. This, however, is to be the result of only the *first* of several large quakes, to bring about the subsidence of even larger sections of land than just the coast.

Robert C. "Doc" Anderson, who is known as the "Georgia Seer," and boasts a prophetic accuracy of 95%, predicted that in the *next decade*, or before 1990, a powerful quake will occur along the San Andreas, seriously damaging both Los Angeles and San Francisco. Ominously, there is only a little time left before Anderson's time element runs out.

More recently, an amateur psychic, Mrs. Diane McLeod, "saw" a seismic scale point to 9.2 Richters on Los Angeles--which would be the largest quake so far ever measured. At the same time, another scale showed 6.9 Richters in Sacramento, and even higher numbers for San Francisco. Many high-rise buildings, Mrs. McLeod envisioned, collapsed into rubble, and not far away, Mt. Shasta stirred and began to erupt. These however will be only the first signals for an even greater disaster, and those who understood the signs would leave in time. In the next quake, soon after the first, the ocean will rush in, covering most of Los Angeles, and other portions of California will similarly flood, with tremendous loss of life.

In March of 1967, a Mr. Jasper Pierce of Sumter, South Carolina, found himself being "taken" to above the Imperial Valley in California, a vantage point from which he witnessed the coast from San Francisco to the Gulf of California collapsing into the ocean, at the same time a

69

tremendous mass of molten rock pushed upward from beneath. Looking eastward, Pierce saw other disasters in progress: The Grand Canyon opening wider, and volcanoes spewed forth fumes which poisoned the entire Southwest; portions of the Rocky Mountains fell toward Colorado; and a wave of water swept over Florida and the Gulf states, as the entire East coast slowly rose 300 feet, as far west as the Mississippi valley.

One evening in September, 1958, Reverend Dr. Lindsey of Sacramento was given a vision, which moments after coming out of, he described in full on a tape recorder, so that he would not forget the details. In his vision, he was given indications that some time "beyond 1968" there would be three signs, just before a superquake is to hit California. First, Australia will suffer the greatest shock ever felt there; second, a volcano will erupt in the Mediterranean sea area, creating a devastating tidal wave; and third, cracks will appear in the city halls of both Los Angeles and San Francisco. These will be the portents that *within one year* a large part of California will fall into the ocean, causing tidal waves 150 feet high to completely circle the earth.

In predictions made only within the last few years, the descriptions for potential disaster have remained remarkably similar. Mr. David Miles, a traveling lecturer for a Washington-based aviation industrial firm, has had a series of "out-of-body" experiences: In the first, while driving in the San Francisco area, he suddenly found himself no longer in his car, but floating at a great height above the California coast. Suddenly, he saw the whole of Los Angeles, San Diego and Santa Barbara disappear beneath an advancing wall of water, as buildings collapsed and freeways swayed and buckled. When the commotion died down, all Miles could see was a vast expanse of water. In his other experiences, the lecturer keeps "seeing" the same huge wall of water bearing down on him, as he drives along the various thoroughfares of Los Angeles.

Danny Henry, a former citizen of Fontana, California, awoke one night in a cold sweat, having had a very vivid nightmare. He found himself atop Mount San Gorgonio,

70

which lies north of the town of Banning. The sun was in the west, and as Henry looked on, the whole country below began to tremble. From the valleys a great cloud of dust rose up, obscuring everything--but not before he saw a great crack appear, and everything beyond the Cajon Pass to San Bernardino quickly drop away. In the distance beyond, Henry saw the ocean coming, what he described as "a silver wave coming toward me." The waters filled up the areas that had dropped off, the waves dashing up against the cliffs left by the great fracture.

The image of a cliff's edge also figures prominently in a vision of Reverend C.F. Harrell of Phoenix, Arizona. He suddenly found himself "transported in the spirit" to a high cliff, and looking down he could see great numbers of people floating about in angry waters strewn with the wreckage of buildings, ships, cars and pavement. A tidal wave suddenly came upon them, and more of the coast was destroyed, the wave completely sweeping away San Bernardino. Elsewhere, other tidal waves caused damage around the world, particularly at Vancouver, British Columbia, and even the Eastern and Gulf of Mexico coasts of America. A voice told Reverend Harrell that the great quake will be preceded by three smaller quakes, as warning signs. The first will shake the entire coast from Mexico to north of San Francisco, and one will see some streets and freeways buckle. Just as this destruction will be cleared away and rebuilt, the second quake will strike; rebuilding will start again--and then the third shock will happen. After that, the superquake will not be far off. The Reverend, in a continuation of his vision, stood on a mountain above Los Angeles, and covered his ears from the roar of the hurricane and tornado winds accompanying the earth movement and tidal wave. In a single minute, he saw, ten million people will lose their lives. The shock and wave will cause the geologic understructure supports along the coast to give way, and all of California west of the San Andreas will slowly tip toward the ocean, then break off, leaving only a cliff wall behind.

Egon Schuetz, of Vancouver, British Columbia in Canada, has had several premonitions about California. First, he says, there is going to be an earth upheaval that will shake an area up to 300 miles in radius from the west coast, centering between Eureka and Los Angeles. Then--due to inherent weaknesses and instability of the Californian rock strata--movement of a great fracture *37 miles deep* will cause the shore all the way inland to the coastal mountains to fall away into the ocean. Cracks will also break up the San Joaquin Valley floor, and it too will be completely flooded.

One of the most dramatic prophecies concerning the future California cataclysm began back in the early fall of 1968, when Reverend Donald Abernathy of Bell Gardens, California had a visionary dream in which he saw fire shooting out all along the San Andreas. He experienced all the sensations of a giant earth tremor, and witnessed the sight of buildings toppling, and thousands upon thousands of people screaming in terror. Finally, mountains began crumbling, and they, together with the entire coastline, vanished beneath turbulent waters. The Reverend, overcome with these scenes of horror, asked the Lord for the time when this disaster will occur. He was not told, but in a second vision was shown a large red sun sinking in the sky--that this would be a sign. Soon after these visions, Reverend Abernathy began preaching what he had seen to his congregation. So clear and powerful was the import of his prophecy, that within three months all the members of his church, and four neighboring churches, moved out of California, and resettled in the East.

Still other premonitions, made in the last few years, have convinced people to also relocate to safer places. Sandra Hayes, the young daughter of Zolton Kurthy of Los Angeles, had a dream in which she found herself on the shore at Santa Barbara, on a clear and sunny day. Suddenly, there was a sound like thunder, and from Santa Barbara to Baja, Sandra saw "a tremendous pulling apart of the earth." Next, she was in Los Angeles, where she envisioned thousands of cars lined up bumper to bumper, barely moving. But out of the west came rushing waters, flooding the city, and piling up the cars into a large heap. The waters continued onward, sweeping through Santa Monica, Hollywood and Crenshaw--and then Sandra saw her own home, along with thousands of others, being

CALIFORNIA

obliterated by the watery waves. Sandra's parents, on the strength of her dream, have moved the entire family out of Los Angeles, to northern California.

There are still other visions which suggest that on the very day the west coast is destroyed, there will be those who will receive a last-minute psychic warning, and will convince others to leave while there is still time. Not long ago, Daniel Carlson of Garden Grove, California had a very clear dream in which he found himself and his family--his wife, two children and his mother-in-law--standing on a high plateau above Los Angeles. Their conversation revealed that on this day he had purposely driven to this spot, so that they could be safe from, and at the same time witness, a great destruction. As late afternoon approached, and nothing happened, Carlson's family became restless, especially his mother-in-law, who thought the whole trip had been pointless and wanted to return home. But suddenly, Carlson stretched out his finger toward Los Angeles, which had momentarily been lost to view in a rising cloud of dust. Despite this--and because the air was unusually free of smog that day-- they were still able to see tall buildings fall over as a huge crack appeared in the middle of the city. Streets and whole blocks tilted downward violently. Finally, a subterranean cave-in occurred, the city fell into the crevice, and within seconds the ocean came roaring in. A few minutes later, no sign of what had been a thriving metropolis remained--no building, tower, road or bridge. The Carlson's left their vantage point, to take a closer look. From a small hilltop near the water's edge, sitting in the ruins of a restaurant, they gazed over the new stretch of ocean, where Los Angeles used to be. Only a few people had escaped--a few, Carlson noted, who like himself had heeded their own prophecies and premonitions, and had left in time. These had endured ridicule by those who would not believe them, many of whom had been friends and relatives. Now those alive could only stand about, and mourn the tragic passing of those who had not listened.

21. THE "SOURCE" SPEAKS OF THINGS TO COME

Reverend Paul Solomon, of New Market, Virginia, has been called the "second Edgar Cayce." For the past several years since 1972 he has been the voicepiece of highly spiritual messages which bear resemblance in language and accuracy to the "sleeping prophet" of yesteryear. The Fellowship of the Inner Light is an organization which has grown up around Solomon, and has been actively promoting and publishing his words which they term "The Source." Among the "Source's" many teachings, ranging in subject matter from health and diet to spiritual growth and meditation, are interspersed warnings of events to come in our immediate future, with the promise of a better Age to be established in more distant times. Here is a brief survey of future events Solomon has foreseen:

We are about to enter a seven year period of famine, of which three "peak" years will be bad. People will fight in the streets over a scrap of bread, and currencies will have no value. This is the time, the Source suggests, to get out of large cities and coastal areas.

After the famine, there will be a very brief stabilizing period, but this will not fully develop, since we will then be entering into a time of war. This will be around the mid-1980's. Our nation, weakened by economic chaos and internal divisions, will be "attacked by another" world power or powers, who will attempt to "break in upon our shores." The fighting and destruction will be so serious that the Capital will be moved, to a Northern or Northwestern site.

The Source also reveals that America will some day be troubled by civil war brought about because of religious belief. Brother will oppose brother in the streets everywhere, much like the conflict presently going on in Northern Ireland. This too will contribute to the general weakening of this country as a great power.

There will also be a series of catastrophic earth changes to trouble America and the world, which will peak in the years 1982-1984, and even more disastrously about May 5, 2000, coinciding with certain planetary alignments at those times. In the Western Hemisphere, earthquakes will begin on the west coast of South America and progress northward, increasing in intensity as they move. Around 1984, the West coast of this nation will be struck, with several hundreds of miles eventually disappearing into the waters of the Pacific. Alterations on the East coast will follow, with portions of New York, Long Island, Connecticut and Massachusetts dropping off, and Florida cut off from Georgia by a strait of water. Meanwhile, land will rise both in the Pacific and Atlantic, forming new continents. The disasters on the West and East coasts will be caused by North America "folding" like a closing book, with the fold centering in the Mississippi valley. This entire region will be flooded by the waters of the Great Lakes, which will empty into the depression.

Other areas earmarked to suffer similar alterations will be many: Like Cayce, Solomon foresees Japan to slide into the sea, and changes to transform the face of northern Europe. Britain will someday be covered with polar ice. The biggest geological upheavals are scheduled for the second peak, in 2000. Strains on the earth's magnetism will cause a shifting of the poles, and wide displacements on the surface, so that it will take on a new shape and form.

Along with the dramatic alterations in the material world will occur parallel transformations in the spiritual realm, also affecting mankind. There is to be a spiritual polarization: On one side, there will arise a leader who in Italy will seize the Spear that pierced Christ as his power, and espouse the cause of the poor and the church, so that many will think he is the Christ returned. Even many well-versed in metaphysical teachings will make the mistake of casting themselves at his feet. But the Source identifies him as the Antichrist. Eventually, he will be the instigator of "infamous deeds" that will make those perpetrated in Germany during the last war "pale by comparison." In sharp contrast, another man will come forth who is a teacher of true spiritual wisdom. According to the Source, he is alive today, living somewhere in the Middle East, as a modern Hebrew, and we will begin to hear of his work beginning in 1980 or 1981. The Source calls him John "Peniel"—John who has "met God face-to-face." He will come to this country to bring his message of true love and brotherhood, and farther on, he will possess the Holy Grail as his power, ultimately defeating the Antichrist leader, in order to prepare for the Second Coming of the true Christ. On that day--during a horrendous battle among the nations the Source identifies as Armageddon--John will point to the sky, and everyone will behold the Light of the Divine One. The veil separating the physical and spiritual will be parted, and spiritual forces will join in the conflict. Those upholding the "Law of One" will be victorious--and "there will be set in motion that new system, that new order of all that is to be " The Source sums up what is to come in these words: "This ball of earth will be smashed flat and reformed into the birth of a new earth and reign of peace."

22. THE MONARCHY OF MOROCCO IS ABOUT TO BE OVERTHROWN

The Middle East and North African nations comprising the modern Arab world are not known for any degree of political stability. One notable exception has been Morocco, situated on the Atlantic coast, south of Spain. The King of Morocco--Hassan II--has done much to westernize his country, and has offered strong security for national and foreign business and industry. But according to one of Nostradamus' prophetic poems, the present Moroccan government's days may be numbered. Nostradamus, writing in 1558, said:

Au point du jour au second chant du coq,
Ceux de Tunes, de Fez, et de Bougie,
Par les Arabes captif le Roi Maroq,
L'an min six cent et sept, de Liturgie. VI, 54.

At daybreak, at the second crowing of the cock,
Those of Tunis (Tunisia), of Fez (northern Morocco) and Bougie (Algeria),
By these Arabs the King of Morocco will be captured,
Sixteen hundred and seven years after the development of the Liturgy.

The interpretation is pretty self-explanatory: Arab forces from Tunisia and Algeria, and guerilla forces from northern Morocco, will conspire together, and overthrow the Moroccan monarchy, making the King their prisoner. In the Mediterranean latitudes, the "second crowing of the cock" occurs soon after three o'clock in the morning. As for the date in the last line, it is usually understood to refer to the years transpired since the inception of the French Liturgy, by Auxentius some time between A.D. 355 and 374. "Sixteen hundred and seven years" from these dates gives us 1962 and 1981. So far the event has not been fulfilled--but there is still time left on the seer's prophetic clock. Between now and the end of 1981, watch your newspapers for what is happening in Morocco.

23. IMPERIAL ROME AND MODERN AMERICA--IS HISTORY REPEATING ITSELF?

Historical philosophers are prophets in their own right, for while the future may not be revealed to them by extrasensory means, they do receive important insights by finding parallels and cycles in the past which are often repeated in modern times--and could be repeated in times to come. There are, for example, many fascinating parallels between the history of the United States and ancient Rome. Like Rome, America already has: rejected a monarchy and become a republic; been involved in several wars not of her making, but from which in the end she always emerged victorious and stronger; tried to keep peace in the world by stationing her armies among her allies and territories under her protection; and now begins to show signs of weakness and instability from her overabundance of wealth and lack of further purpose. If we look at what happened to Rome in her twilight days, and use her history to extrapolate a future history for the United States, we might expect the following list of events to occur. Some of these, you will notice, are happening now, or at least have a potential of taking place in the not too distant future:

1. The President of the United States will gain greater powers, especially through the exercise of his being

Commander-in-Chief in times of war, and chief diplomat abroad.

2. Congress will become more and more ineffective in passing meaningful legislation, the powers of directing national policy falling solely to the President, with Congress remaining as a body of wealthy yes-men exercising petty individual politics only. Corruption and scandal will be the order of the day.

3. Real political influence will be held in the hands of powerful advisors, Cabinet members and various Pentagon and national security officials surrounding the President, who will be constantly involved in intrigues, vying with one another for Presidential favors and policy making. Eventually, these groups will have the power--like the Praetorian Guard of old--of presenting their own candidates for President to the people.

4. The nation will become a giant welfare state, with production left to the slaves of the modern age--the computers and machines. To keep idle Americans preoccupied, the government will sponsor "media events"--sports spectaculars, entertainment extravaganzas, political rallies, and even space shots.

5. Americans will become more concerned with security, and will even give up individual freedoms to attain it. Policing action and law enforcement will be left to private semi-military groups, and to a more powerful National Guard, backed by federal intelligence and security agencies. The armed forces will be composed of professional soldiers hired for pay--both American and foreign.

6. Production will fall, and America will become more and more dependent on imported goods. As a result of foreign markets being subject to revolutions, wars, embargoes and failing economies, Americans will have to put up with periodic shortages of luxuries and even essentials, disrupting the national economy.

7. American currencies will repeatedly be devalued--as Roman coinage was debased--and this will lead to a fixing of prices (as happened under Emperor Caracalla). Jobs will also be fixed, with no one allowed to change their profession, once chosen.

8. In the midst of increasing decadence, the American government will drop the seperation between church and state, and American leaders in a stand for conservatism, will attempt to become the nation's moral and spiritual leaders as well. Eastern religions will have great success among the masses, competing with the established yet languishing Christian churches. Eventually, the churches will compromise the basic principles of both Christian and Eastern beliefs, by creating a synthesis--a new form of religion that some day will have more influence than the failing American government.

9. America will see herself as the bulwark of civilization against the modern "northern barbarians"--Russia. But her repeated clashes with this power will leave both weaker (the Cold War, Korea, Vietnam). Eventually, the two will ally and join forces against the threat of the present-day Huns from the East--China.

Are these events going to happen, even as they happened to ancient Rome? The path we are on, and the direction we are heading, suggests they are. Perhaps the old saying is right: Where we have not learned the lessons of history, we are doomed to repeat those lessons.

24. THE COMING AVATARS--MESSENGERS OF HOPE

Among every people who believe in the God-Spirit, there are prophecies of the advent of a true Savior, or Avatar, who will guide mankind in the next Age.

Gautama Buddha, founder of the largest religion in the east, gave this prophecy before his death: "I am not the first Buddha who has come upon the earth, nor shall I be the last. In due time another Buddha will rise in the world, a Holy One, a supreme enlightened one, endowed with wisdom auspicious, embracing the Universe, an incomparable leader of men, a ruler of gods and mortals. He will reveal to you the same eternal truths, which I have taught you. He will establish his Law, glorious in its origins, glorious at the climax and glorious at the goal in the spirit and the letter. He will proclaim a righteous life wholly perfect and pure, such as I now proclaim. His disciples will number many thousands, while mine number many

81

hundreds. He will be known as Maitreya." Maitreya means "World Unifier," and Buddha further predicted that he and his followers will come to India "from the west, from the mountains."

Two Westerners who traveled through central Asia forty years ago--Professor Nicholas Roerich and Josephine St. Hiliare--noted several prophecies concerning the coming of Maitreya and the events to precede his appearance: "First will come an unprecedented war of all the nations. Brother shall rise against brother. Oceans of blood will flow. And the people shall cease to understand one another. They shall forget the meaning of the word Teacher. But just then shall the Teachers appear and in all corners of the world shall be heard the true teaching. To this word of truth shall the people be drawn. Already, many warriors of the teaching of truth are reincarnated. Only a little time more will elapse before everyone shall hear the mighty steps of the Lord of the New Era. And one can already perceive unusual manifestations and encounter unusual people. Already they open the gates of knowledge and ripened fruit are falling from the trees. And the Banner of Shamballa, the spiritual kingdom, shall encircle the central lands of the Blessed One. And the warriors shall march under the banner of Maitreya."

In the same regions of central Asia, it is also reported that even the tribes of the steppe country are discarding their ancient gods and are awaiting the soon arrival of the "White Burkhan," who will offer them and the entire world a spiritual rebirth.

Among the many schools of Mahayana Buddhism, there are prophecies of the coming Bodhisattvas--enlightened beings who by choice have denied themselves ascension to higher planes in order to help humanity as a whole struggle out of their material bonds. The next great Bodhisattva who is to incarnate on earth will be called Amida, and he is described to be Christ-like in his message and life.

A key figure who has popularized Tibetan Buddhism in the West is T. Lobsang Rampa, the mystic author of several books, including *The Third Eye* and *Chapters of Life*. According to Rampa, already many of the disciples and forerunners of the next Messiah have been born, the first of these in 1941. Before the birth of the Messiah himself, his coming will be preceded by geological upheavals, and an increase of the earth's heat, causing catastrophic reduction in rainfall, beginning in 1981. The Messiah will be born in 1985, and after an early life filled with special training, he will revolutionize the world spiritually beginning in 2005. During the next millenium following, his message will bring about a new way of life, with mankind evolving into fantastic and unexpected dimensions of being.

The second largest religion in the East is Hinduism, and among its adherents there is anticipation for a new *avatar* or savior. We are approaching the end of an Age of Darkness, and this period--as predicted in the *Vishnu Purana*--will be marked by a steady decline of human values coupled with rampant materialism and violence. But just before the cycle ends, divine influences will be felt that will lead to a complete transformation of the human spirit, readying it for the commencement of an Age of Light. Instrumental in this transformation will be the next avatar whose name shall be Kalki, or Javada, and he will be the ninth and last reincarnation of Vishnu, the god of Peace. His appearance (like Maitreya) will be from the west. In his last incarnation, as Lord Krishna, he spoke these words, recorded in the *Bhagavad Gita*: "I have been born many times and I remember my past lives. When righteousness is weak and faints, and unrighteousness exults in pride, then I return on earth. For the salvation of those who are good, for the destruction of evil in man, for the fulfillment of the kingdom of righteousness, I will come to this world, as in ages past."

Moving to the Middle East, we find the Moslems too await a spiritual leader, called by them Muntazar. He will be a successor of Mohammed, and will bring understanding to all the races of the world, beyond the end of time. Their cousins, the Jews, still await the coming of their Messiah, a Messenger from the God of their fathers who will restore His people to the blessings of the Chosen Race. And in the Christian New Testament, which had its origins in the Middle East, the second coming of Christ is mentioned over 300 times, more than any other topic or doctrine. For each time salvation is mentioned, the second coming is spoken of twice; where the apostle Paul speaks of baptism only 15 times, he alludes to the advent 55 times. If a message is to be considered by Christians important because of its prominence in the Scriptures, then the return of the Christ stands second to none.

Other religions, as well as various mystic and psychic sources, also foresee the coming of a promised Man of Peace. The Zoastrian Vestas of Iran believe that the present world will last for a period of twelve thousand years. The great spiritual leader Zarathustra came at the end of the ninth millenium, and that another like him--the Vestas predict--will be named Saoshyant, and will come at the end of the twelfth millenium to unite the world. Historians date Zarathustra as having lived about 1000 B.C., which means that Saoshyant is due to appear after A.D. 2000.

Helena Blavatsky, founder of theosophy, declared in the last century that we are at the very close of the cycle of 5,000 years of the present Kaliyuga or Dark age, which will be succeeded by the Satyayuga, or Age of Light. With the advent of every Age, the "Masters of Wisdom," adepts of higher spiritual knowledge, send forth a Messenger to teach the nations. The next great Messenger, Blavatsky predicted, will appear soon after 1975, and will begin guiding mankind when he reaches full maturity at the close of the twentieth century.

The Coptic Fellowship, founded in America in 1927 by Master Hamid Bey of the venerable Coptic Order of Egypt, honors the birth of the New Messiah as already taken place. Hamid Bey was an eye-witness to the event, as were twenty-one other Masters from many nations, gathered near Mt. Shasta, California on November 11, 1949. At that time, the child was taken away to a secret place, to begin learning, and prepare himself for his sacred mission. Today, as a man, he now walks the earth *incognito*, gathering his disciples from about the globe, and the Coptic Fellowship prophesy he will fully make his presence known to the world when the time is right, which could be around 1984.

84

Psychic Frank Bowman, in a book entitled *The Coming World Unifier*, written in 1944, did not forecast any specific time as to when the new Avatar would be born, but did feel that he would reveal himself for the first time near Benares, India--an event that will be missed entirely by the press. But as the movement surrounding him grows, he will soon after travel to the United States, and there on the West coast, his message will be clearly heard by all. He will gather about him those who had prepared the way--even many who have died, he will resurrect to join him. The first of these "servers," according to Bowman, was born as early as 1878.

One of America's most famous psychics, Edgar Cayce, gave several trance readings regarding the advent of the new Messiah, and other spiritual leaders. In 1936, when asked what changes we should expect by the year 2001, the slumbering Cayce said that a great spiritual outpouring promised by the prophets of old was already happening at that time, and that "soon there will appear in the earth that one through whom many will be called to prepare the way for His day on the earth"--in other words, a forerunner will come to gather the growing number of spiritual people to meet the coming Savior. Cayce, in another reading, called this forerunner "John Peniel." As to when the Savior himself is made known, the sleeping prophet indicated several times that this will happen at the very end of a period of earth upheavals, in 1998. At that time, "His light will be seen again in the clouds," or a sign will be given that the Christ is here, and--as Cayce described it--"begins then the *reign* in '98." At the same instance, many other spiritual leaders of the past will be reborn to aid in humanity's spiritual formation. One of these will be Cayce himself. Before his death in 1945, the prophet gave a reading concerning his future self, and communicated these words: "As this priest may develop himself to be in that position to be in the capacity of a liberator of the world in its relationship to individuals in these periods to come; for he must enter again at that period, in 1998." Beyond, in the 21st century, the coming Messiah and his helpers will inaugurate an age of human transmutation. Cayce foresaw: "He will walk and talk with men of every clime. Then, in groups, then masses, they shall reign for a thousand years, for this is when changes materially come."

Predictions of a coming Savior to the world have been made through the ages. The 12th century king and spiritual leader of Indonesia, Djojobojo, received a vision which to a large part has already been fulfilled to an amazing degree of accuracy. Looking from his own time, Djojobojo foresaw that after a few centuries had passed, his native islands would be conquered by a strange race of white-skinned, blue-eyed, fair-haired men. They were to rule the islands for three and a half centuries. The Dutch--who fit Djojobojo's"strange white race" perfectly-- colonized Indonesia from 1610 to 1942, a period of 332 years. Djojobojo next prophesied that the Dutch would be driven out by another race of men, these to be slant-eyed, yellow-skinned and dwarfish, to come from islands to the northeast. They were to stay in Indonesia for a very brief period of time. In 1942, the islands were invaded by the Japanese, who ruled over them only until 1946. After they had abandoned the islands, Djojobojo foresaw that Indonesia would once again be governed by its own people, but this would be a bad period, because there would be much division between brothers, between religions and races. Blood will flow, predicted the king, but soon after a great Spiritual leader will come from the west and unite the warring factions into a single peaceful world. Indonesia, as well as the rest of the nations, are indeed suffering from the division prophesied by Djojobojo, and will continue for years to come. But then the "Spiritual King" will enter, and in his advent he will fulfill the last segment of Djojobojo's prophecy--and the hopes of mankind.

Among many of the Indian tribes of Central and North America are prophecies concerning the arrival of a great Man of Understanding. Moctezuma, king and priest of the Aztec Indians, made this prediction to his daughter in 1519, the year that Cortéz and his Spanish conquistadores decimated Mexico and the Aztec civilization. In a vision given to him before his death, Moctezuma foresaw that other peoples would occupy his realm and these would establish a religion of Priests and a Cross. The Priests would carry out persecutions worse than the Aztecs ever inflicted on their neighbors. But after eight great cycles were to pass a great change was to come. Within and toward the end of the ninth cycle would be a brief Age of Battles, the Priests will disappear, the Cross remain and in the place of the Priests a man will arrive from the east representing true freedom and Faith. In Aztec chronology, a great cycle was fifty-two years long. The first cycle began in 1519; the ninth will end in 1987. This correlates with Tony Shearer's predictions in his book *"Beneath the Moon and Under the Sun"* (Sun Books, 1975).

Long before white men invaded their land, the Hopi Indians of the Southwest United States were told of the coming of white-skinned intruders who would treat them and their land with contempt. But these will meet with a terrific destruction at the hands of the "nations of ancient wisdom"--China, India, Egypt, and the Middle East. After the destruction will be rebuilding, and after the rebuilding there will eventually come a spiritual rebirth, and a light will appear to the Hopis out of the east, in the form of the True White Brother. He will wear a red cloak or red hat and will bring with him sacred signs. Accompanying the True White Brother will be two helpers, one with a Hindu swastika and a cross, the other with a sign of the sun. These three will together shake the earth and purify it, and make it once again a fit place to live.

The great Holy Man of the Ogalala Sioux, Black Elk, prophesied the coming of a spiritual Message from the east in the form of a man. Like the Hopi White Brother, this man will also be dressed in red, and Black Elk further described him to have long, flowing black hair and to be of a race different from either the white men or the Indians. The Message which this man will proclaim will spread like fire and encompass the world.

In 1912, many of the holy shamans among the Eskimo tribes of the far north received dreams, all picturing the same coming of a Prophet to their people. He will be light-skinned, but not entirely white; he will have a long-flowing beard and long hair; he will come from the east.

The Iroquois in Ontario, Canada were left with the tradition of the seer Deganawida, who died before the arrival of the first European settlers. Deganawida predicted that his people would face a time of great suffering at the hands of a giant white snake. Eventually, however, after the white snake will be engaged in a battle with a red snake, a period of peace will ensue in which the Indians will no longer be bothered by the white serpent. This period of peace, Deganawida further foresaw, will be marked by a great light to come to his people from the east. That light, he said, would be himself, reincarnated, to bring hope to all peoples and represent the spirit of peace.

25. THE SIXTH TRUMPET--A PROPHECY OF WAR FROM THE EAST

In the Book of Revelation, written by the apostle John at the beginning of the Christian era, we find these words in Chapter 6, describing a coming world conflict:

"Then the sixth angel blew his trumpet, and from the four horns of the altar of gold which stands before God, I heard a solitary voice saying, to the sixth angel who had the trumpet, Liberate the four angels who are bound at the great river Euphrates. So the four angels, who had been in readiness for that hour in the appointed day, month and year, were liberated to destroy a third of mankind. The number of their troop of cavalry was twice ten thousand times ten thousand (200,000,000); I heard what their number was. And in my vision the horses and their riders wore breastplates the color of fiery red and sapphire blue and sulfur (brimestone) yellow. The heads of the horses looked like lions' heads, and from their mouths their poured fire and smoke and sulfur. A third of mankind was killed by these three plagues of fire and the smoke and the sulfur that poured out from the mouths of the horses" (Amplified; Living).

There are a number of interesting points to consider here. First, the strange forces under the Sixth Trumpet are to originate "at the great river Euphrates," the major river system of the Mesopotamian valley. This river often represented the entire East in prophecy, for it was the barrier separating the West from the Orient. Second, the number of the troops mentioned under the Trumpet--200 million--is a number of only very modern proportions. Several Bible commentators have noted the disturbing fact that China today has a standing army of over 200 million men. It is also clear that the so-called "cavalry" has nothing to do with real horses and riders: Rather, the description of breastplates, and fire, smoke and sulfer fumes issuing from the "horses'" mouths, sounds like a modern tank or mobile artillery or rocket-launching vehicle, heavily armored, highly maneuverable, and quick to attack, the shells or rockets it fires leaving their deadly mark in the form of explosions of smoke, fire and fumes. Lastly, we may note the Revelation reference to the three colors--red, blue, and yellow. Nineteenth century Bible prophecy scholar Uriah Smith, a proponent of the historicist school of interpretation, noted that these three colors were predominant among the Arabs, Turkish and Mongol military dress and banners, during their conquests of North Africa, Spain and southeast and central Europe in ages past. Today, they are still to be found in most flags of the Middle East and Oriental nations. According to the futurist school, the Arabs and Chinese are to arise again, in a war of conquest as of old, and once more threaten the forces of the West with destruction.

26. "DECADES OF CATACLYSM"--EARTH DISASTERS FOR THE 1980's AND 1990's

Jeffrey Goodman, who has been a pioneer researcher and author in a promising new field called "psychic archeology," has also done ground-breaking investigation work into prophecies about upcoming world geologic alterations. In his book, *We Are the Earthquake Generation* (Seaview Books, 1978), Goodman tells how over the past few years he contacted a number of established psychics living all across the United States, and by personally testing them, has verified their high degree of prophetic accuracy. Going a step further, Goodman next asked the psychics in his test group--each one seperately and independent of one another--what earth changes we should expect both in this country and abroad, in the near future. The result of Goodman's queries was astounding: The outline of things to come that each psychic gave agreed with everyone else's, to a degree of exactness far above and beyond what the laws of chance would have permitted. Not only this, but the individual psychics also offered their own personal insights which, when added to the general framework, gives us a very detailed look at the future indeed. Here, then, are the catastrophes we can expect, as foreseen by Goodman's group:

From 1980 to 1985, the big news will be a series of large quakes to strike Alaska, western Canada, and the U.S. West coast. The recent violent eruptions of Mt. St. Helens in Washington, and the rising temperatures in the waters of Crater Lake, in California, are the first signs. Changing the way a modern map of these areas look: The Aleutian islands off Alaska will begin to disappear one by one; land will rise in the Bering Straits, eventually creating an Alaskan-Siberian landbridge; Vancouver, British Columbia will be threatened by inundations; a seaway will form through central Oregon stretching as far inland as Idaho; and a large chunk of California will break off into the ocean. Concerning the last disaster, the psychics agree that San Diego, Los Angeles, and San Francisco are to be severely affected, and that the breaking point will occur roughly along a line from Eureka through San Bernardino to the Gulf of California. The one thing the psychics do not see eye-to-eye on is what will happen to the broken "chunk:" Some see the whole thing will simply sink into the Pacific, but others think it will remain "afloat" as an island or series of islands, located off the new coastline. As warning signs that this major earth movement is to take place, the Colorado river will change its course, and the Imperial valley in southern California will begin filling with water.

Meanwhile, in the same five-year period, other catastrophes are predicted. A strong shock is to hit New York City, with sympathetic quakes damaging the East coast from Washington to Philadelphia. In New York, the lower part of Manhattan will completely vanish. The Midwest will also be plagued by disturbances--the Great Lakes and St. Lawrence river are to swell in size from faulting, while the first warning quakes will shake St. Louis and Memphis. These disasters, understandably, are foreseen to cause food shortages, and the American government will be barely able to aid the millions of victims in so many destroyed areas.

For the following half decade, 1985 to 1990, the cataclysms begin expanding in scope. The period will open with a well-defined chain of events around the world: First, India will be struck by tidal waves and quakes, and it will lose its coastlines and southern tip; second, Japan will suffer the same fates; third, an eruption of Vesuvius in Italy will trigger a shock wave felt as far as France and Scandinavia; fourth, Mount Pelee in the Caribbean will then erupt; fifth, following in three months, California will again be cursed with massive faulting, plus a shift in the Japan Current on the coast; and sixth, three more months later, what is left of New York City will be wiped out. This time, it appears, America will not be alone in receiving the brunt of the disaster--Europe and the Mediterranean area are also going to be shattered: Portions of the Irish and English coasts will sink away; massive shocks will strike in Italy, Greece and Turkey; and the Black Sea will expand as a result of a collapse of the Dardenelles, causing a subsidence and flooding in the Ukraine and Caucasus. Tremors will also affect Syria, Iraq, and Israel, and the western outlet of the Mediterranean shall be blocked by a rising around Gibraltar. So severe will some of these disturbances be, that the Earth's axis will tip a degree or two.

The picture of earth changes for the 1990's does not get better--in fact it gets far worse, as the cataclysms reach new dimensions of mass destruction. So great will the coming alterations be, that the psychics predict that the Richter scale, which measures degrees of earthquake intensity from 1 to 10 (each number representing ten times the destructive power of the previous number), will have to be revised to include *an 11 and a 12*. Once again, California will be shaken, and new portions of the coastline will start dropping off--but this time the fallings and landslides will not stop until the Pacific waters *reach Nebraska*. The new coastline formed will follow closely a line from Vancouver through Seattle eastward to Sheridan, Wyoming and continuing as far as North Platte, Nebraska, where it will swing south through west Kansas to Amarillo, Texas, then at El Paso return west, bypassing Phoenix and Yuma, returning to the present coast just south of San Diego. Putting it in starker terms, a third of the country will vanish. At the same time, however, most of the other two-thirds are not predicted to fare too well either: The entire coast from Massachusetts to the Carolinas will be inundated; the Great Lakes will be displaced, flooding the Mississippi valley; and large portions of Georgia, Alabama and Florida will also submerge. Elsewhere, in Europe, English lands will disappear, with the waters of the Atlantic to "lap at the door" of London; parts of Norway, Sweden and Finland are to break up; and Denmark will become an island, with Copenhagen forced to relocate. New lands will rise in the Atlantic and Pacific, including an island west of Britain, a 100-mile uplift off the California coast, and islands off western South America. The latter will cause western South America to be rocked by massive shocks, and the southern portion of the continent will break away. On the other side of the world, Russia's northeastern coast will sink away; China's land will also fault, with large lakes forming west of Peking; Indonesia's volcanoes will all explode at once; land will rise south of India; and Japan and Hawaii will almost completely disappear.

At the end of this last period, about the year 2000, the psychics foresee that the mounting world disasters will directly affect the Earth in the severest of ways, causing the globe to shift on its axis again, only this time the poles will completely change positions. The planet will literally "tumble over" for several days, but eventually stabilize once more. New climates and geographies will then be established, and the psychics agree unanimously that afterward, mankind will be given the opportunity of creating a new civilization that will not repeat the mistakes of the Present Age.

THE FOURTH THUNDER

27. DARK DAYS FOR THE PAPACY AHEAD

Over the past few years, Washington seeress Jeane Dixon has received psychic impressions and visions concerning the future of those who sit in the Chair of St. Peter, as head of the Roman Church -- and what she foresees is ominous indeed. By the end of the century, she predicts, one Pope will be wounded and another killed. The latter, Mrs. Dixon forecasts, will come to power as a result of a very controversial Papal election. He will not have the approval of the majority of his fellow Churchmen, and at the end of his brief rule, he will die violently--a death which will involve a number of Cardinals. With the end of his reign, there will be a complete restructuring of ecclesiastic power, and thereafter, a board of powerful Cardinals shall rule the Church.

Mrs. Dixon has linked her prophecy of the coming papal assassination with the mysterious "Prophecy of Fatima." In 1958, while attending Mass in St. Matthew's Cathedral in Washington D.C., the seeress received a vision in which an image of the Virgin Mary appeared before her. To the right and above the apparition, mists were brought together that formed the word "Fatima," and below it she saw the throne of the Pope. The throne was empty, but off to one side she saw a Pope with blood running down his face and left shoulder. The picture of the stricken Pope vanished, but the throne remained empty. Hands reached out for it, but no one sat in it, even though the throne continued to radiate a strong light. Mrs. Dixon interpreted the vision to mean that the long-kept secret "Prophecy of Fatima" had been revealed to her: A future head of the Holy See will be assassinated while away from the seat of power, in Rome. Thereafter, the Church will have a new kind of leadership, different from the Papacy.

The story of the mysterious "Prophecy of Fatima" began in the Cova da Ira, a dale not far from Fatima, Portugal. Here, three small children tending sheep were visited by the spirit Virgin Mary, and given a number of prophecies. One of these prophecies has yet to be divulged. On one appearance of the spirit, the children received a most important prediction which one of them--a girl named Lucia--sealed in an envelope and sent to the Bishop of Leira. Later, in 1927, another spirit appeared to Lucia, instructing her that the unopened prophecy was to be kept secret until 1960, and was to be sent to the Pope. The envelope was finally opened in the appointed year by Pope John XXIII--who, witnesses to the event testify, turned pale when he read its contents. Unfortunately, Pope John saw fit that the prophecy remains secret. Jeane Dixon believes the secret of Fatima was revealed to her, and it describes the violent death of the Successor of Peter in the near future, and the decline of Papal authority as the center of the Church.

Another modern prophetess, Chicagoan Irene Hughes, claims that the secret of the "Prophecy of Fatima" was also revealed to her psychically, and she too believes it pertains to a future reorganization of the Church hierarchy that will greatly affect the office of the Holy See. She predicts further that in the very near future the "Prophecy" will be released to the public, not on purpose, but by accident.

The wounding of one Pope and the murder of another, and the events surrounding these tragic acts, were also prophesied by Nostradamus in the sixteenth century. In several of his prophetic quatrains, he described how one day Rome will be attacked by Eastern powers using terrible weapons which will cause fire and disease, and that as a result the Pope will be stricken, and led out of Italy in captivity. Shortly thereafter, the surviving Cardinals, having moved the seat of Church power elsewhere, will elect a "caretaker" pontiff who will greatly antagonize them:

Very near the Tiber (Rome) will threaten the Libyans (the Arabs),
Shortly before there will be a great flood,
The sacred Chief (the Pope) will be captured, and imprisoned,
The castle (San Angelo) and palace (the Vatican) in flames. II, 93.

In the places put to fire, they will flee because of disease,
The weather fickle, the wind brings death to three leaders,
Great thunderbolts will fall from the sky, devouring the estate of the Shaven Ones (the Cardinals; the Vatican),
The Great One (the Pope) nearly killed, his successor will barely rule. Presage 98.

Through fire from the sky, the city almost burned, consumed,
At the same time there will be tremendous flooding,
Sardinia will be vexed by the North African (Arab) fleet,
And the Church will vacate her seat of power. II, 81.

The great star (Halley's comet?) will burn for seven days,
The cloud will cause two suns to appear (atomic explosion?),
The great dog (siren?) will howl all night,
When the great Pontiff will be forced to change country. II, 41.

By the power of three nations at war,
The Holy See will be moved elsewhere,
Where a new Pope will receive the spirit,
And the Church will have a new center. VIII, 99.

    The future scene of a Pope having to leave the Eternal City amid great destruction is one that has been shared by others with psychic foresight. In the 13th century, John de Vatiguerio envisioned that one day, at a time "the world is grievously troubled," "the Pope will change his residence," and there will be no rulership and no Pope of the Church of Rome "for twenty-five months." One hundred years later, John of the Cleft Rock prophesied, "Towards the end of the world, the Pope and his Cardinals will have to flee Rome in tragic circumstances to a place where they will be unknown. The Pope will die a cruel death in his exile." Nicholas of Fluh, in the 15th century, likewise foresaw a time when the Church will be left desolate "without Peter or his successors," while the ancient "Prophecy of Premol" portended the day when "Rome will collapse in tumult, and the King with the Cross and Tiara (the Pope) shall wipe the dust of debris from his shoes, before hastening in his flight to other, distant shores."

In the last century, the Catholic visionary Helen Wallraf foretold that "some day a pope will flee from Rome in the company of only four Cardinals." Her contemporary, the Augustinian nun Anna-Katerina Emmerick, received clear pictures of a pope in hiding, who will be very weak, and exhausted by many sorrows and tribulations. This will occur at a time when the Vatican has been engulfed in flames from top to bottom, and only the Sanctuary and the Main Altar will survive. Planks of wood will be erected to block off the destroyed section, so that Mass may again be performed. But for the exiled pope, there will be little hope--he will be ill-fed, weakened, allowed to have only an aged priest at his side. Finally, the pontiff's head will nod to his chest, as he dies, sitting alone in a large chair....

In 1874, the mysterious Church mystic Don Bosco wrote a letter, still kept in the Vatican archives, in which he warned Pope Pius IX of a time when a brilliant light would suddenly flare up in the sky, while a great battle waged round about. At that instance, a Pope and a procession of his priests will come out of the Vatican and slowly walk through a square "covered with dead and wounded, who appear to be crying for help in a loud voice." Not only in the city of Rome, Don Bosco declared, but the whole "countryside and landscape will be much denuded of population, the ground churned up as if by a hurricane, and there will be a heavy shower of hail." For "two hundred sunrises," he further predicted, the Pope and his small retinue will be forced to wander, and in strange, foreign lands.

A strikingly similar vision was given to Pope Pius X, in 1909. During an audience of the General Chapter of Franciscans, the Pontiff suddenly slumped forward for several minutes, and upon regaining consciousness, rose from his seat in agitation. "What I have seen is terrible," he said. "Will it happen to me? Will it happen to my successor? What I know for certain is this: The Pope will one day have to quit Rome, and in leaving, he will have to be carried out, and over the dead bodies of his priests. He will be taken away in disguise some where, and in forced retirement, he will die a miserable death."

While the wounded Pope remains a prisoner in enemy hands, according to Nostradamus, those Cardinals who will escape the holocaust will elect a new Church head--only his election will be a stormy one, eventually leading to his assassination by certain ecclesiastic officials:

The great Pontiff taken captive,
The Great One succeeding will fail the Clergy disasterously,
He will be elected while absent from his ruined estate (Rome),
Where his favorite ministers will have been slain. V, 15.

The great fishery (the Church) will complain and weep,
Over the choice it has made, deceived about his vitality,
He will want to remain with them little, and will travel far,
Plotted against by those of his own tongue (Latin). VII, 35.

The last but one to be called Pope,
Will work and rest by the light of the moon,
He will wander far, his head filled with distractions,
Seeking to deliver his great people from oppression. II, 28.

Elected as Pope, he will be mocked by those who elected him,
Unexpected, sudden, prompt and timid,
With too much good nature; he will be murdered,
And night shall see the deadly embrace of his death. X, 12.

He who will have the government of the Great Cloak (the Papacy),
Will be pressured to perform several deeds,
Twelve ones will come to stain the cloth,
Under murder, murder will come to be perpetrated. IV, 11.

Roman Pontiff, beware of traveling near
The city that two rivers flow through,
Near there, your blood will spurt,
You and others, when the Rose will flourish. II, 97.

The Royal Priest (the Pope) bowing low (during Mass),
A great flow of blood will come out of his mouth,
The Angelic realm (the Church) believing itself saved from danger,
And its former ruler, still alive, will die in Tunis (North Africa). X, 56.

When the sepulchre of the famous Roman is found,
The day after a Pontiff will be elected,
Approved by the Senate of Cardinals by a slim majority,
He will be poisoned, his blood found in the sacred chalice (of the Mass). III, 65.

In the last verse, the "sepulchre" or grave that will be discovered on the day after a Pope to be murdered is elected, seems to have been of special interest to Nostradamus, for the prophet devoted fragments of four quatrains in giving clues as to how, when and where it will be unearthed. Here are the fragments:

When the new sect of believers is founded,
The bones of the great Roman found,
A sepulchre covered by marble will appear,
The earth to quake in April, poorly buried. VI, 66.

The bones of the Triumvir will be found,
While some look for a deep, enigmatic treasure,
Those from thereabouts will not rest easy,
Digging for this thing of marble and metallic lead. V, 7.

Torrents of water will open the tomb of marble and lead,
Of the great Roman with the Medusine device. IX, 84.

A deep column of fine porphyry found,
Under the base inscriptions of the Capitol,
Bones, twisted hair, Roman, forced open. IX, 32.

The ancient remains, Nostradamus stipulated, will be
of a "Roman Triumvir." There were only six such famous
men in ancient Rome: Julius Caesar, Pompey, Crassus,
Octavius Augustus, Marc Antony, and Lepidus.

At the time of the Pope's assassination, Nostradamus
predicts that the Church's new seat of power will be in
America:

Not long happy, he will be abandoned by his followers,
In the year disease strikes, the Sacred One (the Pope)
struck down,
When the Great Lady (the Church) will be in the Elysian
Fields,
And the greater part of fruits left unpicked because of
disease. Presage 61.

In Greek mythology, the Elysian Fields were equivalent
to Paradise, and were located in the far west, across the
Ocean.
During its American sojourn, and soon after the murder
of the Pope, the Church will come under the influence of
American clergymen, who will act to eliminate the office
of the Papacy as the sole rule of the Church:

After Libra (the astrological sign for the Roman Church) has been desolated and abandoned,
And the successor of the Great Pontiff will wander far,
He will be struck down by those of Septentroinale (the New World),
By those who eventually will possess the Chalice (Church power). VI, 82.

The eldest daughter of the British Isle (America),
Born fifteen years before her brother (France; 1776-1791),
By promise a procurement verified,
She will succeed to the kingdom of the balance (Libra; the Church). IV, 96.

Libra (the Church) will see the Hesperians (Westerners, Americans) govern,
Holding the monarchy of heaven and earth (the head of the Church),
No one will see the forces of Asia perishing,
Seven will no longer comprise the Hierarchy, the Church order. IV, 50.

Seven is the present number of ecclesiastic positions in the Church--the last line in the last verse predicts that this power structure-- which includes the Papacy--will be dissolved.

In one of the Nostradamian quatrains noted previously, we read that when the last Pope is murdered, "the Rose will flourish." The "Rose" appears to be a Church leader who will head the board of ruling Cardinals, who will eventually lead the clergy back to Rome when the war with the East comes to an end. Here again, we find references to the fact that while the Church will survive the conflict, the office of the Pope will not:

Into the Antique land (Italy), fountain of wisdom,
There will return the Rose,
The Papacy ruined, no longer pre-eminent,
It will be overthrown, Peter's bark a wreck amid the waves. V, 31.

The "Rose" Churchman, however, will institute changes that will lead to the greatest disaster for the Church of all:

In the middle of the world (Rome) shall rule the Rose,
Because of new edicts, blood will be publicly shed,
To speak the truth, everyone will shut their mouths,
Then at that time will the *Awaited One* come forth. V,96.

What is to happen in the Church at this point finds an historical analogy in the French Revolution. The French people overthrew the Bourbon monarchy of Louis XVI in order to gain liberty--but in the end all they succeeded in accomplishing was to clear the path for the rise of a greater and more powerful dictator, Napoleon. In the same way, the Church clergy may one day feel it will be time to do away with the Papacy, and the concept of a sole absolute ruler. But by so doing, they will open the door to one who will step in to dominate the Church more completely--and ultimately to its utter ruination. In the verse above, Nostradamus called this coming man the "Awaited One:" in the following quote, taken from the prophet's letter to Henri II, he describes this person in greater detail:

"There will come forth one who will reorganize the whole of Christianity. A great peace will be enforced, with union and concord between those of opposite beliefs and philosophies overseen. And thus the universal kingdom of the Furious One--who will counterfeit and impersonate the Sage (Christ)--will be consolidated."

Nostradamus is predicting here that a Savior figure will appear who will claim to fulfill Messianic hopes, and will offer his brand of peace to a war-weary world. He will reorganize the Church, and consolidate Christianity and the other major religions into a One World Church and a One World Religion. The world's inhabitants will give him the power to enforce a universal Pax in Terra, a Peace on Earth, in the political and international realms. He will claim to offer hope, but in actuality he will be the Antichrist, a false Savior.

In a concluding verse, Nostradamus prophesied:

In the world there will be one Ruler,
A peace, but not for very long,
When the fishing bark (the Papacy) is lost and gone,
The Church then ruled to its great destruction. I, 4.

The false Savior will usurp power in the Roman Church at the time the Papacy no longer exists. He will institute a forced World Peace, but it will only last a short time, and the "Savior's" policies will eventually prove disasterous for both the Church and the world....

28. A VISION OF WORLD-DEATH AND WORLD REBIRTH

One of the most dramatic prophecies of the ending of the Present Age and the dawning of the New comes to us from Scandinavia, its origins lost in the dim mists of prehistory. It is called the "Ragnarok" or the "Dusk of the Gods," and captures the tragedy of the world lost, and the triumph of a world revived to new life:

In mid-air sang the Vala, a prophetess who knew of the end of all things--the destiny of the gods and men, the last terrible war and Odin's death, and the coming of Surtur, whose flames shall one day engulf the world. Odin sat on his golden throne and listened in silence to what the Vala said, for he already knew what was to come. From his youth he had foreseen the "Ragnarok," and now he had grown old.

The Vala lifted her voice at high noon, and spoke: The Age of Evil has come to the world--the Age of Knives, Battle-axes and Split Shields. The warlike fall upon the peaceful, brothers kill brothers, and even children spill one another's blood. Everyone steals and hoards great wealth, and sensual sin prevails. The end of the world is nigh--yet men are hard and cruel, and listen not to the doom that is coming.

Now follows the Age of the Northern Winds. Swords clash against an ever-darkening sky. Fierce beasts, in terror, leave their habitations in forests and mountains and deserts to seek their prey among men. No one heeds the cries of his neighbor, or lifts a hand to save.

Fimbul Winter now comes. All over the world, the heavens are filled with falling snows, and the ground is covered with killing frosts. The sun is dimmed, it offers no gladness, while never-ending storms blow and devour the crops. In vain do men await the coming of summer. Three times winter follows winter over a world imprisoned in snow and ice, yet despite these perils, men still wage war, blood is shed, and Evil grows still greater.

Now, at the appointed time, the Midgard serpent is shaken with tremendous rage. It trembles and quakes on Ocean's slimy floor, so violently that its motions cause waves to sweep across the Midgard earth, as high as the mountains. It raises its terrible head out of the sea--fire and fumes it shoots forth. At the same time, the world's mountains shake and the rocks tremble, and the giant maidens are stricken with terror. Mortal men in Midgard are killed in great numbers, and their shades crowd the path to Hela. The sky begins to stretch, and finally breaks in half, because Surtur now comes forth....

On the plain of Vigrid is the last battle fought. It is a hundred miles by a hundred miles, enclosing the forestlands of Vidar the Silent, where Odin is doomed to die. From the east drives Hrym, his defender covers him with his shield, and his hordes follow him. The hosts of Evil now clash against the godly host of Asgard.

Suddenly, in the skies, a disaster occurs. Closer and closer the wolf Skoll has crept toward the sun, and finally devours it. The heavens are blackened at noon, the earth turns red with blood, and the seats of the mighty giants drip with gore. The moon, too, is swallowed, by Hati-Managarm, and the stars vanish from the sky.

Now Surtur finishes the end of creation. He aims his firebrands against the last warring gods, and they are burned up. The Midgard earth is swept with fire, and the smoke curls about the mountain peaks. Even heavenly Asgard is scorched, the flames enveloping the withering world trunk of Ygdrasil. Earth, smoldering and blackened, sinks into the Ocean, and the waves slowly cover it....

Yet now, when all seems lost, miraculously a new dawn has come. The sun shines bright again, for Balder the Peaceful has returned. Earth rises a second time from the sea, clad with green pastures and forests--a thing of beauty to behold. The morning air is filled with the sounds of falling waters.

In this new Earth, Evil has ended and every ill has ceased. Balder the Peaceful has indeed returned, and together with Hodur the Faithful, he takes up residence in the empty and silent halls of Odin. Lifthraser and Lif, and their offspring, who are the regenerating race, come out of their hiding places in Mimer's subterranean realm, to inhabit the Midgard earth. Pure are they, the members of this new race, and without stain. The food they share with one another in Time's second morning is honey-dew, and their children shall overspread the earth. And at the center of the world the elders of the new race shall dwell in their hall which is called Gimle. It shines brighter than the sun, with a roof of pure gold, and it rises as high as the heavens. Here indeed shall the holy ones live in peace and eternal joy forever more....

29. SABATO--THE PROPHET EXTRAORDINAIRE

A living Frenchman, Mario de Sabato, is fast becoming one of Europe's most widely recognized professional clairvoyants. In 1971, he published a list of predictions for the world--and many have already come true with amazing accuracy. For example, his list forecasts that Italy would suffer from earthquakes and left-wing agitation; Portugal (which in 1971 had a stable government) was to become "avant-garde" with a "leader of the opposition;" a "restoration of the monarchy" will happen in Spain; a coming sudden fall of the monarchy in Iran; a revolution in Ethiopia; an international crisis in Angola; and the end of American involvement in Vietnam, with the country "eventually completely communist," and "then a new war brought about by China" will occur--fulfilled in the subsequent Chinese border invasions.

For the near future, Sabato foresees that the United States will be plagued by a "severe economic crisis," and "one man's folly will endanger peace." Beyond, America will join in collaboration with a "capitalist" Soviet Union in a conflict with China. The warning signs will be political crises in Turkey, Pakistan, Taiwan, and Korea, and escalating Sino-Indian border skirmishes. The Chinese, Sabato portends, will invade into Europe, not to be halted until they reach eastern France. The war will also involve the Middle East, where oil wells are to be ignited across the entire Sahara. Eventually, the Chinese will be defeated, and Peking completely destroyed. Following will come a "short period of world harmony," with Paris becoming the capital of a United Europe, the Soviet Union joining in "cooperation with Christianity over the reorganization of Eurasia," Brazil chosen as the leader of a United South America, and the United States absorbing the Central American states.

Further in the future--after the year 1993--a true Golden Age will dawn, with a "new evolution of man in every sense." The Age will begin with a "Progressive" period lasting 170 years, also with a 370-year period designated "Prophetic," with special emphasis placed on the era from 2547 to 2737. Between 2003 and 2031, a "mysterious man" will arrive, a Christ figure who shall "settle the problem of good and evil and also the whole system of the after-life, the discarnate and reincarnation." Other Messiahs will also come forth, some from other worlds, and their teachings will reveal how the human race will be able to advance tremendously in only a few years. "Wretchedness will no longer exist," Sabato promises, and the concept of the "end of the world" will finally be understood as having been "merely a kind of purification." In the centuries to come, man will achieve "complete freedom of conduct," and will be able to visit other worlds and other, more advanced spiritual civilizations, to evolve and expand awareness still further. At the close of the Golden Age, the Earth's atmosphere and sky will turn a bright orange, and around the year 2800, an even better age, of higher dimensions for mankind, will begin.

30. WILL YOU BE READY FOR THE GREAT BLIZZARD OF 1981?

Astrologers who specialize in weather forecasting recognize that there are certain planetary aspects which bring on unusually hot summers and droughts, or on the other extreme, terrible winters of freezing temperatures, high winds and heavy snowfalls. One aspect, by itself, is a portent of some proportion; two coinciding together indicates an unusually severe condition. But when *several* aspects suddenly loom on the astrological horizon in a very short time of each other, then the predicted weather will be more than something to sit up and take notice of--it will be an event people will need to make special preparations for. The winter of 1981-1982 is going to be such an event. According to the astrologers, at that time 1) Saturn will be on the celestial equator, creating cloudiness, low barometer readings, and greater snowfall; 2) Saturn-Uranus conjunctions indicate long cold spells; 3) a Mercury-Uranus conjunction in late 1981 will be the harbinger of high winds and extreme low temperatures, with special warnings of severe conditions for the American Northeast and Northwest; 4) Jupiter and Saturn will both be in conjunction and parallel, and will produce violent storms and blizzards; and 5) negative positions between Jupiter and Uranus will bring hurricane-like winds and freak electrical storms. These aspects, in turn, are part of a much larger configuration involving almost the entire solar system: In late 1981, a grand configuration will be shaping up, with the Earth and Moon situated on one side of the Sun, and Mercury, Venus, Mars, Saturn, Neptune and Pluto on the other side, across 85 degrees of celestial longitude. This, the weather astrologers warn, will help accentuate an already terrible winter. There are some indications, in fact, that this grand aspect will also be felt during the *previous* winter, beginning about Christmas, 1980, peaking about January 25, 1981, and not ending until March.

The years 1980 and 1981 will not be the only future years to see radical weather aberrations, for other years beyond are also earmarked for trouble: In 1986, Mars will be in perigree and at one of its nearest approaches to the Earth, plus at the same time Halley's comet is predicted to return to our skies. Some forecasters believe that the combination of Mars' and the comet's aspects will produce a cataclysmic heat wave. Two years later, in 1988, three consecutive conjunctions of Uranus and Saturn in the last degrees of Sagittarius will create extreme drought, especially in February, June and September. This aspect, coupled with Neptune and Mars in southern parallel of declination, indicates a winter that will be even worse than the one predicted for 1981. Surviving this, we can look forward to 1993, when a powerful Uranus-Neptune conjunction in Capricorn will occur in February and March, and again in September, October and November, producing yet another especially bad winter.

Each of these times of erratic weather--especially for 1980, 1981 and 1988--the astrologers forewarn have the potential to break all existing records, and could bring in their wake great property damage, suffering and loss of many lives. What is very alarming is that if the present energy crunch and oil shortages continue to grow, we will be in an even worse shape to face the first of these "terror winters," only a very short time away. More than this, if adequate preparations are not made beginning *now*, we could face a real economic crisis, and even food shortages, due to the destruction of crops and livestock. We have the warnings--what will happen depends on how well we listen to them.

31. THE STORY OF THE OLD INDIAN

On a blistering hot summer day in 1958, a minister named David Young was driving along a highway that stretched through desert country, not far from Taos, New Mexico. Toward noon, he saw an elderly Indian walking on the road's gravel shoulder, and knowing he must be suffering from the heat, Young stopped and asked him if he would like a ride to the next town. The old man nodded, and got in.

For several minutes, the Indian said nothing, but then he finally spoke: "I am White Feather, a Hopi of the ancient Bear Clan. In my long life I have traveled through this land, seeking my brothers, and learning from them many things of wisdom. I have followed the sacred paths to my people, who inhabit the forests and many lakes in the east, the land of ice and long nights in the north, the mountains and streams of jumping fish in the west, and the place of holy altars of stone built long ago by my brothers' fathers in the south. From all these I have heard the stories of the past, and the prophecies of the future. Today, many of the prophecies have turned to stories, and few are left--the past grows longer, and the future grows shorter.

"And now White Feather is dying. His sons have all joined his ancestors, and soon he too shall be with them. But there is no one left, no one to recite and pass on the ancient wisdom to. My people have tired of the old ways--the great ceremonies which tell of our origins, of our Emergence into the Fourth World, are almost all abandoned, forgotten. Yet even this has been foretold. The time grows short."

The old Indian fell silent again, but after a minute spoke once more: "My people await Pahana, the lost white brother, as do all our brothers in the land. He will not be like the white men we know now, who are cruel and greedy. We were told of their coming long ago. But still we await Pahana.

110

"He will bring with him the symbols, and the missing piece of that sacred tablet now kept by the elders, given to him when he left, that shall be restored to the tablet and make it whole. This shall identify him as our true white brother."

Turning to Young, he said: "You are much like Pahana, and not like other white men. You stopped to give an old man a ride, to lighten his burden. That is the way of Pahana. He will come soon, for the prophecies are nearly done."

Resting a moment, the Indian found his breath, and then continued: "The Fourth World shall end soon, and the Fifth World will begin. This the elders every where know. The Signs over many years have been fulfilled, and so few are left.

"This is the First Sign: We were told of the coming of white-skinned men, like Pahana, but not living like Pahana--men who took the land that was not theirs. And men who struck their enemies with thunder." Young later realized this is how the Indian prophets would have described gunpowder.

"This is the Second Sign: Our lands will see the coming of spinning wheels of wood filled with voices. In his youth, my father saw this prophecy come true with his eyes--the white men bringing their families in wagons across the prairies.

"This is the Third Sign: A strange beast, like a buffalo, but with great long horns will overrun the land in large numbers. These White Feather himself' saw with his eyes--the coming of the white man's cattle.

"This is the Fourth Sign: The prairie will be crossed by snakes of iron...." At that moment, Young slowed his car to drive over a railroad crossing--and this time it was his own eyes, looking down miles of winding track, that saw how the prophecy had been fulfilled.

"This is the Fifth Sign: The land shall be criss-crossed by a giant spider's web." The Indian stopped, and glanced for a second upward at the telephone and electric lines that flashed past alongside the highway.

"This is the Sixth Sign: The land shall be criss-crossed with rivers of stone that make pictures in the sun." The

Indian paused again to let Young puzzle over the meaning of his words. Suddenly, he understood, for he was seeing it right in front of him: The concrete road stretched ahead, and in the distance, the shimmering heat waves produced a mirage, an image of the road itself just above the surface. The Indian nodded and went on.

"This is the Seventh Sign-- and it is the first that is yet to come: You will hear of the sea turning black, and many living things dying because of it.

"This is the Eighth Sign: You will see many youth, who will wear their hair long like my people, come and join the tribal nations, to learn of their ways and wisdom.

"And this is the Ninth and last Sign: You will hear of a dwelling-house in the heavens, above the earth, that shall fall with a great crash. It will appear as a Blue Star. Very soon after this, the ceremonies of my people will cease.

" These are the Signs that great destruction is coming. The world shall rock to and fro. The white men will battle against other peoples in other lands--with those who possessed the first light of wisdom. Terrible will be the result. There will be many columns of smoke and fire such as White Feather has seen the white man make in the deserts not far from here"--Young immediately knew he meant the atomic bomb tests. "Only those which come will cause disease and a great dying. Many of my people, understanding the prophecies, shall be safe. Those who stay and live in the places of my people shall also be safe. There will then be much to rebuild. And soon--very soon afterward--Pahana will return. He will bring with him the dawn of the Fifth World. He shall plant the seeds of his wisdom in their hearts. Even now the seeds are being planted. These shall smooth the way to the Emergence, into the Fifth World.

"But White Feather shall not see it. I am old and dying. You--perhaps you will see it. In time, in time...."

The old Indian's voice faded, and then went silent. They had arrived at his destination, and he pointed to the corner where he wanted to get off. Young stopped the car, let the old Indian out, and watched him slowly disappear down the street. Then Young continued on his trip--he never saw the old man again.

Over the years, however, the minister never forgot the prophecies told to him by the Indian, and kept a careful watch for their fulfillment. The seventh prophecy, he believed, described the big oil spills in the early 1970's, that ruined the ocean coasts and killed wildlife in many parts of the world. The eighth prophecy he identified as the mid-1970's youth movement back to nature, and their increased interest in the simplicity of the Indian's life on the land.

In 1976, David Young died. He did not live to see the last of the prophecies, but if he were alive today, he would have known that the ninth and last prophecy has happened now too. "You will hear of a dwelling-house in the heavens, above earth, that shall fall with a great crash." On July 11, 1979, the United States orbiting space platform, Skylab, re-entered the earth's atmosphere, and its remnants were scattered across the central and western deserts of Australia. The prophecy also said it would appear as a "Blue Star:" Eye-witnesses to the event said that many of the Skylab pieces streaking through the night sky left "a bluish tail of flame behind them."

A third aspect of the old prophecy forecast that soon after the "crash" of the heavenly "dwelling-house," the ceremonies of the Hopi Indians would cease. At the present time, the progressives among the Hopis are working to convince their people to become U.S. citizens, in order to gain from the benefits. But as the traditionalist Hopis point out, such a move would also do away with the reservation, and threaten their sacred shrines, so important to their ceremonies. Yet they know, despite their resistance and their warnings, that the progressives will eventually win. As one traditionalist spokesman recently put it: "The land base of Indian tribes which is tied to religious sites will no longer be protected, and religious ceremonies will soon die away. Hopis know this will come to pass as foretold by our prophets. Pahana has accomplished his purpose of educating us in this way."

Now that the Ninth and last Sign has been and is being fulfilled, what of the fiery catastrophes that are predicted to follow soon after? The old Indian, White Feather, gave us a few clues--but other Indian prophecies are far more

explicit. The Hopi shamans foretell that the United States will be partially destroyed in a war begun by "the old countries, which first received the light of knowledge"-- the Middle and Far Eastern nations. The home of the Hopis, in the American Southwest, will be one of the few "safe" lands, from which refugees will eventually return to rebuild the land.

Similarly, Sun Bear of the Chippewa Bear tribe received a vision as a child in which he saw the white man's land devastated by droughts, severe energy shortages--and saw the burnt and cratered shells of what are now major metropolises.

The holy man of the Canadian Iroquois, Deganawida, also had a prophetic dream long ago, in which he saw the coming of a "white serpent"--symbolizing the coming of white men--who would at first offer the Indians signs of peace, but then would turn on his people and "choke their life blood." This situation would continue, Deganawida foretold, until one day when the white serpent will be threatened by a red serpent. The white serpent will release its strangle-hold on the Iroquois people so as to concentrate his energies against the red serpent, and the Iroquois and other Indian tribes will escape to a hilly country and unite there in safety. So terrifying will the conflict between the two serpents be that--as Deganawida described it--a great heat wave will cause mountains to crack and rivers to boil, and certain regions will for a long time be left with no grass and with no leaves on the trees. Both serpents will be sickened by the stench of death. Eventually a black serpent will enter the battle, the white serpent will be greatly weakened but victorious, and an age will then ensue of peace and tranquility in the world.

These, then, are the prophecies. The signs are finished, and we now stand at the doorstep of momentous events, that shall bring about the ending of one world, and the beginning of a new one.

32. PYRAMID PROPHECY--MAN'S SPIRITUAL PROGRESSION TO THE 83RD CENTURY

On the rocky plateau called Giza, situated just west of Cairo, stands one of the greatest enigmas of all time--the Great Pyramid. Just what purpose it is supposed to have served has never fully been answered. Conservative scholars are convinced it was a pharoah's tomb, though no mummy or funeral markings were ever found in it. Others claim it accumulated or generated strange, unknown energies they call "pyramid power." Still others give evidence it was built by the lost civilization of Atlantis, that wished to leave behind to future ages a lasting testimony of its existence and knowledge. And then we have what is probably the most ingenious interpretation of all--that the Pyramid is a "prophecy in stone," showing by the positions and measurements of its internal passages and chambers, a complete outline of man's spiritual history, from the dim past to the far future.

This school of interpretation, called pyramidology, is by no means new, having been first proposed by an English mathematician, John Taylor, in the early nineteenth century. Later, his protege, Charles Piazzi Smythe, a Scottish scholar, spent several years at the Great Pyramid itself, measuring its every nook and cranny, so as to establish more precise time-lines in the Pyramid's prophetic message. The structure contains its own measurement, called the "pyramid inch," which is about one-one thousandth of an inch off the British inch. The proponents of pyramidology believe that this pyramid inch represents one year in the structure's prophecy--and that all one must do is simply mark off the number of inches along the passages and chambers, and one will find the story of the past, and what is to come. Recently, Peter Lemesurier, in a provocative book entitled *The Great Pyramid Decoded* (Avon, 1977), has refined and updated the last century and a half of pyramidology's discoveries, as well as offering a detailed projection of the future, of what is in store for mankind and his spiritual development. According to Lemesurier, the Pyramid's message can be summarized this way: It tells the story of the repeated appearance of a Messiah figure or "Great Initiate" who will lead men--the "lesser initiates"--along many spiritual paths through many ages. He will be the perpetual example to them--but it will finally be by means of their own free will that men shall choose either total Perfection or total Imperfection, as they achieve or cast off enlightenment in a succession of lifetimes.

The date for when the Pyramid's prophecy begins is 4000 B.C., and it is called by pyramidologists the "base-line" date, marked by the extension of the first or descending passage on a bisection with the Pyramid's foundation. This date is thought by some to represent the time of the beginning of the Present World Age. The entrance to the Pyramid gives the date of the summer solstice of 2623 B.C.--which may have been the time of the origins of Egyptian monotheistic religion in its purest form, the awakening to the concept of a relationship with a singular Divine entity. From here on, various markings, blocking stones, passage entrances, steps and hanging lintels delineate these important dates and events:

2141 B.C., spring equinox--This corresponds with the birth of Abraham, the father of the Jewish nation, and monotheistic religion in the Mesopotamian area.

1453 B.C., March 30--The date of the Exodus from Egypt; the inception of a new upward path.

2 B.C., September 27--The birth of the Christ; the first recorded entrance of the Messiah into the earth plane.

A.D. 29, October 14--Baptism of the Christ, beginning of His Ministry.

A.D. 33, April 1--The crucifixion; the Enlightenment fulfilled.

1223 to 1228--Franciscan and Dominican reform in the Church; the Messianic teachings revived.

1440 to 1521--The Renaissance of learning, and the Reformation beginning with Martin Luther; the second Messianic teachings revival.

1844--Beginning of the "Final Age," the end of 2,300 years in Bible prophecy (Daniel 8:14, historicist).

1914, summer--World War I starts; the beginning of the Age of Hell on Earth, during which all discarnate enlightened return in a universal reincarnation--the population explosion mushrooms.

1933--The return of the Christ-spirit; initial preparations made for the New Age; first awareness of New Age consciousness.

1967 (plus or minus 3 years)--Beginning of a spiritual and moral decline in the world.

1971 (plus or minus 3 years)--First global crises: pollution, famine, material shortages.

1977/1978 (plus or minus 3 years) to 2004 (plus or minus 3 years)--Rapid decline and collapse of materialist society.

1985, November 30--An outpouring of powerful spiritual energy surround the enlightened.

1999, February 21--Establishment of a true kingdom of the Spirit. Lemesurier describes it to be,"a separate and unique form of human society based solely on allegiance to the spiritual."

2004 to 2025--Materialist society remains in desolation.

2034, October 31--The "forerunner" of the Messiah appears.

2039, October 21--The second recorded entrance of the Messiah on earth begins.

2076 (plus or minus 3 years)--Beginning an era of greater awareness; consciousness is expanded, and mankind is raised to new levels of experience.

2116, March 28--The Messiah departs this plane of existence.

2132/3 (plus or minus 3 years)--Spiritual escape closed to those who remain unenlightened.

2134, summer--The third entrance of the Messiah on earth begins; the enlightened can no longer fall back into spiritual darkness.

2238, autumn--The Messiah departs this plane of existence; the foundations of human life are reaffirmed.

2264, summer--The fourth entrance of the Messiah on earth begins.

2279--The partially enlightened are initiated to higher learning.

2368, autumn--The Messiah departs this plane of existence.

2394--The fifth and final entrance of the Messiah on earth begins.

2422 to 2477--Last efforts to reform the totally unenlightened.

2499--The Messiah departs this plane of existence.

2499, February 21--The enlightened depart the material plane, entering into spiritual reward, though they are still bound to the earth.

2569--The unenlightened exiled to lower worlds, to begin again in a new cycle of existence toward an upward way.

2989, July 2--Beginning of the First High Millenium; the enlightened are reborn into the physical plane for the last time, in preparation for escape from the earth plane.

3279--End of the initiations of the partially enlightened; they now enter into the physical plane experience as newly enlightened.

3989, June 30--End of the First High Millenium; the returned enlightened depart the earth forever, and enter into the first of the purely spiritual planes; the newly enlightened remain for further physical plane experiences.

6225, midsummer--The newly enlightened depart the material plane and enter into a spiritual reward, yet are still bound to the earth.

7276, spring--Beginning of the Second High Millenium; the newly enlightened return to the physical plane one last time to prepare for the final escape from the earth plane.

8276, spring--End of the Second High Millenium; the newly enlightened depart the earth forever, joining their fellow enlightened souls in the first of the purely spiritual planes.

84th century to Beyond Time--The earth, empty, passes out of existence; the spiritual souls of mankind continue to progress through timeless, spaceless dimensions, through five levels of spiritual experience, ultimately arriving at the final step. The Messianic plan for the evolution of Man will be fulfilled as the souls of humanity pass from the finite into the infinite, back whence they came--from the very mind of God.

33. PROPHECIES OF ERRATIC WEATHER AND COMING FAMINE

In the last few years, headlines around the world have announced an alarming condition--our weather for some reason is going haywire. Dry and moderate areas are suffering from extreme drought, while other places, normally wet, are plagued by too heavy rains and flooding. The real worry is that these weather changes will steadily increase, and severely hamper world food production. The prospects are very disturbing: With the majority of people on this planet on the brink of starvation as it is, a general failure of global crop production because of bad weather would lead to greatly inflated food prices, and world famine. Several psychics and seers, both of times past and times present, have foreseen that our fears are justified--the weather and food situations are not going to get better in the immediate future, and those who can prepare by storing food, or buying land to grow their own staples, had better begin doing so now.

The French seer, Nostradamus, offered us several prophecies about what is going on, four centuries ago. This poem of his forecasts present and future weather conditions:

Par quarante ans l'Iris n'apparaitra,
Par quarante ans tous les jours sera vu:
La terre aride en siccite croitra,
Et grands deluges quand sera apercu. I,17.

For forty years the rainbow will appear in some places,
During the same years it will be seen not at all in others,
Here, the parched earth will wax dry,
There, great floods will accompany the rainbow.

A strict translation of the first lines reads thus: "For forty years the rainbow will not appear; for forty years it will be seen every day." Most interpreters have assumed that what is predicted is a 40-year period of drought, followed by another forty years of rain. But the two events appear rather to be intertwined, for their description is intertwined in the verse--lines 1 and 4, and 2 and 3, should be read together, respectively. Such a construction strongly suggests that the two elements-- drought and deluge--are to occur concurrently, within the *same* 40 years designated. This interpretation also best fits the characteristics of climatic aberrations we are now experiencing. In the United States, for example, the combined effect of repeated droughts in the West and Midwest, with large snow and rainfalls in the East, have in the last few years begun to affect food production and the economy. Add to this the recent severe drought in Central Africa, the rain shortages in Europe, and higher precipitation levels in Russia, South America and eastern Asia, and the world picture reveals the beginnings of a truly global climatic crisis.

In line 1 of the verse, the prophet used the term "Iris" for the rainbow; Iris, in Greek mythology, was personified by the rainbow, and acted as an intermediary between heaven and earth. She was personified as a winged messenger with the power to traverse the world and penetrate to the ocean depths. Nostradamus, by using the Iris symbolism, may have hinted at some universal element of world weather mechanics as being the cause for the world changes--perhaps the evaporation of atmospheric moisture levels above the oceans.

It is noteworthy that American seer Edgar Cayce, about fifty years ago, prophesied a 40-year period of progressively increasing geological changes to occur beginning in 1958, with truly cataclysmic events to begin after 1978--the period we are in now. Plagemann and Gribben, in a revolutionary study entitled *The Jupiter Effect* (Vintage Press, 1974), have demonstrated that there is a definite relation between earthquakes and climate, the two being linked with changes in sunspot activity, which in turn is influenced by the positions of the planets. The two researchers warn that we have entered an era between now and the end of the century when the planets will join in a number of unusual configurations. These will place tremendous pressures on the sun, and ultimately on the earth, especially from 1982 to 1984. We should expect a marked increase in severe earth upheavals and erratic weather. These will certainly have their effects on food production, and the economy: Edgar Cayce, when asked in a trance state in 1943 if we would have another Depression-style disruption in economic exchange, warned; "There may indeed be another (disruption) over just such conditions," with "hardships" and "extreme periods," though this would come "in the next generation"--our generation. A year later, in another psychic reading, he foresaw there would come "more and more upsetting in the monetary units of the land." He also predicted "hardships which have not yet begun in this country, so far as supply and demand for food is concerned. Anyone who can buy a farm is fortunate, and buy it if you don't want to grow hungry in days to come. Hold on to acreage, for that may be the basis for the extreme periods through which all portions of the country must pass-- for production of self as well as those closer associated with you."

In a second verse about our immediate future, Nostradamus warned:

La grand famine que je sens approcher,
Souvent tourner, puis etre universelle,
Si grande et longue qu'on viendra arracher
Du bois racine, et l'enfant de mamelle. I,67.

The great famine I sense approaching,
Often reversed, then to become universal,
It will be so long and so great,
That they will eat the roots of trees, and newborn babes.

In the early and mid-1970' s, the famines of Biafra, India and Central Africa were offset ("reversed,' ' line 2) by aid from the breadbaskets of the world--the United States and Canada in particular, which harvest one-third of global wheat production. Today, however, the increasing destruction caused by drought and heavy precipitation is reducing world surplus stockpiles of food to a bare minimum. When the next big famine occurs--probably in South America, southern and eastern Asia or in Africa--there may no longer be relief available. Two very sobering reports issued not long ago by the American CIA warn that, because of weather changes and crop failures, famine for four-fifths of the world's population is imminent. And if the failures continue beyond, even the agricultural centers of the world will feel the pinch. In the last line of the verse, the French prophet predicts that in certain areas the situation will become so critical that people will eat anything that is alive--stripping trees bare, and even digging up their roots for nourishment. Finally will come the unspeakable, ultimate act of desperation: Men will steal away children from their mothers, to be killed and feasted upon so that they may survive.

A third Nostradamian poem reiterates this grisly picture:

La voix ouie l' insolite oiseau,
Sur le canon du respiral etage:
Si haut viendra du froment le boisseau,
Que l' homme d' homme sera Anthropophage. II,75.

The call of the unwanted bird,
Will be heard on the chimney stack,
A bushel of wheat will rise so high in price,
That man will eat his fellow man.

The meaning of the first two lines is rather obscure, and modern interpreters have offered a variety of ideas. The "l'insolite oisseau" of line 1 might be a vulture, which feeds on dead flesh; or it could be an owl--in divinatory terms, the sign of ill-omen and death. A strict translation of the second line reads: "On the pipe of the air-vent floor" ("respiral"--Old French, air vent). This line is thought to be a cryptic description of a chimney or smoke stack--a fitting symbol for urban or heavily populated places. The fact that vultures or owls would be found in urban areas portends that death tolls from coming starvation will be greatest in the cities. Another interpretation sees the bird that builds its nests in chimney tops as the stork, by tradition the bringer of children. That the bird is "unwanted" might imply that having children will one day be considered too

123

burdensome--which in a time of famine would be understandable. Perhaps this may be interlinked with the last line of the last verse quoted above, in which Nostradamus warned that children will one day be stolen for food. These prophetic scenes are certainly linked in turn with elements in the last line of the verse here, which (strictly translated) reads: "That man-to-man to become a Man-eater;" that is, populations are to degenerate to the level of cannibals in their desperate search for food.

Line 3 is predicted to be the cause of the situation: "A bushel of wheat will rise so high in price." This implies that crop production in the agricultural nations of the world will be diminished to such a degree that prices will be purposely over-inflated to protect what remains for themselves. As a result, the non-agricultural nations will no longer be able to afford the cost--and for them the resulting famine will lead to scenes of horror.

The third line is also an echo of a similar prophecy, found in the Book of Revelation, written by the apostle John almost two millenia ago. In the vision of the third of the Four Horsemen of the Apocalypse, John hears a voice that tells him, "A quart of wheat for a denarius (a whole day's wages), and three quarts of barley flour for a denarius, and there is no oil or wine" (Amplified and Living Versions). Most commentators of the Apocalypse consider this to represent a severe world-wide famine being prophesied here. Is this a symbolic warning for our present world? Other seers and prophets, of yesterday and today, say yes. The hoofbeats of the Third Horseman are now beginning to be heard in the streets--it is up to us whether or not we acknowledge what is coming, and whether or not we try to ready ourselves for it....

34. SIGNS OF THE AGE OF THE SPIRIT

Giaocchino de Fiore, an austere Cistercian monk who lived from 1130 to 1202 in Calabria, Italy, authored many commentaries on prophecy, from the Sibylline oracles and Merlin's portents, to the Revelation apocalypse of the apostle John. These works and their interpretation in turn helped Giaocchino formulate his own version of the future--a vision which there is good reason to believe will see its fulfillment in our lifetimes.

The Italian monk taught that there will be a total of three Great Ages, corresponding to the Father, Son and Holy Spirit. In his famous work, *Vaticini del Vangelo eterno* (*Prophecies of the Eternal Gospels*), first printed in 1484, Giaocchino described the Old Testament era as the Age of the Father: A time of the law and fear, servile slavery, tradition, and the domination by the old. With the advent of Jesus of Nazareth and on to the present, we have been living in the age of the Son: An era of faith, grace, symbolism, liberty and youthful vigor. Today, however, we are fast approaching the last, the Age of the Spirit, wherein we shall see the exercise of mutual love, communal friendship, complete freedom, rebirth, spiritual contemplation, charity and transcendence. According to the monk, the Christian Church of his day, and ours, is a bulwark of symbolism. But symbols are only a temporary reflection, and must give way to a new form of actualization, one of spiritual realism. The Latin Church, Giaocchino wrote, "is only a pale and wan prologue of the coming revelations of the Holy Spirit." He also exclaimed, "Peter will disappear in front of John, because the reign of the Holy Spirit will be the reign of the free."

The coming transition, however, will not be easy. The Italian monk foresaw that the dawning of the Third Age would be preceded by a short period of "persecutions and calamities," that will only end with a great downpour of the Spirit from Heaven. As the Father brought a Flood of waters to destroy the wicked in Noah's day, and the Son sacrificed a surge of blood to give men an understanding of faith and liberty, so the Spirit will bring about a deluge of fire, love and justice. With this, the whole concept of the Church will be metamorphosed into a way of living, of spiritual action and being. All fear will be erased and, as Giaocchino called it, it will not only be the beginning of the Age of the Spirit, but also the Age of Perfection.

There is not a day that goes by when the newspapers or media do not report on some act of violence some where in the world, the work of political or radical organizations bent on making a name for themselves, and drawing global attention to their cause. Among the most active of these, has been the Arab terrorists, in particular the Palestine Liberation Organization. At the present time, their activities are limited to sabotage, hijacking, planting bombs on crowded streets and machine-gunning innocent people. But there are indications they may move on to more infamous deeds--namely, the kidnapping of prominent persons and important dignitaries. In 1558, the French seer Nostradamus foresaw a threat made by modern terrorists toward the Roman Catholic Church. He wrote:

Par mer le rouge sera pris de pirates,
La paix sera par son moyen troublee:
L' ire et l' avare commettra par feint acte,
Au grand Pontife sera l' armee doublee. V,44.

On the sea a red one will be taken by pirates,
Because of this action, peace will be troubled,
Through a feigned act he will reveal his captors' anger and greed,
The great Pope will double his guards.

In line 1 of this prophecy we are informed that, "On the sea a red one will be taken by pirates." Nostradamus frequently used the phrase "red one" to denote a Cardinal of the Church, with their prominent red garb. By "pirates," the French seer meant the Moslem corsairs of North Africa, who greatly hindered traffic throughout the Mediterranean in the prophet' s day. The prediction here, then, is that a Cardinal will be captured and held at sea by Arabs. Today, we would identify these kidnappers as Arab terrorists. Because of the captured "red one," "peace will be troubled." The captured Church official it appears will stir things up because of his actions: "Anger and greed he will expose" on the part of his captors, "through a false act" of his own, not described further. Without a doubt, this flagrant action on the part of the Arabs will not help relations between Catholic Europe and the Middle East. The last line suggests that the kidnapping will so concern the Vatican that the Pope himself will order an increase in the protection of all Church officials, as a precaution against further terrorist attempts.

THE FIFTH THUNDER

36. A SIXTEENTH CENTURY ACCOUNT OF WORLD WAR III

The following is a series of verses taken from Nostradamus' monumental work on prophecy, *The True Centuries*. These verses appear to describe the details of a coming war that will involve nations the prophet called the "two brothers" or "two masters" of "Aquilon" (the North)--the modern United States and the Soviet Union. These two will be attacked by the "Orient," who will be allied with the "Arabs," and together will also invade and devastate Europe. As you read these poems, notice the repetition of many of the events described, which directly link these verses together. Also take note of the ominous illusions to nuclear and germ warfare. The various astrological configurations suggest this tremendous conflict could take place in the next decade: These configurations have taken place before and will happen again, separately--but only in the 1980's will they *all* occur in a short period of each other. As for the rest of the details, let the reader interpret these for himself:

The scythe (Saturn) joined in the water sign (Scorpio) near Sagittarius,
At the midpoint of its ascendant,
At that time disease, famine, death by military action,
Near when the world will approach the time of its renewal. I, 16.

128

(Note: Saturn will be in Scorpio from December, 1982 to November, 1985. The midpoint will be in May, 1984).

One day two masters will be friends,
Their great power will be increased,
The New World (America) will then be at its high peak,
The bloody one will weigh the number killed by attacking them. II, 89

The leader long awaited will never come
Into Europe; he will appear, to unite Asia instead,
One issued of the great league of Hermes (god of negotiation),
He will dominate over all the Rulers of the Orient. X, 75.

Throughout Asia there will be great political restriction,
Even in Mysia, Lycia and Pamphilia (all in modern Turkey),
The Yellow King filled with evil doings. III, 60.

Only for a short time will there be Temples of all colors (U.N.?),
White and black will intermix,
But the red and yellow races (Middle and Far East) will leave,
Then will lands suffer from blood, disease, famine, fires and floods. VI, 10.

When those who share communications over the Arctic Pole are united together,
There will be great terror and fear in the Orient,
The newly elected leader, though strongly supported, will tremble also,
At the same time Rhodes (Greece) and Turkey are stained with Arab blood. VI, 21.

A nation surrounded on three sides by water (America),
One that will make Thursday its holiday (Thanksgiving),
Its fame, praise, rule and power will grow,
By land and sea, it will appear as a tempest to the Orient. I, 50.

By the two will the peaceful rule be established for a short time,
After three years and seven months, they will be involved in conflict,
Two powers to rebel against them,
Occupation of Armenia (east Turkey) by the younger. IV, 95.

At sunrise one will see a great fire,
The noise and light aimed toward Aquilon (the two powers of the North),
Within the lands bordering on the Arctic Circle one will hear cries of death,
Through instruments of steel, death will come from fire and famine. II, 91.

They will fail because of absence of purpose, all in discord,
One will suddenly be placed back in power,
When toward Aquilon will come a very loud roar,
Many casualties from pointed weapons crossing, from above, Presage 26.

From the air sign (Libra) near the Urn (Aquarius) Saturn retrogrades,
Mars held in fire sign,
Toward Aquilon southward (from the Pole) will come a great conflagration,
The Russian, the Leader of the East will seek to capture. Presage 8

(Note: Saturn will retrograde from Libra and Mars will be in the fire sign of Leo in July-August, 1983. A later possibility will occur in February, 1988).

There will be triggered a living fire, a secret, unseen form of death,
Horrible and frightful, it will be enclosed in containers,
Launched from a fleet of ships, in a single night it transforms a city to dust and vapor,
The city glows, the enemy demands terms. V, 8.

When evil (Saturn) and war (Mars) are in fire signs,
Others grouped in an air sign, and a long-tailed star
(comet) seen,
Through secret fires a great place will blaze with intense
heat,
Little rain, hot blasts, wars, invasions. IV, 67.

(Note: In February, 1986, Mars and Saturn will be in
the fire sign of Sagittarius, and the Sun, Venus, Mercury
and Jupiter will all be in the single air sign of Aquarius. In
the same year, Halley's comet is scheduled to reappear).

The populated places will be uninhabitable,
Great disorder, people trying to obtain food,
Areas governed by incapable officials,
Among the great brothers, chaos and death. II, 95.

From beyond the Black Sea and Mongolia (from China),
There will be a King who will travel in the direction of
France (westward),
He will pierce through Alania and Armenia (southern
Russia),
And in Turkey he will leave the mark of his bloody rod. V,
54.

From the Orient will come the cold-hearted,
To vex Venice and the inhabitants of Rome (Italy),
They will be accompanied by the Libyan (Arab) fleet,
Malta will tremble, the neighboring isles emptied. I, 9.

The Oriental will leave his seat of power,
He will pass the Apennine mountains (in Italy) on his way
to France
He will transpierce through the sky, over seas and
mountain snows,
And everyone will be struck with his rod. II, 29.

From Fez (North Africa) the invaders will penetrate into
Europe,
Whose cities will be ablaze, whose inhabitants will be
murdered,

131

The great leader of Asia will come by land and sea with a great army,
Uniformed in blues and grays, they will pursue those of Christendom (Europeans) to death. VI, 80.

Death will be arrayed in the seventh house (Libra),
A portent of coming hail, tempest, evil disease, and great fury,
Because of the King of the Orient, all the Occident (Europe) in retreat,
He will subjugate his former conquerors. Presage 40.

(Note: The three death signs, Mars, Saturn and Pluto, will be found together in Libra in early 1982).

Aquilon will use the wind to break its encirclement,
Beyond their defense lines they will launch forms of dust,
Rain will also disseminate it, which was once used against them,
This will be a desperate effort against their frontiers. IX, 99.

A great force will come out of Slavonia (Russia),
The Oriental destroyer will see his ancient city (Peking) destroyed
He will see his empire desolated,
And he will not know how to put out the great fire. IV, 82.

Twice raised up, twice lowered,
The Orient will threaten the West,
Its adversary after several battles,
Only to be defeated at sea, and ultimately fail again. VIII, 59.

The royal bird (eagle) seen over the city of the sun (Rome),
It will appear as an omen that seven months later,
The Oriental defense will fall amid lightning and noise,
For a week the enemy will directly attack its cities. V, 81.

(This quote, taken from Nostradamus' "Epistle to Henri II," also contained in the *True Centuries*, prophesies the fall of the East:) "The leaders of Aquilon, two in number, will be victorious over the Orientals and so great a noise and tumult of warfare will they make that all the Orient will shake with terror because of these two brothers, who are not yet. The chief of the Orient will be vanquished by the Northerners (those of Aquilon) and the Occidentals (Europeans), and the people they had stirred to war and had united with them, will be put to death, and scattered, and their offspring made prisoners."

(After the defeat of the Orient, Nostradamus foresees the Western powers joining together to liberate occupied Europe:)

Fire from the sky will be seen over the shores of the Occident (Europe),
And in the South (Africa and Asian nations), even in the Levant (the Middle East),
Half of them will die before they can find shelter,
It will be called the Third Age of Mars the Warrior (World War III)
The Firelighters will come forth to ignite the conflageration,
It is the age of (Nuclear) Fire, and its end is famine. Sixain 27.

Like a winged griffon will come the commander of exiled Europeans,
Accompanying him will be the commanders of Aquilon,
They will lead a great troop of red and white,
And they will go against the commander of Babylon (the Middle East) X, 86.

After the cold-hearted powers are destroyed in the Orient,
The empire that included the river Ganges (India), Jordan (Middle East), the Rhone and Loire (France) and Tagus (Spain), will soon be lost,
The hunger of the conqueror will be glutted,
Then the fleet will scatter him, blood and bodies will float in the seas. II, 60.

133

The two wicked ones in Scorpio,
The Sultan of the Middle East murdered in his command
post,
The Church troubled by its new ally,
Europe occupied by those from the North. I, 52.

(Note: The "wicked ones," Saturn, Mars and Pluto, will
be in Scorpio within a short period: Mars will stay
between February and August, 1984, Saturn conjoins in
1983-1985, with Pluto entering in 1984-1985).

37. WHAT THE HEAVENS PREDICT

While the fast-moving inner planets and their
constantly changing positions effect the everyday lives of
men, it is the outer orbs--Uranus, Neptune and Pluto--that
move more slowly, and rule the rise and fall of nations and
mass movements. These will be the bodies that will
oversee the end of the Present Age according to
astrologers, and will help usher in the New Age to come.

In 1975, Uranus entered Scorpio, which is the sign of
death and regeneration. New Age stargazers foresee this
period--to last until 1982--will mark the beginning of new
ideas and the destruction of the old needed to sweep aside
the Piscean Age, and prepare entrance into the Age of
Aquarius.

Moving into Sagittarius, in 1983 to 1990, Uranus is
predicted to spark a re-interest in religion, and bring
about new religious ideas. Forecasters warn, however,
that Uranus will be afflicted, or will be at odds with other
planets in many charts, which could cause eccentricity and
fanaticism in religious dogma, resulting in some negative
spiritual development. As a counterbalance, more
cooperation and synthesis will take place among truly
Spirit-centered individuals of diverse beliefs and
philosophies.

For 1990-1997, Uranus will be in Capricorn, and the
period will ultimately see a complete reversal of existing
government and other power structures. There will be a

strong desire among some to overthrow what is established, and begin anew.

When Uranus enters Aquarius in 1997-1998, many astrologers believe this will herald the beginning of the Aquarian Age. The configuration will see a return to exploring and discovering Spiritual truths and employing mental energies to an extent never before attained.

The planet Neptune also exerts a powerful influence, especially in the mass consciousness of mankind. In 1970-1984, Neptune will be in Sagittarius, and we are already seeing the consequences: A turning to new religions and cults. In favorable aspects, it is a "pre-dawn" period for the New Age, when interest is growing in ESP, reincarnation, and most significantly the importance of man's Higher self. But the position of Neptune, when afflicted, will also bring about in some an aimless wandering, with an acceptance of false prophets, Messiahs and fanatical adherents. The tragic Jim Jones cult was a real fulfillment of this kind of influence.

Neptune will pass into Capricorn from 1984-1998, and this, astrologers predict, will bring in chaos and upheaval in governments and economies on a world-wide scale. Out of the suffering, those who are strong and Spirit-centered will learn spiritual responsibility and self-discipline. Toward the end of the period, with the world undone, these individuals will emerge to attain higher spiritual awareness, and help establish a new and better way of life.

Like Uranus, Neptune will also enter Aquarius about the year 2000, as a sign of a new beginning. It will bring the founding of a new civilization based on enlightened humanitarianism, and knowledge will be used for only constructive purposes. The psychic abilities of people are also forecast to be heightened, as well as the growth of universal brotherhood among all mankind. The promise of a rebirth of Spiritual leaders at this time is also indicated.

Pluto, the farthest planet out, is the planet of change--and the alterations its positions in the heavens portend, for the next 25 years, will be literally earth-shattering. The planet will be in Libra from 1972-1984, and, as already seen in such mass movement

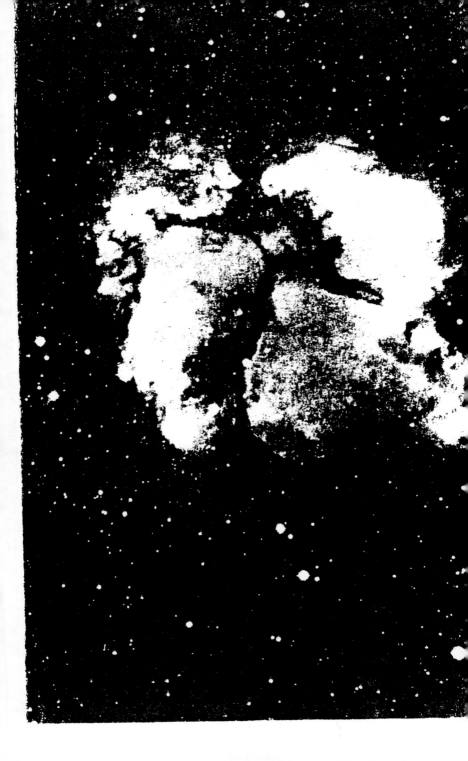

concerns with war, the environment, and political corruption, the alignment has triggered interest in justice and moral questions. There will be many more changes in concepts of law, marriage, and established practices and institutions. A danger exists, however, to "moralize," to over-define and turn dogmatic in terms of what is "right" and "wrong."

Pluto next enters Scorpio, from 1984-2000, and this configuration foreshadows global destruction and conflict. Many astrologers foresee the same horrors described by visionary prophets and psychics, for this period: famine, disease, nuclear and germ warfare. The influence will be very potent, and mankind will be plunged into the deeps of the most terrible period of death and chaos ever experienced. But hope will come eventually--and man will emerge to greet the New Age.

Pluto passes into Sagittarius in 2000, marking an era of Spiritual regeneration, and the discernment of deeper Spiritual values. Man will learn how to communicate with God through his intuition, and will be taught by many reincarnated Spiritual leaders in new interpretations of himself in relation to the universe about him.

According to the stars, then, the next few years of Tomorrow will be difficult and trying, but with the Day After Tomorrow comes hope and peace...

38. A "WATERGATE" IN THE SUPREME COURT?

It has been said that the United States is ruled by five men--the majority vote among the nine judges who sit on the Supreme Court. This saying reflects the realization of how powerful the Court is: The Supreme Nine can strike down any law passed by Congress or signed by the President as unconstitutional, and its only check is that the President has the power to appoint the judges. But this may change in the near future. Past American political history reveals that scandals have from time to time plagued the Capitol and the White House--but as yet there has never been a scandal in the Federal Courthouse. Writing four centuries ago, Nostradamus foresaw that the Supreme Nine will no longer be immune--and their transgressions will lead to a number of mandatory removals from the bench. The prophet's poem reads:

D'humain troupeau neuf seront mis a part,
De jugement et conseil separes:
Leur sort sera divise en depart,
Kappa, Theta, Lambda, morts, bannis, egarez. I, 81.

Nine set aside from the rest of humanity,
Removed, having divided all by their judgements and
counsel,
Their fates will be determined on their departure,
K, Th, L--dead, deported, led away.

This is a fascinating verse in many respects. Nostradamus
begins by describing nine men who are "set aside" from
the rest of mankind. Why? The second line offers the
answer: They will be known for their "judgements and
counsel;" that is, the nine are judges, and being "set
aside" suggests their office is the highest one, placed
above all others. This is of course an excellent description
of the United States Supreme Court. It is interesting that
at no other time in history, in all the days since
Nostradamus wrote, has the number nine designated the
number of men of a highest court, who hold such great
legal power and influence.
   The second line implies that the Court will make a
series of bad judgements, and this will in time result in a
major scandal--the forced retirement of certain members
of the judicial body, and their prosecution. In line 2 the
word "separes" can mean either "divided"--refering to the
judgements--or "removal," pointing to those who will
make the judgements. Line 3 suggests further that
sentences will be passed against those leaving,
"determined on their departure" from their office. Line 4
offers clues as to the identities and destinies of three of
the Justices who will face sentences for certain scandalous
activities. First, they will have, or be associated with,
three initials--K, Th, and L. The order of the sentences is
very probably linked with the order of the initials: "K"
will "die," "Th" will be "banished" or deported from the
country, and "L" will be "led away"--presumably to prison.
The word "egarez" also has the connotation, "led astray,"
suggesting that the last person will be involved with

others in conspiracy, and his actions will have become misdirected, contrary to the integrity of a high office.

39. THE THREE DAYS OF UNKNOWN DEATH

Throughout history, there have been many instances recorded of the sky suddenly blackening, of the sun "going down at noon," and terrified inhabitants lighting their lamps in the midst of the day. But there is another "time of terrible darkness" forecast to come—one which will cover not just a small area, but will envelop the entire earth. And with this darkness will come death and dying for many.

In the apostle John's apocalyptic visions, we find this description of the Fifth Plague, foretold to be directed against the wicked of the earth in the last days: "And the fifth angel poured out his vial on the seat of the Beast; and his kingdom was full of darkness, and they gnawed their tongues for pain."

The seer Nostradamus, in this prophetic verse of his, captured the same scene, and predicted further the time of year the great darkness will take place:

Near the twentieth day of the sign Taurus (or about May 10), the earth will tremble mightily,
A theatre (arena, colliseum, circus) filled to capacity shall be ruined,
Everyone amazed at the darkening of all the air, the sky and earth,
Which will cause the unbelievers to call upon God and his saints. IX, 83.

In a similar fashion, a number of Church mystics of the last century have also received foresight of the strange, death-dealing blackness. In 1819, Marie Julie Jahenny de la Faudais recorded she witnessed a vision of three days and nights of continuous darkness. It would begin, she said, with a blood-red cloud covering the sky, causing the earth to tremble like thunder, and the waves of the sea to grow violent. The cloud would then grow thicker, with rays and flashes of lightning destroying many buildings, while people caught outside will succumb to noxious fumes. Soon the sun and moon will be blotted out, and the pitch blackness will be so great that only candles will penetrate the void, with all other forms of illumination failing. When finally the clouds disperse, the bodies of the dead will cover the entire planet. The majority of mankind will not have survived.

Less than twenty years later, in 1837, the blessed Anna Marie Taigi repeated the same warning: She too envisioned the horrible blackness to last for three days, and forbade the pious to open their windows or go into the streets--or they would drop dead on the spot. The air, she said, shall be "laden with pestilence," and will not descriminate between the holy and the unbeliever, taking the lives of each equally.

In the very same year that Anna Marie Taigi received her impressions, St. Gaspare de Bufalo, of the Congregation of the Most Precious Blood, had a startling revelation in which he likewise saw *three days* of darkness, and weeping of survivors as they mourned over bodies strewn over the surface of the earth.

Finally, in 1878, Sister Marie of the Crucified Jesus reiterated the same portent of three awful days of darkness, only she added the sobering prediction that only *one-fourth* of mankind will survive.

In our present century, the prophecies of coming darkness continue: In 1943, a revelation of the Madonna given to Berthe Petit of Belgium included this warning: "The punishment will approach like a cloud, which will increase in size and spreads out until it will cover everything. Sparks will then descend out of it, annihilating people by fire and blood." Today, the modern psychic Criswell, of California has foreseen a remarkably similar scenario. Time and again, he claims, he has dreamed of a day when people will speak to one another, and when they will talk about tomorrow, nothing will come out of their mouths. That same day, Criswell predicts, what he calls a "black rainbow" will encircle the earth, and will slowly suck away most of the air in the atmosphere. Men everywhere will die in the streets. But the disaster will last only a short while, with survivors

140

coming forth afterward to rebuild the earth. And the date for this horrendous event? Criswell says--August 18, 1999.

40. DANIEL'S PROPHECY OF A MIDDLE EAST WAR

A detailed account of a war involving the Arabs and Europe, was written by the Hebrew prophet Daniel, more than 2,600 years ago. The story is found in the Book of Daniel, Chapter 11, verses 40 through 45. The interpretations of this prophecy have been many and varied in recent years, especially as a result of the crises that have developed in the Middle East between Israel and her Arab neighbors. Here is one interpretation that satisfies all the symbols of the prophecy:

Verse 40. "At the time of the end shall the king of the south push at him; and the king of the north shall come against him like a whirlwind, with chariots, and with horsemen, and with ships, and he will enter into the countries, and shall overflow and pass over."

This verse gives us the entire story of the conflict: In the last days of the Present Age, the "king of the south," or a dominant power in the Middle East, will attack the "king of the north," or Europe and her allies. The northern powers will counter-attack and eventually defeat the Arabs. Verses 41-45 now give the particulars:

Verse 41. "He (the king of the south) shall enter into the glorious land, and many countries shall be overthrown: but these shall escape from his hand, even Edom, and Moab, and the chief of the children of Ammon."

The war will begin when the Arabs successfully conquer Israel ("the glorious land") and several other nations. Edom, Moab and Ammon are now a part of Syria, Transjordan and Arabia, all to become unified in a confederated Arab empire--and thus not to be among those to be attacked.

Verse 42. "He shall stretch out his hand also upon the countries: and the land of Egypt shall not escape."

The Arabs will extend their policy of unification in North Africa, and pro-Western Egypt will be overwhelmed.

Verse 43. "But he shall have power over the treasures of gold and silver, and over the precious things of Egypt: and the Libyans and Ethiopians shall be at his steps."

The Arabs will have "power over gold and silver," or great economic strength--which they have already through control of most of the world's oil. The "precious things of Egypt" may be Egypt's hidden oil reserves. The Arabs will also unify North and Central Africa under their control.

Verse 44. "But tidings out of the east and out of the north shall trouble him: therefore he shall go forth with great fury to destroy, and utterly take away many."

Events in other parts of the world--in the Orient and among the superpowers of the northern hemisphere, the United States and Russia--will trouble the Arabs, and they will drive to consolidate their positions.

Verse 45. "And he shall plant the tabernacles of his palace between the seas in the glorious holy mountain; yet he shall come to his end, and none shall help him."

"Tabernacles" are tents--an appropriate symbol for the Arabs. They will attempt to establish and defend themselves in Israel--between the Mediterranean and the Dead and Galilee Seas--and in Jerusalem, "the glorious holy mountain." But as already predicted in verse 40, the powers of the north (Europe and her allies) will defeat and destroy them, bringing this future war to a close.

41. EARTHQUAKE AND FIRE--THE FATE OF NEW YORK CITY

While on a visit to New York City in 1904, prophetess Ellen G. White, founder of the Seventh-Day Adventist Church, had two visions about the future of the great island metropolis of the East coast. In the first vision, she described how "building after building arose, higher and higher," constructed by men of wealth and power as symbols of themselves, competing with one another for the highest and most expensive structure. The great buildings, she predicted, would be declared "fireproof and perfectly safe." What is fascinating is that Ellen White wrote these words at the turn of the century--several

years before the first Manhattan skyscrapers were designed and erected. "Suddenly," as her vision of the future progressed, however, "there was an alarm of fire." "The firefighters will be unable to operate their engines." The tall buildings, each and every one, had burst into flame, and burned with such an intensity "as if made of pitch." It is noteworthy that Ellen White foresaw the *skyscrapers* on fire, but not the *city*--indicating that the fire is not to originate from below, but rather from the sky. In her second vision, the prophetess witnessed another type of destruction to severely affect the very same high buildings she had seen: "One word from the Lord," Ellen White warned, and these structures will fall to pieces, and be swept away, as if the Almighty had brushed them aside with His hand. The scene of a great shaking and collapse of New York's skyscrapers suggests an earthquake of great severity to strike the city.

This double prophecy, of fire and quake, finds a significant parallel in the prophetic poems of Nostradamus, written in the sixteenth century. In one verse, the French seer forecast:

From forty-five degrees the sky will burn,
The descending fire will approach the great New City,
In an instant, a great scattered flame will leap up,
Testing them to the fullest extent. VI, 97.

Many interpreters believe the "great New City" is New (York) City--and here, as in Ellen White's vision, we find a description of the metropolis suffering from fire, from the sky. The question is, what will cause the "sky to burn," as Nostradamus depicted it? One feasible answer is nuclear weapons. In a recent report made by Pentagon experts, it was disclosed that one of the most efficient methods of utilizing nuclear weapons is to coordinate the simultaneous detonation of several devices in a relatively small area--within 20 to 50 miles of each other--and at a high altitude anywhere from 50 to 150 miles up. The result of all these explosions taking place close to one another and in thin atmosphere is that the air between and surrounding them will be ignited, or "ionized." This mass

144

of super-heated gases, several thousands of degrees in temperature, would descend to ground level, burning everything in its path. The scene would literally look like "fire falling from the sky," and the Pentagon report mentioned that such a nuclear cluster-detonation would burn out, "an area the size of New England." This example is a prophecy in itself, for New England appears to be the region to one day be so affected: The modern Californian seer, Criswell, has forewarned that in the 1980's the United States will be attacked by "a foreign power" with missiles, and several nuclear explosions will take place over the state of Vermont. Ionized air originating from these explosions above Vermont most certainly would spread out and threaten New York City, directly to the south, with its fire. In Nostradamus' verse, we read that, "From forty-five degrees the sky will burn." *The forty-fifth parallel marks the border between Vermont and Canada.*

In a second Nostradamian verse, we find indications that the nuclear fire to burn New York may be the trigger to touch off a second disaster--a large earthquake:

Earth shaken, fire from the center of the earth,
Will cause an earthquake around New City,
Two great rocks will grind against each other,
The rivers (Hudson and East) will turn red. I,87.

The first line can be interpreted two ways: First, it can read as it appears above, with the word "terre" in the original interpreted as the "earth" or "ground," in which case the "fire" refers to subterranean tectonic heat. But "terre" can also mean "earth" in the alchemical sense (Nostradamus was a practitioner of alchemy); that is, "substance, the elements, matter." In this case the line could read, "*Matter* shaken, fire from the center of *matter*," will cause the quake. What we have here is a perfect description of the source of a nuclear explosion: It is created when uranium is "shaken" apart, and a portion of its nucleus or "center" is transformed into energy or "fire." If the second reading is taken, then the events described here in this verse are directly linked with the first verse: The nuclear fire that "will approach the great

145

New City," will generate "an earthquake around New City," and the two disasters will occur at the same time.

A third verse by Nostradamus describes the earthquake in greater detail:

The rich agricultural region, near the New City,
On the way to the man-made hollowed mountains (skyscrapers),
They will all be taken and plunged into the bay,
Its people forced to drink poisoned, stinking waters. X,49.

According to the prophet, the towering skyscrapers of New York--which he could only describe in sixteenth century terms as "man-made hollowed mountains"--will be toppled by the coming quake, and their remains will be swept into New York harbor. The quake will seriously affect surrounding farmlands in New Jersey, Pennsylvania and New York state. After the catastrophe, relief will be late in coming, and surviving New Yorkers will be forced to drink water polluted by the floating debris. This is directly related to the last line in the second verse above, which described the nearby rivers to turn red.

42. THE COMING FALSE RELIGION AND MASS PERSECUTIONS

Prophets and visionaries from the past to the present have looked ahead to the time when a New Age will begin, of true Peace and true spiritual Light. But many of these same prophets also have predicted that just before the New Age will come, we will first pass through a short period, that will be just the opposite--a time of terror and spiritual Darkness.

One seer, Nostradamus, wrote several prophecies about the coming rise and fall of a "one World Religion" and a "Universal Church," to dominate the world in the 1990's. He forecasts:

They shall come forth to reveal a false way,
That is buried, they shall profane,
Sects and religious philosophies shall multiply,
Light exchanged for Darkness, ancient wisdom exchanged for the untried. VIII, 14.

146

There will arise a new sect of Philosophers,
Despising death, gold and material wealth,
They will not be those bordering on the German mountains (Protestants),
They will have great power, and crowds will follow after them. III, 14

The adherents of this new religion will initiate radical changes in the Roman Church, throwing out many of its long-established institutions and sacred practices:

They will return to short sacrifices,
Transgressors will be threatened with death and martyrdom,
No longer will there be monks, abbots and novices,
Honey more expensive than wax (no candles used in services). I, 44.

The gray, white and black (orders of monks) changed and put out,
They will be replaced, dismissed, thrown out of their monasteries,
They will be mocked by the ravishers,
And the vestals (nuns) confined behind bars. Presage 65.

Temples will be consecrated in the original Roman fashion,
They will reject the abundant tradition,
Placing first their own laws above men,
And setting up their own cult of the saints. II, 8.

Blinded, eyes opened to antiquated fantasies,
The garb of the monk will be stripped from him,
They will even chastise Rulers in their religious frenzy,
And empty treasures in front of their temples. II, 12.

At the same time, a mysterious new leader will arise in the Church, who will consolidate all of Christianity under him:

147

One will dominate over the Estate of the east (Eastern Orthodox Church),
Yet he will remain standing on the square Stone (of Peter; Roman Catholicism),
He will reach toward the South (Asia) and the West (America),
The crooked staff (Church power) in his hand, silent but persuasive. V, 75.

In Germany will be born diversified religions (Protestantism),
They will approach paganism to satisfy believers,
While the heart remains captive, the returns will be small,
Eventually they will be brought back to pay the true tithe (of the Roman Church). III, 76.

In the last verse, the many denominations of Protestant Christianity are forecast to lose their original spirituality, and one by one their adherents will fall away, leaving them poor and destitute. In the spirit of ecumenism, they will be joined back into the Church, from which the German Luther had once revolted.

The law of the Sun (the Church) and Venus (the East) thought contrary,
Yet both possessing the revealed Spirit,
Not fully understanding one or the other,
The great Messiah through laws will uphold the Sun (the Church). V, 53.

In an effort to force the One Religion upon the peoples of the Middle East, a false "Messiah" will declare that the new religion of the reorganized Church is superior to all other major religions--Mohammedism, Judaism, Hinduism, Buddhism, etc. The truth is, as Nostradamus stressed, the Eastern religions advocate spiritual paths as inspired as Christianity. But such truths will be ignored, and the process of "converting" other beliefs through force will begin.

Ancient spiritual wisdom given substance,
Energy of heaven and earth, hidden gold in the mystic
words,
Body, soul, spirit given tremendous power,
To challenge the rule of the universal church. III, 2.

Despite the enforcement of the One Religion
throughout the world, there will be many who will remain
faithful to their own individual Spiritual belief, whether as
true Christians, Buddhists, Moslems, etc. To them, the
Spirit of God will speak, and they will be given
superhuman strength and wisdom in a time when their
faith will be tested to the fullest.

The student of ancient spiritual wisdom, to him heaven
will touch,
When he cannot be able to proceed in his readings,
Finding secrets closed up in the words revealed,
Then they will spread the meaning far. II, 27.

Those who will study and aohere to the words of those
Writings sacred to the world's religions--the Bible, the
Koran, the Bhagavad Gita, etc.--will be given special
understandings of difficult passages. Given the Light,
they will spread the Light in opposition to the darkness of
religious intolerance.

The resistance of the Spirit-centered against the
dictates of the One World Religion will cause a swift
reaction, and Nostradamus predicts that a terrible
persecution will begin in many places around the world. In
this quote, from his "Epistle to Henri II," the prophet
foresaw mass murders in his native France, under a
future leader named "Ogmios," and further genocide
perpetrated by those of "Aquilon"--the two nations of the
North, the modern America and Russia:

"The French Ogmios will be supported by so great a
number that his Empire (a United Europe?) and his great
law will extend over a large area. For some time the blood
of the Innocents will be shed profusely by the guilty ones
recently elevated to power. Then will occur great floods
and great loss. This will occur to the Aquiloners by the

149

will of God. During great and marvelous events harmonized with the Holy Scriptures, the persecution of the Spiritual people will have its origin in the powerful leaders of Aquilon, who shall dominate also over the Orient. The persecution will last one year, or somewhat less, for then the leaders of Aquilon will die. The same thing will also take place in the South (Asia and Africa), where for the space of three years Spiritual people will be persecuted even more fiercely, by the Apostate seducers who will have absolute control over the Church. The people of God, observers of His wisdom, will be persecuted horribly; the affliction of these Spiritual will be such that their blood will flow everywhere."

In "Aquilon" itself, a leader will receive praise as the greatest murderer of all time:

"One of the horrible leaders of Aquilon will be told by his adherents as an ultimate in praise that he has shed more human blood of the Spiritual Innocents than anyone could spill of wine. This Leader will commit incredible crimes against the true Children of God. Human blood will flow in the public streets and holy places, like water after an impetuous rain, and nearby rivers will be colored red."

Another cruel leader, who Nostradamus likens to Nero, will re-light the crematorium ovens once used by the Nazis, this time to exterminate not just Jews, but the "heretics" of all faiths:

Three times over will one do worse than Nero,
Very much human blood will flow, those valiant will flee,
He will cause the death-furnace to be rebuilt,
Peace dead, the new leader will cause terrible scandal. IX. 17.

The young Nero of the three furnaces,
Will cause those who recite the Ancient Wisdom to be thrown in and burned,
Happy will be those who are far from such practices,
Three of his relatives will finally murder him in ambush.
IX. 53.

The chief instigator of global persecution, however, will be the head of the One World Church--the Antichrist, who Nostradamus describes in these two verses:

Buried in the earth alive, voices of the holy stifled,
When a human flame will declare himself divine (the false Messiah),
He will cause the earth to be stained with the blood of the spiritual,
He will destroy holy places, setting up impure temples instead. IV, 24.

The Antichrist will annihilate three times over,
In the twentieth; for seven bloody years will his persecution last,
Against heretics, dead, captive, exiled,
But then comes blood, bodies strewn in death, waters reddened, hail upon the earth. VIII, 77.

For seven years near the end of the 20th century, will the "Antichrist" or false Messiah personally conduct his campaign of extermination against those who will not conform to his One Religion. In the end, however, his power will collapse amid natural catastrophes and strife, that will portend the end of the Present Age of existence...

43. 2000 PLUS--THE PSYCHICS LOOK AT THE NEW AGE
Psychic investigator Jeffrey Goodman, in a survey among several American psychics, discovered that they all prophesy very similar events for the world in the beginning of the 21st century--events which will be part of a general rebirth and renaissance for human faith and civilization. First, the psychics note that the world of the next century will be a very different place: As the result of the Earth's axis shift about the year 2000, most of the present day continents will change their shapes, with large portions submerged, while new continental masses will have risen in what are now the oceans. The climate

too will be altered, with Alaska becoming more temperate, and Florida turning colder.

The survivors of the axis shift, the psychics agree, will begin rebuilding, with the initial steps taking place in New Zealand, because it will have suffered least during the transformations. This land, they agree, will become a "land of hope and opportunity."

At this time, mankind--having learned what a disasterous course the rank social materialism of the twentieth century has led us--will devote themselves to a true spiritual renewal. Teachers will appear--from this and other dimensions--to aid in this reformation, to "lift the veil from men's minds," and offer new cultural directions.

By the year 2030, new governments and economies will be established but their influences will be of a greatly reduced level, with their guiding emphasis being to promote personal development, and insure fair distribution of essentials. Science, too, will take a more creative direction: Instead of being used for exploitation and regulation, it will explore revolutionary new forms of energy and growth, while remaining in perfect harmony with the earth and its environment. Some of the scientific achievements the psychics forecast are: Using prayer for increasing agricultural yield and controlling weather; tapping the earth's and the sun's electromagnetic field as a universal power source; using color, light and crystals for healing; and finding the secret to limb regeneration.

The psychics ended their vision of the future by saying that it will take some time for the world and mankind to revive after the convulsions of the Present Age--but the rebuilding will eventually lead to higher and nobler planes of human expression and existence, the likes of which we have difficulty in being able to comprehend today.

44. THE FUTURE ACCORDING TO ROSS PETERSON

Ross Peterson is an extraordinary man who, since 1974 after an injury resulting from a fall, has become a "channel" for psychic information. Much in the same manner as Edgar Cayce, Peterson places himself into a trance, and an associate puts questions to him and copies down his answers. He is totally unaware consciously of what he says while giving such a reading--and even if he was, he would not understand it, because the data that comes forth is not of his own, but is from somewhere else--from a dimension which records all past and future events. Most of Peterson's readings have consisted of medical "examinations," whereby he psychically tells what is wrong with a person and prescribes healing measures--most often never even meeting or seeing the person on the physical plane. What is remarkable is that Peterson's accuracy so far has been calculated between 90 and 95 per cent.

Besides medical readings, the psychic has also made startling prophecies about the future. Here is what he has foreseen:

Between 1984 and 1987 there is a likelihood for a nuclear war. But the *real* major disasters will be changes in the earth's crust. Destruction will first affect Georgia and Carolina; then Los Angeles will "plunge under water," with a flooding of the San Joaquin valley, eventually leading to an area as far east as Nevada turning into an inland sea. In 1989 or 1990, a major shock will devastate the Northwest U.S. and southwest Canada, leading to economic collapse. Manhattan is scheduled to disappear by 2006. Before 2030, Ireland and western England will suffer a similar sinking. In the meantime, parts of Spain, Portugal and Italy are to be submerged; a "ring of fire" will bring about the destruction of Borneo, Japan, northern Alaska, Washington, Oregon and California; and the St. Lawrence river will reverse directions, filling and overflowing the Great Lakes into the Mississippi valley, turning Louisiana and Mississippi states into a "great inland sea."

Peterson, however, sees these coming earth changes in a positive light: In one trance he stated that it is only in times of "disruption or chaos that the masses of men begin to turn to that which is within," beseeching God for help, and a "return to the simple ways, the fulfilling of the purpose of life itself." These new realizations, the psychic predicts, will aid in fostering a spiritual rebirth. He foresees, amazingly--yet as has also been prophesied by Edgar Cayce and others--that "the next great awakening of Christianity will be in the land of the Bear, in Russia." But he stipulates that this Christianity will be different from the Christianity we know today: "It will be modified to conform more closely to the true teachings of Jesus, the Master. For ye shall find that the ancient Asian concept of reincarnation will be wedded, as it originally was, to the traditional teachings of Catholicism and from this marriage a new faith will emerge. It will lead to a thousand years of light and love demonstrated in the experience of man." Peterson foresees further that the new spiritual age is promised to begin "in 1998 or 1999," and will be marked by "the second coming of Christ." Peterson explains this event in these terms: "Christ will be defined as a consciousness. The second coming of Christ is when masses and masses of men seek God first. All others second. And this will come, in the midst of the earth's troubles. Men, amid the darkness, will see God's light in the sky."

THE SIXTH THUNDER

45. WILL THE PRESIDENTIAL DEATH CYCLE BE BROKEN?

We are presently in a very special presidential election year--one falling as it does every twenty years at the very beginning of the decade. Because of this there are many who fear that whoever is elected in 1980 will certainly die in office, or be assassinated. Why? Because ever since President William H. Harrison was elected in 1840, and died in office, every U.S. President elected at 20-year intervals from that time has not survived his term. The list reads this way:

Harrison	1840	Died	1841
Lincoln	1860	Assassinated	1863
Garfield	1880	Assassinated	1881
McKinley	1900	Assassinated	1901
Harding	1920	Died	1923
Roosevelt	1940	Died	1944
Kennedy	1960	Assassinated	1963

What makes this occurrence truly remarkable is that of the remaining 27 Presidents *not* elected in the 20-year cycle since 1840, only *one* died in office, and neither did those elected in 1800 or 1820. The "death cycle" thus began in 1840, and according to probability tests, there is

155

1 chance in 2,500 that this cycle is due only to coincidence. But why does it happen?

Astrologers point out that the presidential death cycle has coincided exactly with the great Jupiter-Saturn planetary conjunction, that occurs at intervals of 19.85 years and, since the inception of this nation, falls always on the decade-opening election year. What is equally remarkable is that only since 1840 has the conjunction been taking place every time in an earth sign--Taurus, Virgo or Capricorn--and will continue to do so until the year 2080. But there is one important exception: In 1980, Jupiter and Saturn will be meeting in an air sign, in Libra. For this reason, astrologers are predicting that the man elected in 1980 will *not* die in office this time. In fact, they go on to forecast that the presidential winner is destined to become one of the most universally popular American leaders in our nation's history.

46. FOUR NOSTRADAMUS PROPHECIES ON COMING REVOLUTION AND WAR IN RUSSIA

These poems, written in the year 1558, tell of an event that has the potential of being fulfilled in the very next few years. The first line reads:

The law of Thomas More (communism) will decline,
Acceptance of another philosophy more appealing,
The Dnieper river (in western Russia) will give way first,
Given goods by another nation more attractive. III, 95.

Sir Thomas More's *Utopia*, published in 1516 and read by Nostradamus as a young man, advocated the communal sharing of wealth. The Dnieper river, which flows through the Russian Ukraine, rises in the Valdai hills near Moscow. The prophet predicts here that Communism will fail in Russia, to be replaced by another ideology, probably capitalism. The last line some interpreters see being the United States, and its recent trade agreements with the Soviets. In the second verse:

156

At the places and times of religious abstinence (during Lent),
The communal law will be opposed,
The old leaders will strongly support it, then all removed,
"Loving of Everything in Common"--Communism--to suffer setback. I, 14.

In the spring season, there will be a major upheaval in the government of the Soviet Union. The aging political bosses of the Kremlin will be forced out of power, and a new rulership will be established. As a result, the principles of Communism will remain in name only. Verse three:

From the Slavish people (Russia) will come songs, slogans and threats,
But then their Leaders and Statesmen placed in prisons,
The pronouncements of these headless idiots,
Will have been received as divine utterances. I, 14.

Nostradamus forecasts here that someday Russia's present administrators will find themselves confined to their own Gulag camps. The use of propaganda and fear tactics will come to an end. Verse four:

After coldness, rivers overflow (in the spring), when idiots are expelled from power,
The Northern Bear in confusion, opposed by the Orient,
Poisoned, the land encircled, they will be driven from their City,
Joyful return, the new philosophy no more. Presage 21.

Once again, we find reference to the springtime as being the time of the revolution, and to "idiots" who will be overthrown. The "Northern Bear" is an age-old symbol for Russia. Dipping farther into the future beyond the coming revolution, Nostradamus foresaw that the Soviets will one day be attacked by China. They will invade, using germ warfare, and the conflict will be so serious that the Russians' "City"--probably Moscow--will be for a time abandoned. But the verse says they will return in victory,

157

and in the rebuilding of their capital and government, the last vestiges of Communism--the "new philosophy"--will be swept away.

47. THE FOUR HORSEMEN OF THE APOCALYPSE--A MODERN INTERPRETATION

Nearly two thousand years ago, the apostle John had a remarkable vision of the future, and wrote what he saw in a lengthy document, which has come down to us today as the "Book of Revelation," or the "Christian Apocalypse." In Chapter 6 of the prophetic book, John described the appearance of four horses and their riders, each with distinctive characteristics, symbolizing four successive periods of trouble and woe for the world. While Bible commentators over the past two millenia have given many different interpretations for these Horsemen, there is one application that is seeing a disturbing fulfillment in our modern age--and offers us a warning of what is yet down the road.

According to a new, updated system of interpretation, the Four Horsemen represent major events taking place in the world from 1881 on. In that year, on January 9, the Sun officially left the sign of Pisces, and from that date to the year 2000 (when the Age of Aquarius will begin), is the "time of change."

The First Horseman, the Messenger of Subjugation, is pictured riding a victorious white steed, and he holds a bow and wears a crown. John wrote, "and he went out conquering and to conquer." The modern interpretation sees this rider as representing global imperialism by the Western powers from 1881 until the early years of the twentieth century. The Second Horseman is the Messenger of War: He is astride a crimson, blood-hued horse, and is given a large sword, so that he may, "take away peace from the earth, so that men should slay one another." Within the first three-quarters of the twentieth century, the world passed through a period of global warfare and international crises of such magnitude as never before experienced: The Russo-Japanese War, 1904-1905; World War I, 1914-1918; World War II, 1939-1945; Korea, 1951-1953; Vietnam, 1966-1974, plus innumerable smaller conflicts. The Third Horseman is the Messenger of Famine--and he represents the period many believe we have now entered. He rides a black, sackcloth-colored horse, and holds a pair of balances in his hand. John tells how during the times of this horseman, a handful of wheat and barley will cost a whole day's wages, and oil and wine will not be available--meaning that food and other essentials will be scarce, and prices will be greatly inflated. Surviving this, we look forward to the Fourth Horseman, who is the most feared of all. He approaches on a deadly pale, venom-spotted horse; the rider's name is Death, and Hades--the ruler of the dead--accompanies him. John portends that this messenger of Destruction will be "given power over a fourth of the earth, to kill with a sword, famine, pestilence and wild beasts." We may note that this rider carries a sword, like the Second Horseman of War--meaning that what is forecast here is another global conflict, only one far worse than any in the past. According to the prophecy, one-fourth of the world's population will be severely affected, and in the near future, this will mean *over one billion people*. The one consolation is that the Fourth Horseman is the last one John foresaw. Beyond, the apostle prophesied other difficulties and calamities, but eventually these will pass, and an age of a "new heaven and a new earth" will someday dawn. From our perspective today, however, only two Horsemen have passed by--we have yet to face the forebodings of the remaining two....

48. WHEN BRITANNIA WILL SINK BENEATH THE WAVES

There exist many disturbing prophecies, made by living psychics, and seers of the past, that tell how a major geologic upheaval is going to occur soon, that will transform most of the island of Britain into ocean. The suddenness with which this cataclysm will occur was attested to by Edgar Cayce, who prophesied that northern Europe is to be "changed in a twinkling of an eye."

English psychic John Pendragon, who died in 1970, foresaw London to be partially submerged, and the lowlands of his native nation to be covered with water.

Madame H.P. Blavatsky, mystic and psychic, wrote in 1882 that the British Isles would be the first among many victim nations to suffer from earth upheavals and vast floodings.

A seventeenth century prophet, Friar Balthassar Mas, saw in a vision an island overwhelmed by a deluge and swallowed by the sea. Soon after the terrible tragedy, Mas wrote that he saw the waters begin to recede, little by little, and the upper portions of sunken towers and buildings appeared once again. The voice in his vision told him the island was England.

Nostradamus, in his prophetic poems written four hundred years ago, also forewarned the future English submergence, and offered several interesting details. In one verse, designated Century III, Quatrain 70, the French seer portended that, "Great Britain, comprising England, will be flooded very high with waters." The only area indicated to be affected will be England, and this is reiterated in another verse--X, 66--where Nostradamus envisioned, "The *island* of Scotland will suffer from frost." Scotland today is not an island--but would become one if England, to its south, were to disappear. If we look at a topographical map of Britain showing the various elevations, we can see that the land of England proper is generally lower than its neighbor, Scotland. In the very same verse, the seer predicted further: "The chief of London will reside in America" (in the original French verse, the name clearly appears--"L'Americh," America). It appears the sinking disaster will be so great that the British government will be forced to temporarily move to the New World. In a parallel poem--II, 94--Nostradamus foresaw: "The maritime Lion (Britain) will be in hopeless terror, people will flee over the sea in countless numbers, but a quarter of a million will not escape." These words are very ominous, for it warns that over 250,000 Englishmen will die as a result of this mass evacuation. And this may be only the casuality list over and above that created by the disaster itself. In Presage 12, Nostradamus wrote: "Cities will fall into the Thames

river, the noise will claim a fourth of those who are asleep." The "cities of the Thames" center about one of the largest metropolises in the world, London, and the disaster--a great subterranean "noise" or vibration that will cause buildings to collapse--is mentioned to occur at night, and will claim one-fourth of all of London's population, or several million. In yet another verse--IX, 31--we read these lines: "In the tin island (Britain was a tin supplier in the days of the Phoenicians), Saint George (England's patron saint) will be half submerged, The temple at Easter, great cracks will appear." Other verses--VIII, 53 and VI, 22--identify this "temple" as being a "heavenly temple" or "temple of the sun" situated "at London." This is Westminister Abbey in London, built upon the former site of a temple to the sun-god Apollo--which itself was destroyed by an earthquake in A.D. 154. According to the prophecy, the coming earth upheaval will occur around Easter season, and the floor and walls of the Abbey are going to be ripped apart by the convulsions. There appears to be a depression along the northern Thames bank which passes beneath the city of London along Strand, Fleet Streets and Cornhill. If enough pressure were exerted upon this depression by an earthquake, the bed could give way and buckle, causing the damage to London and its Abbey as predicted.

Despite the great quake, and the flooding of London, Nostradamus indicates in one more prophecy that London will survive, to become an island city. In verse IX, 48 he wrote that, "The great city of the maritime ocean (London), Will be surrounded by a crystalline swamp"-- that is, shallow waters covered with ice. This is reminiscent of the Nostradamian poem we read above, that described the "*island* of Scotland will suffer from *frost.*" In the verse here, the seer goes on to say that, because of the new island city is now standing in the middle of ocean waters, it will be exposed to the harsh Atlantic weather: "In December and in the spring, It will be tried by violent winds."

Thus--according to the prophets of the present and past--Britain, which in days gone by once ruled over the waves, is destined to someday tragically rule under them as well.

162

49. A DREAM OF THE TWENTY-SECOND CENTURY

On March 3, 1936, while sleeping aboard a train en route from Detroit to his home in Virginia Beach, Virginia, Edgar Cayce had a strange dream--a dream that catapulted him into the far future. In the year 2100, he foresaw, he would return to a new lifetime, in what is now Nebraska. Though today the place is near the center of the nation, in that century the Nebraskan city he will be born in will be on the Pacific coast--the entire western portion of America having disappeared. His family name, Cayce heard in his dream, will sound strange to him. At a young age, he will remember his former life as Edgar Cayce from two hundred years before, and several scientists will come to visit him and study his story. He described them as being mostly bald, long bearded, and wearing flowing robes and strange glasses--glasses that may be used to "read" a person's aura, electromagnetic field, psychic energy centers, and life rhythms. These scientists will take the young boy on a trip across the country, and he will clearly point out to them all the places he had lived and worked in his former life--in Kentucky, Alabama, New York, Michigan, and Virginia. Cayce remembered in his dream that they traveled about in a "cigar-shaped, metal flying ship which moved at high speed."

As they journeyed, Cayce saw many unusual things. The houses of the 22nd century were mostly of glass. Industries were small, and scattered here and there--not concentrated in large cities. Indeed, most cities of our present age were gone--New York, he noted, had been destroyed by both war and earthquake, and only by that time was it safe enough for its former inhabitants and their descendants to begin rebuilding. Water, he also foresaw, will cover most of Alabama. And what is now Norfolk, Virginia will become an immense seaport, filled with international traffic.

As a result of their excursion, the scientists and the young "second" Cayce rediscovered and collected many important records of Cayce's work in the past life. Nebraska, it appears, will become a major center of learning by the 22nd century, for the scientists, Cayce envisioned, returned there with him, to do an intensive study of their findings. Cayce, in later years, grew up and again lived as a great psychic and devoted healer--only in this new life, he will be far more respected, for the intellectual and spiritual climate of the future will have advanced to learn not to ridicule such abilities, but to study them as a significant source of information. The Cayce of 200 years hence, the Cayce of the past foresaw, will enjoy a long, peaceful and much celebrated life. And with that happy note, his dream of things to come, came to an end.

50. "PROPHETECY" AND ITS OUTLINE OF THINGS TO COME

In the studies being presented, we have been looking at the messages of many prophets, and identifying parallels between them. One modern researcher, Thomas Dimanne, has coined a word to describe such a study as "prophetecy." The root of the word is the Greek "prophetes," which was the name given to a group of priests who interpreted the utterances of the ancient Oracle of Delphi. Thus, prophetecy does not refer to the ability to prophesy, but means, as Dimanne defines it, the "science of *interpreting* prophecies of the future." More than just interpreting, Dimanne has gone one step beyond--to formulate a synthesis of the works of hundreds of seers and seeresses through the ages. Here are the high points of this "prophetetic" picture:

I. Period of Disintegration: Hyperinflation and depression, leading to the collapse of interdependent world economies. Increasing centralization of power, with initial steps taken toward Huxlian-Orwellian totalitarian government. Old ideologies (Democracy and Communism) remain in name only. Polarization of the world nations into two opposing power blocs: The Far East, Middle East, non-white, newly developed nations *versus* the Western and Soviet, white, over-developed nations. Progressive dissolution of Western Civilization: Rank materialism, sensationalism, nihilism. Ecumenism of the Christian churches. Radical changes in church doctrine, organiza-

164

tion and function. Government support and authority given to church programs for the restoration of "moral" and "religious" standards amidst increasing decadence. In counterbalance, increasing spread of "New Age" spirit and practices.

II. Period of Catastrophe: Ecological disasters on land and in the oceans. World-wide imbalances in nature. Crop failures and severe food shortages, due to global weather alterations. Limited nuclear-bacteriological, and all-out conventional, World War between the East and West power blocs. The collapse of Western civilization. The destruction of the past two thousand years' artistic and scientific achievements. Chaos and revolution. Government breakdown and a brief period of local autonomous rule based on survival needs. Total pessimism, leading to mass movement toward religious revival. Increasing messianic hopes. Rise of religious leaders and aggressive new forms of church power as the nuclei for restoration. Counterbalance: The appearance of teachers of true Spiritual wisdom, who give comfort to the suffering, but reject power.

III. Period of Restoration: Economic recovery, with new economies and economic centers established. Gradual control of world economy by the new churches. Re-establishment of governments, weak but totalitarian, dominated by religious leaders. Global religious and conservative consciousness. Strong desire to end the world's ills through unity and collective controls. Initial steps taken toward the creation of a one-world religio-political monopolist government. Emergence of the "Babylon Civilization:" Ideational, pseudo-mystic, monastic, mass-hypnotic, irrational salvationism. Collapse of traditional Protestant-Orthodox structural organization, and a synthesis of the fragments into a Global Church. First steps toward forcing the Eastern religions to disban, or compromise their Spiritual teachings, and be absorbed by the Global Church. Realization of Messianic hopes through the initial appearance of a World "Savior" figure. Counterbalance: True Spiritual teachers begin going underground, giving their "New Age" message in secret meetings, and preserving and hiding sacred writings of the Ancient Religions. The teachers warn that the World "Savior" figure is without inner Light.

IV. Period of Domination: World economy stabilized, totally controlled by the Global Church. Totalitarian governments control regional and continental populations, yet are dominated by the dictates of the Global Church. Universal Peace, but at the price of individual freedom. Political and religious power maintained through economic and psychological mass controls. Opponents labeled as "heretics" and "antichristians." Flourishing of the "Babylon Civilization:" Ideational, but with increasing tendencies toward materialism. Forced "conversion" of all religions and philosophies in the name of world peace. Establishment of a One Global Religion and One Global Government as the only acceptable universal authority. Death sentences given to those who do not conform. Ascendancy of the World Savior figure as the object of global worship. Counterbalance: True Spiritual teachers, and their disciples, continue to give their message, in the face of mounting persecution. Despite the enforcement of the One Global system, many remain faithful to their own Spiritual beliefs. Continued study in secret of the Ancient Religions and the sacred writings.

V. Second Period of Disintegration: The Global Church becomes wealthy and materialistic from its world economic controls. A new wave of world ecological and geological disasters causes economic depression, but the Global Church continues to grow rich through unequal distribution of economic goods. Revolt of the world leaders. Destruction of the Global Church as a unifying power. The Babylon Civilization ends: Realization of spiritual corruption, hypocricy, universal despair. Counterbalance: Victory of the Spiritual over intolerance. Teachers of the Light warn of the coming "cleansing" and lead their disciples to places of safety.

VI. Period of Termination: Global chaos and disorder. Counter-revolution begun by the World Savior figure and remnants of the Global Church. Conflicts among various factions for world control. Preparation for World War. Spiritual forces of Light and Darkness are seen fighting in the heavens. The earth shifts on its axis. Mass destruction. Warring forces on the earth are annihilated. Triumph of the Light.

VII. Period of Re-Creation: The Spiritual folk, the Teachers and their disciples, emerge from hiding. Rebuilding is begun, in harmony with the earth. Founding of the Aquarian Spirit-Age. Present forms of religious and political power are abandoned and forgotten. The New Civilization of Light emerges: Spiritual, intuitive, supersensory, transcendental. The appearance of True World Saviors. The brotherhood of man, and the communion with the Godhead, and Spiritual progression continues unlimited....

51. VISIONS OF ENOCH THE PROPHET--THE FINAL TRANSCENDENCE OF MAN

The person of Enoch has always fascinated Bible scholars, because he is one of the few patriarchs named in the Old Testament who led such a spirit-filled life that he did not die, but was "taken to heaven" before it was his time. The *Book of Enoch*, which is often classified as second century B.C. Jewish pseudographia but nevertheless contains curious elements suggesting a much greater antiquity, records how the prophet of old made many visitations to higher spiritual realms before his final departure from the earth. In one of these, Enoch was given a prophecy that tells of a future time when mankind will no longer exist on the material plane, but will be joined in the same infinite dimension as the Divine:

And it came to pass that my spirit was translated
And it ascended into the heavens:
And I saw the holy sons of God,
They were stepping on flames of fire:
Their garments were white,
And their faces shown like snow.
And I saw two streams of fire,
And the light of that fire shone like hyacinth,
And I fell upon my face before the Lord of Spirits.
And the angel Michael seized me by the right hand,
And lifted me up and led me forth into all the secrets,
And he showed me all the secrets of righteousness.

And he translated my spirit into the heaven of heavens,
And I saw there a structure built of crystal,
And between these crystals tongues of living fire.
And I saw angels who could not be counted,
A thousand thousands, and ten thousand times ten thousand,
Encircling that house.
And they came forth from that house,
Raphael, and Michael, and Gabriel, and Phanuel,
And with them the Head of Days,
His head white and pure as wool,
And his raiment indescribable.
And I fell on my face,
And my whole body became relaxed,
And my spirit was transfigured;
And the angel came to me and greeted me and said to me:
"This is the Son of Man who is born with righteousness;"
And he said to me:
"He proclaims unto you peace in the name of the world to come;
Far from hence has proceeded peace since the creation of the world,
And so shall it be unto you forever and ever.
And in that day all shall walk in his ways,
With him will be their dwelling-places, and with him their heritage
And the righteous shall have peace in an upright way,
In the name of the Lord of Spirits forever and ever."

52. TWO MORMON PROPHECIES ABOUT THE FUTURE OF AMERICA

America has not only been the home of many new and diverse political ideas, but has also seen the birth of several new religions and sects. And not a few of the founding fathers of these American religions have been inspired with visions of the future of their land. Two visions were given to leaders of the early Church of the Latter-Day Saints, or the Mormons. Brigham Young, who led his people to settle in Utah, delivered this forecast of things to come in 1869, at a time when his people were suffering the intolerance of others: "All that you now know can scarcely be called a preface to the sermon that will be preached with fire and sword, tempests, earthquakes, hail, rain and fearful destruction. You will hear of magnificent cities now idolized by people, sinking into the earth and entombing the inhabitants. The sea will heave itself beyond its bounds engulfing many cities. Famine will spread over the nation, and nation will rise against nation, kingdom against kingdom, states against states, in our own country and in foreign lands."

Orson Pratt, another Mormon leader, had an even more detailed vision of America's future troubled times. Writing near the end of the last century, he foresaw: "What then will be the condition of the people when the great and dreadful civil war will come? It will be very different from the war between the North and South. It will be neighborhood against neighborhood, city against city, town against town, state against state, and they will go forth destroying, and being destroyed. Manufacturing will almost cease, great cities will be left desolate. The time will come when the great city of New York will be left without inhabitants."

53. IS AN ATTACK COMING FROM OUTER SPACE?

One of the agreements signed by the United States and the Soviet Union in recent years involves the ban of sophisticated weaponry from space. Fascinating is the fact that the use of such weapons to attack earthly nations from the heavens above was the subject of a prophecy over four centuries old. In 1558, the French seer Nostradamus wrote these words:

Si grand famine par onde pestifere,
Par pluie longue le long du pole arctique:
Samarobryn cent lieues de l'hemisphere,
Vivront sans loi exempt de politique. VI, 5.

A great famine created by a disease-producing wave,
Carried by a lengthy rain from the Arctic Pole,
Samarobryn one hundred leagues from the hemisphere,
Living without the laws of war, exempt from agreements.

The key line here is line 3, "Samarobryn one hundred leagues from the hemisphere." Analyzing one element it contains at a time, we can find what the subject matter of the whole verse is about:

1. "One hundred leagues"--In sixteenth century Europe, the measurement of a league varied considerably, from 2.5 to as much as 4.5 miles. In another of his poems, however, Nostradamus makes mention of a convent named Saint-Paul-de-Mousole, situated outside the seer's birthplace at Saint-Remy in southern France. He described the convent as being "three leagues from the Rhone." By modern measurement, the convent is a fraction over eight miles from the banks of the Rhone river, making Nostradamus' three leagues about 2.7 miles each. "One hundred leagues," then, would be equivalent to 270 miles.

2. "From the hemisphere"--This is a most interesting phrase, because in order to be 270 miles from all points of the "hemisphere" of the earth, one would have to be orbiting at that distance out in space. In modern astronautical terms in fact, the prophet's use of the word "hemisphere" is the most correct, since someone or something a certain distance from merely the "earth" on one side would be that much farther away from the other side of the earth at any given moment.

3. "Samarobryn"--This word is composed of two word segments: "samara," or seed pod, and a form of the Latin verb "obire." The latter of these means, "to wander, to travel, to *encircle*," and as an intransitive verb is used specifically to describe a celestial body, "something which has the appearance of a *heavenly object* setting in the sky." As to a description of the object itself, the first word segment, "samara," may be a clue. More accurately speaking, a samara is the seed of an ash, elm or maple tree, and is comprised of a central pod with one or two projecting leafy wings.

171

Putting all the elements together, we find that the prophet was attempting to picture an object spherical in shape, having wing projections (solar panels?), and circling the earth at an altitude of 270 miles. In modern terms, this would be a satellite or space platform. It is noteworthy that 270 miles is considered an ideal orbital altitude--it was in fact the orbit of ill-fated Skylab.

But in Nostradamus' prophecy, this orbiting space vehicle is the source of the disaster described in the first two lines: It will inject a "disease-producing wave" into the Arctic region, that will be carried by a "lengthy rain," and produce a great famine. Now the Arctic is a barometric pressure region where storms originate and move southward. If someone were to seed the Arctic atmosphere with deadly bacteria that uses water vapor as a carrier, the storm clouds would spread the germs and disperse them over Canada, the United States, the Soviet Union and Europe. The prophet describes the pestiferous attack to create a "famine," suggesting the bacteria will be directed toward destroying the agricultural crops of these nations, precipitating severe food shortages. The one world power that has the means of carrying out such an act, that would profit by a general weakening of the West and the Soviet Union, and yet would not itself be affected by the attack--is China. The Chinese presently have the technology to create offensive bacteria weapons and--in the early 1980's--place such weapons into space, into a circumpolar orbit. Since China's weather consists of eastern and western monsoon wind patterns, its territory would not suffer from an Arctic-originating germ dispersal. Nostradamus' last prophetic line alludes that the "laws of war"--the rules of the Geneva Convention which forbid the use of germ warfare--will be completely disregarded, and that China will also act outside any agreement on space weaponry ban made by the United States and the Soviet Union. We should remember, too, that we have the means today of detecting the presence of nuclear weapons in outer space--but we have no method of detecting bacteria weapons.

THE SEVENTH THUNDER

54. THE PHILOSOPHERS AND THE FUTURE

It is significant that the most prominent among historical philosophers in this century--Spengler, Sorokin, Toynbee, etc.--all agree that Western civilization is presently showing all the signs of decay and disintegration exhibited by other pasᴛ civilizations before their collapse. But while it took several centuries for such civilized centers as Rome and Athens to fall, modern technology has speeded up the pace of our present day history, so that the collapse of our civilization will be quicker and more tragic. Our culture, the philosophers believe, could very well die amid the chaos of a terrible war to come.

What, then, will emerge once Western Civilization has passed from the world scene? Arnold J. Toynbee suggested that the next logical step will be the establishment of a global state under the dominance of a universal Church.

Toynbee takes as one past analogy the fall of the Roman Empire and the rise of the Catholic Church. Civilization disintegrates by jolts, or "rout-rally-rout" as the historian called it. For Rome, the jolts were a series of internal wars, misgovernments, and barbarian assaults that finally culminated in a near collapse, in the third century. In the last "rally" before the final collapse, the Christian Church--which had previously suffered persecution but

173

had nevertheless grown to a position of power--was accepted and taken in by the Roman Emperors as a partner in government, as a reinforcement against the loss of control. When the Empire finally went to pieces in the fifth and sixth centuries, the Church was left as the beneficiary, filling the vacuum left and becoming sole ruler. Toynbee noted that the same relation between a declining civilization and a rising religion can be seen in a dozen other historical instances.

So far, Toynbee observed, we are following along a similar pattern: Rout--World War I; rally--League of Nations; rout--World War II; rally--United Nations. Today, the ecumenical movement among the Christian churches, as well as a growing new revival in organized religion, is a portent of things to come: After the final rout, in a next World War, the seeds of religiosity now being planted in the present will prosper, and a "new Christianity" as Toynbee called it will fill a new power vacuum, to become the inheritor of Western civilization. But, as Toynbee noted, the "new Christianity" will not be anything like the Christianity of today. Just as early Catholicism, in its zeal to convert pagan Europe incorporated many pagan practices into its framework as a compromise, so the "new Christianity" will "graft" on elements of all other existing philosophies and religions in order to become a global system. What Toynbee failed to foresee, however, is that, while Catholic Christianity became heir to only Roman Europe, and because of its limited extent was forced to tolerate the existence of other major religions in areas beyond its domain, the "new Christianity" will become the beneficiary of the entire world--and the other major religions will not be able to escape its intolerance. The future world religion will be in a position of absolute power: What beliefs or philosophies will not be joined into it by compromise will be pressured in by force--or threatened with extermination.

A Russian philosopher, Nicholas Berdyaev, writing in 1923, captured the spirit and atmosphere of the coming universal religious state, in these words:

"Now is night upon us. We are going into a period soon of senility and decay. There may be a new chaos of peoples; the feudalism of Europe may be a possibility. A terrible home sickness has taken hold of the better part of mankind. It is the sign of the approach of a new age of religion.

"The new Middle Ages will be, inevitably and in the highest degree, 'of the people'--and not in the least democratic. Power will be strong, often dictatorial, for the people will invest men of outstanding merit with the sacred attributes of power.

"The notion of progress will be discarded as camauflaging the true ends of life: There will be a life, there will be a creation, there will be a turning to God--or to Satan.

"This process of unification and universalization will strike hardest at the chosen individualist who belongs to no group or collective. We are witnessing a reversion to the herd instinct, but in new, civilized and technicalized forms.

"Mass movements always demand a unifying and strength-giving symbol, which also becomes the test for orthodoxy. All who do not accept the symbol are accursed and cast out as heretics. And in our day, the categories of heresy and orthodoxy have already become very important social factors. The domination of the mass over personal conscience has again become a decisive factor. This is clearly a reversion to the Middle Ages."

After this gloomy forecast, Berdyaev--as if speaking to the people of the New Age that will dawn once the future "Middle Ages" pass--remarked: "To accept history is to accept revolution as well. Those who disavow revolution and consider it a crime, forget that to a large degree history is a crime. He who does not approve of crime, should strive for the realization of the true Kingdom of the Spirit."

This very same sentiment was shared by Toynbee, who after predicting the future rise of a universal church, realized that such an institution will in no way be able to satisfy mankind's spiritual needs. He wrote:

"The replacement of a multiplicity of civilizations by a universal church would not have purged human nature of original sin; and this leads to another consideration: So long as original sin remains an element in human nature, Caesar will always have work to do, and there will still be Caesar's things to be rendered unto Caesar, as well as God's to God, in this world. Human society on Earth will not be able wholly to dispense with institutions of which the sanction is not purely the individual's active will to make them work, but is partly habit and partly even force. These imperfect institutions will have to be administered by a secular power which might be subordinated to religious authority but would not thereby be eliminated. And even if Caesar were not merely subordinated but were wholly eliminated by the Church, something of him would still survive in the constitution of the supplanter."

A universal church, based on secular power, then, will ultimately fail. But the answer to man's ultimate quest, as Toynbee saw it, will come only when "human nature itself undergoes a moral mutation which will make an essential change in its character"--in other words, there is a truly spiritual change, within each individual. And to accomplish this, there must come a very real synthesis among the world's religions--not a compromise enforced by a single authority which demands conformity to a narrowly conceived vision of reality based on power, but an honest and earnest re-examination through divine guidance, to re-affirm and practice the essence of each religion's sacred truths. The major religions of mankind are already integrated at the summit where true mystics of each are recognized and influenced by one another, across the barriers of doctrine, ritual and observance. Only when this integration becomes a part of the awareness of mankind and is universally accepted, bringing in its wake a spiritual rebirth on the personal level, then and only then will a real positive transformation take place--and there will be, as Toynbee described it, "a four-part spiritual symphony" leading the way to the true harmony of humanity.

55. THE AMAZING DREAM OF A SEVENTEEN YEAR-OLD BOY

In 1937, a young boy named Joe Brandt suffered a head concussion from a fall he received while horseback riding. For three days afterwards, Joe lay in a Fresno, California hospital, drifting in and out of consciousness and delerium. During this ordeal, however, he also had a strange and terrifying dream that kept recurring and continuing--something so vivid and clear that upon recovering he immediately wrote down everything he had experienced. Today, over forty years later, the pages of Joe's journal are yellowed with age, and the ink is starting to fade, but the import of his dream is still as startling as the day he set it down on paper--perhaps more so, because the particulars he envisioned are now being fulfilled.

The first thing Joe remembered after being thrown to the ground from his horse was suddenly finding himself in Los Angeles. But he recognized that it was not the Los Angeles of 1937, for the city was much larger in size and more crowded than he knew it to be. Everywhere, he saw people riding about in buses and "odd-shaped cars," the latter, he remarked, being smaller and faster than those of the 1930's. He called one a "baby half-sized thing," and noted the various vehicles were not mostly black, as in his day--they were all brightly colored.

Next, Joe found himself standing on Hollywood Boulevard. But again he found that the scenery in many respects was very different. To his delight, the girls were all good looking, and wore "real short skirts and pants." Their hair, he described it, was "all frowzy," or frizzled and puffed up from their heads. To his consternation, however, the young men he saw pass by --most of them Joe's own age--had beards and wore earrings. He wrote that this seemed utterly ridiculous to him: "Nobody in the future on Hollywood Boulevard is going to be wearing earrings--and those beards. I don't think anything like that could ever happen." Joe also noted that all the youth "slouched along" and did a "crazy kind of walk," like a strange new dance-step. Joe tried to imitate them, but found he could not. He called to them, to show him how it was done, but discovered that no one could hear him, or even see him.

177

As Joe walked down the street, he observed several things about the strange futuristic place he was in. He noticed that everywhere he smelled sulfur-like fumes that seemed to hang in the air like a faint fog. The theatres he passed by were showing movies mostly preoccupied with sex: One marquee showed a giant picture of a seductive blonde with six-foot long bared legs--something Joe had never seen advertized in 1937. Joe also walked by a place where famous actors and actresses had written their names and impressed their hands and feet in cement. A few of the names he recognized--but most of them he had never heard of before. Next, Joe found a newstand, and took a look at the front page of a newspaper. He wrote that he could not see the date very well: He thought that the year ended in either a "6" or a "9" but could not make out the decade. There was a picture of the President in the headlines--only, as Joe described it, "It surely wasn't Mr. Roosevelt: He was bigger and heavier, with big ears."

As Joe continued to stroll about in his vision, he slowly became aware of a growing feeling that something momentous was about to happen. The first sign he noticed was that, as he walked through a residential area two blocks north of the Boulevard, there were no birds in the trees. This was very strange, Joe thought, because the day was relatively clear and sunny, and he figured the season was early spring. But no birds sang--anywhere. In fact, he became aware, above the din of traffic, there was a swelling silence, as if all Nature was standing still in anticipation of an imminent event. Joe returned to the Boulevard, and the climax came as a nearby store clock showed the time as five minutes to four in the afternoon. The ground began to vibrate a little. Up and down the street, people stopped and looked at each other wide-eyed. One of the bearded youth Joe overheard tell an earringed lad, "Let's get out of here. Let's move back East." But it was too late--in a matter of seconds, Joe saw sidewalks being pushed up by invisible underground forces, while "those funny little cars" began jumping about and up onto the sidewalk. The middle of the Boulevard split in two, a great crack appeared down the center, and gushing water shot out from broken water mains. Everywhere, people were hanging on for dear life,

179

wailing and screaming in terror. Joe tried to cover his ears, but to no avail: The rising combination of rumblings from below, car horns blowing, sirens blaring, explosions and fires, buildings rattling, and millions of people crying, created a deafening roar.

Amidst this chaos, Joe found himself lifted up into the air, and saw that the disaster was not just happening along the Hollywood Boulevard, or even just in Los Angeles: Slowly, almost imperceptibly, the whole area from the San Bernardino mountains to the coast was tilting toward the ocean. At first, Joe witnessed, most of the Los Angeles buildings stood firm in all the shaking, and many people, to escape the cracking streets, crawled into them for safety. But then, almost all at one instance, the buildings collapsed into rubble, killing their occupants. Elsewhere, hundreds of "little" cars traveling large highways--highways wider and busier than Joe had ever seen before--were slipping and sliding into each other, jumbled into heaps, as the concrete roadways began dissolving into large chunks. Finally, Joe could see the ocean slowly coming in, "moving like a snake across the land." Looking back down at where he had stood on the Boulevard, he noticed the store clock--the time was now 4:29 PM.

The scene of destruction was so overwhelming that Joe had to divert his gaze away from it. As he did so, however, he was shown other catastrophes to take place in other parts of the world. Joe felt that these would happen not at the same time as the California quake, but some would occur earlier, and others later. He saw:

An upheaval beginning in the Grand Canyon, spreading as far as Reno, Nevada and Baja California, with the Boulder Dam to be severely damaged.

Volcanoes erupting in both Colombia and Venezuela, South America.

Japan disappeared into the ocean in so short a time that the Japanese people had only enough time to show an expression of surprise on their faces, before going under.

Hawaii will be destroyed by a giant tidal wave.

A flooding of Istanbul will occur as the Black Sea rises.

Sicily will be devastated, as Mount Etna erupts with unrecorded violence.

The Suez Canal will suddenly dry up.

Huge flooding in England, Ireland and Scotland, at a time thousands of people are in church, praying and holding candles.

In New York City, people will go crazy as the water level rises dangerously--kids will run into restaurants and eat everything in sight, stores will be sacked, fuel will be scarce, and mobs will run aimlessly through the streets as radios and sirens blast away, and searchlights light up the night sky...

Suddenly, Joe found himself back in California, standing on Big Bear mountain. He could see the clock which still read 4:29, and the California coast was still tilting slowly into an encroaching ocean. The very air was disturbed, tossing about out-of-control airplanes and other strange aircraft Joe could not recognize. And in the middle of the mounting disaster, Joe heard hundreds of radio ham operators yelling into their sets to the very last minute, warnings and messages for those to the east: "This is California. We are going into the sea. This is California. We are going into the sea. Get to the mountains. Nevada, Colorado, Arizona, Utah. This is California. We are going into the sea."

At this point Joe's vision ended, as he recovered from his concussion. He wrote that he left the hospital--but for many days afterwards, all he could hear ringing in his ears were those final words: "This is California. We are going into the sea...."

56. FORECASTS BY A POLISH MONK

About the year 1790, an unknown Polish monk wrote down the particulars of a premonition he had received about an age distant to him, but not to us today--the twentieth century. The original Latin work was lost, but a copy in German, printed in 1848 at Leipzig, still exists, so we are certain the prophecy is at least a century old.

The monk began his prophetic treatise by stating, "So remarkable has each century of the world been, so will especially the twentieth of that name, and I have seen the destinies that shall befall the inhabitants of the world at that time." First, he warned, beginning in 1900 and for several decades beyond, "In many nations the princes of power will revolt against their fathers, citizens will rise against their kings, children against their parents, and the human race against each other." The first twenty years beyond 1900 saw the end of most monarchies in Europe, and the Great War, the first truly global conflict involving almost the entire "human race." For the year 1938, the monk foresaw the beginning of another "universal war in the whole world," whereby "many of the greatest and respected cities" will be "desolate, empty of their inhabitants." The prediction was off by one year the start of World War II.

Beyond 1938, the monk warned of yet another global conflict, only one far worse than any previous. First, as a prelude to this war, he said, "financial disasters and ruin of property will cause many tears to fall." Then the blow will come: "Almost all the world will be turned upside down. Men will be without mind and without piety. There shall be poisonous clouds, and rays which can burn more deeply than the equatorial sun, armies encased in iron on the march, flying vessels full of terrible bombs and arrows, and flying stars with sulfuric fire which destroy whole cities in an instant." But, the monk wrote, by the year "1986 once again peace will be accomplished, yet it will last only a few years." What will disturb this peace the Pole indicated in the next line: "In 1988 a terrible comet will be seen in the skies, which shall cause a horrific blow to the earth, raising waters from the seas and drowning many lands." Another disaster is scheduled less than a decade later--"In 1996 a quake will shake the whole world, and parts of Italy, Naples, Sicily, Portugal and Spain will disappear into the earth." Finally, the visionary saw, "There shall come in the year 2000 the day of the Lord, who will judge both the living and the dead. Stars and comets will fall from above, the earth will be set afire with lightning, and the old earth will pass away." But all will not be totally lost, for the monk recorded that, "The history of the world goes on," and the new earth beyond will be a place "wonderful for the righteous" who will live in it, in the beginning of the twenty-first century.

57. THE SIBYLS SPEAK OF THINGS TO COME

The ancient Sibylline prophecies, much studied and respected in classical Rome, spoke tersely of the fate of the modern age. The wrinkled pages of the written oracles of Cumae foresaw: "There shall be no end to war in this world. They shall all slay one another." Another fragment minces no words as to the end-time itself: "Then shall the elements of all the world be desolate, air, earth, sea, flaming fire, and the sky and night, all days to one fire, and to one barren, shapeless mass to come." the Roman playwright, Seneca, borrowing his words from the sibyls, wrote this concerning the destiny of the materialistic world:

A single day will see the burial of mankind,
All that the long forebearance of fortune has produced,
All that has been raised to eminence,
All that is famous and all that is beautiful,
Great thrones, great nations--
All will descend into one abyss,
All will be overthrown in one hour.

In contrast, however, the Sibylline oracles also prophesied of an age beyond the great destruction--an age of Peace and Understanding:

No more will treacherous gold and silver be,
Nor earthly wealth, nor toilsome servitude,
But one fast friendship and mode of life,
Will be with the glad people, and all things
Will common be, and equal right of life.
And wickedness from earth in the vast sea
Shall sink away. And then the harvest-time
Of mortals is near. Strong necessity
Is laid upon these things to be fulfilled.
Not then will any other traveler say,
Recalling, than men's perishable race
Shall ever cease. And then o'er all the earth
A holy nation will the sceptre hold
Unto all ages with their mighty sires.

The sibyls also foresaw in the coming future age:

"The Kingdom of God shall come upon good Men; for the Earth, which is the producer of all things, shall yield to Men the best, and infinite Fruits. And the Cities shall be full of good Men, and the Fields shall be fruitful, and there shall be no more Wars, nor Drought, or Famine; nor Hail to waste the Fruits; but there shall be great Peace in all the Earth, and one King shall live in Friendship with another, to the end of the Age; and the Immortal who lives in the Heavens adorned with Stars, shall give common Law to all Men in all the Earth, and instruct Men what things must be done; for his is the only God, and there is no Other; and he shall burn the great Strength of Men with Fire. Then he shall raise a Kingdom forever over all Men, when he has given his Holy Law to the Righteous, to all whom he promised to open the Earth; and the World of the blessed, and all Joys, and an Immortal Mind, and Eternal Cheerfulness. Out of every country they shall bring Incense, and Gifts to the Houses of the Great God, and there shall be no other House to be enquired for by the Generations of Men that are to come, but the faithful Man has given to be worshipped for Mortals call him the Son of the Great God; and all the Paths of the Fields and rough Shores, and high Mountains, and the raging Waves of the Sea, shall be easily passed, or sailed through in those Days. And there shall be just Riches for Men, for the Government of the Great God shall be just Judgement."

58. ARMAGEDDON--THE PRESENT AGE'S RETRIBUTION

The apostle John, in the Revelation, offers a detailed prophecy of a coming corrupt One World Church, and its ultimate destruction. In Chapter 17, a "Harlot" appears seated on a "beast" with seven heads and ten horns. The harlot woman represents a false religious system, the beast the political powers she will dominate, and the ten horns--verse 12--are, "ten rulers who will receive power and authority for a single hour with the beast." Toward the end of the Chapter, John envisioned that these "ten rulers" will eventually "hate the whore, and shall make her desolate and naked, and shall eat her flesh, and burn her with fire." John depicts the stricken Harlot as "Babylon the Great" and the seven heads she sits on are "seven hills"--the Seven Hills of Rome. In Chapter 18, the apostle details the destruction of "Babylon" or Rome, when the earth will "bewail her and lament her, and they shall see the smoke of her burning." She and her dominion will also suffer from "plagues," an allusion to the Seven Last Plagues of Revelation Chapter 16.

This future destruction of Rome as the seat of a false religious power finds interesting parallels in the prophecies of Nostradamus, who identified the leader of the revolt as a ruler of "Aquilon"--the nations of the North, America and Russia. In the prophet's "Epistle to Henri II," we read:

"On the eve of the desolation of the world, when the Woman (the One World Church) is atop her most high and sublime dignity, a number of the leaders and warlords will confront her, and take away her power, leaving only the empty insigna that had once attracted them. The people will go to the right (self-control) and will not wish to submit to the opposite extreme (government control)--to those who salute, march and drive spurs of subjection into them. And thereupon will come one born of a branch long sterile who will attempt to deliver the people of the world from slavery by enforced peace to which they will have voluntarily submitted. He will be protected by Mars (arms and weapons), stripping Jupiter (paganized Rome) of its honors and powers, and will establish himself in a liberated city between two rivers. Government leaders will be cast out and executed, surprised by the conspiracy directed by the second Thrasibulus (who restored freedom to Athens), who will have worked a long time toward this end."

In a second quote from the "Epistle," the prophet further describes the leader of the coming world revolution:

"The third leader of Aquilon (America-Russia), hearing the lament within his rule will raise a very mighty army, and defying the system established by his predecessors, will attempt to return things as they once were, and place the Vicar of the Hood (the Pope) back in his former position and power. But he will find the Church desolated, abandoned by the Spirit, destroyed by pagan corruptions, and the Old and New Testaments thrown out and burned."

Several of Nostradamus' prophetic quatrain poems also describe the future global revolution against the One World Church, the death of its priests at the hands of the common people, and a military assault on Rome:

In the Temples scandals will be perpetrated,
Those reckoned as honors and commendations,
They will engrave holy statues of gold and silver to each other,
Their end will come in great uprising. VI, 9.

Knowledge of the past and present,
Will be interpreted and controlled by the great Jovialist.
(paganized Church),
Time very late, the world will tire of its authority,
And will become disloyal, and chastise the clergy. X, 73.

The world held in peril by its Leaders suddenly allied,
Stirred up against the Shaven Ones (Cardinals) of powerful counsel,
The people will soon be irritated by these Kings of the Church,
And one afterward to gain what he was denied. Presage 99.

The blood of the Church people will be poured out,
In as great an abundance as water,
For a long time it will not be stopped,
Woe, woe for the clergy, utter ruin and wailing. VIII, 98.

Mars (war) will menace with his bellicose face,
Seventy days he will cause blood to flow,
Rise and fall of the clergy complete,
And more for those who would not listen. I, 15.

The false union will be of short duration,
Some powers transformed, others reformed,
In the vessels (churches) people will be suffering,
Then against Rome will come one like a Lion. VI, 20.

A leader will be angry with those who destroyed the Holy
See (Papacy)
And who outlawed the arms of war,
And who mixed poisoned faith with the sweet (the
corrupted One World Religion),
He will murder many, others drowned at sea, calling for
aid from land. VI, 94.

Times will change radically, discord suddenly to emerge,
Counsel of war to change back what had been changed,
The Great Female (the One World Church) will die, lost
through conspirators come by water,
The Great Rebellion, by the great one plotted. Presage 93.

When Mars and Mercury are conjoined in Pisces,
One will go forth to do battle,
His fleet will travel swiftly by sea,
And he will appear before the Latins (Rome). II, 5.

The City (Rome) beseiged, assault by night,
Few will escape, the enemy will come from the sea,
So few survivors that a woman will faint to see her son
alive,
Saturn and Mars in Aries. I, 41.

In the last two verses, two astrological configurations
are given that indicate a possible time for these two
events to happen: The first will occur in February and
March of 1998; the second will take place in April, 1998. It
is significant that this time period also conforms to other
astrological predictions of future conflict. Modern
stargazers have recognized that the entrance of Mars in
Leo and Jupiter in Aquarius have always, in this century,
portended the advent of world war. The configurations
took place in May, 1914 and in September, 1938--on the
eves of World Wars I and II. The next alignment will
happen in August-September, 1985--a date, as we have

seen from many seers' predictions, that coincides with the coming of World War III. Toward the end of the century, Jupiter will be in Aquarius in January-February, 1998, and Mars will be in Leo in September-October, 1998. That year and the following, 1999, figure prominently in many prophecies of yet another war--and the end of the world.

The assault on Rome, according to Nostradamus, will only be the first phase of an escalating world disaster. Once again quoting the prophet's "Epistle," we find:

"There will commence a tribulation of the Church the like of which will never have been seen. At the same time, such plagues will arise that more than two-thirds of the world will be affected. Such confusion will arise that the ownership of land will be in question, and weeds will grow higher than the knee in the middle of cities. For the clergy there will be utter destruction. There will also ensue the most horrible pestilence or plagues, made worse and more stupendous by a famine that will precede it. Such great tribulations will never have occured since the first foundation of the Christian Church. It will cover the Latin regions (southern Europe) and it will leave its traces in the countries of the Spanish (Central and South America). And at that time the Antichrist will become the Infernal Prince of the Dark forces, and will make all nations tremble, even those of the infidels (Arabs), in the Twentieth for the space of five years. Wars and conflicts will suddenly become grievous, and towns, cities, fortresses and other structures will be burned, desolated, and destroyed, with effusions of blood, women raped, and tiny children dashed and broken against walls. By means of the Prince Infernal, so many evils will be committed that all the world will find itself undone, and desolated. Before these events, birds will be seen, crying in the air: Today, Today! and then will vanish."

Here, Nostradamus predicts a counter-revolution will begin, led by the false "Savior" or Antichrist of the broken One World Religion, and his struggle against the world revolutionary forces will plunge the entire world into the worst chaos ever seen. At the same time, diseases and natural catastrophes will grow in number, adding to the global disaster. Governments will break down, all commerce will cease, order in cities will collapse, and everywhere revolutionary and counter-revolutionary factions will fight each other and commit horrible atrocities. A spiritual sign will then be given in the sky that the end of the world is near.

The Revelation of John, as we noted earlier, calls the diseases and catastrophes to come at the end of the century the Seven Last Plagues. In the Sixth of these, we find a forecast of the beginnings of a world war: "And the sixth angel poured out his vial on the river Euphrates, and its waters were dried up to make ready the path for the kings of the East. And the spirits of devils, working miracles, went forth to the kings of the earth, to gather them to battle together in a place called in the Hebrew tongue Armageddon." Armageddon is identified to be the plain of Megiddo, in northern Israel, the scene of many battles among ancient nations of the past. It is noteworthy that for an invading army from the Orient to reach this location, as John's prophecy foretells, the most direct route would be through Syria and Iraq, where the Euphrates valley is located.

Again, several Nostradamus quatrains tell of the same war and its particulars:

Dark forces will make it appear to men,
That they are the instigators of the coming conflict,
Weapons suddenly seen gathered in the peaceful sky,
Great warfare approaches from the East. I,91.

As the fighting and confusion among the revolutionary and counter-revolutionary forces grow, the call to War will be heard everywhere, and the nations will begin gathering arms for a major confrontation. The Orient will threaten the West once again. But the coming struggle will involve not only the material world, but the spiritual world as well, as forces of Darkness and Light also gather for a decisive battle.

The year 1999, in the seventh month,
There will appear in the heavens the sign of the King of
Terror,
When the great leader of the Mongols (Orient) is reborn,
And Mars (war) reigns supreme once more. X, 72.

The War of Armageddon, according to Nostradamus,
will climax in July, 1999. On earth, forces from the East
will attack, plunging the globe into another World War. In
the sky, strange sights will be seen, portents that spiritual
forces will also be locked in battle. The finale will come
when the heavens reveal the image of Christ, the
God-Spirit, who will appear as a mighty Warrior. John
prophesied the same scene in Revelation Chapter 20:
"And I saw heaven opened, and behold a white horse, and
he that sat upon him was called Faithful, and True, and in
righteousness he judges and makes war. His eyes were as
flames of fire, and on his head were many crowns. And he
was clothed in a robe that dripped blood. The armies
which were in heaven, clothed in dazzling brightness,
followed him. And out of his mouth goes forth a sharp
sword and with it he slays the nations. He had a name
written on his robe-- 'King of Kings and Lord of Lords.' "
    With the appearance of this astral spectacle, John next
predicted the warring forces on earth would be slain by a
terrible hail storm: "And there fell upon earth a great hail
out of heaven, every stone about the weight of a
talent"--over 50 pounds. Nostradamus envisioned the
event this way:

A swift and severe rain,
Will abruptly halt two armies,
Celestial hail and descending fires will cover the sea with
pumice,
Death on seven lands and seven seas (the world) sudden.
II, 18.

A streak of light will split the sky,
Death in mid-speech, great extermination,
Stones from heaven embedded in trees, proud nations
collapsed,
Great thunder, the monsters of humanity purged. II, 70.

Besides the great hail, John foresaw that the Seventh Plague will include a tremendous earth movement: "There followed lightning flashes, loud rumblings, peals of thunder, and a tremendous earthquake. Nothing like it has ever occurred since men dwelt on the earth, so severe and far-reaching was that earthquake. The mighty city fell apart, and the cities of the nations fell. And every island fled away, and the mountains were not found." In the Sixth Seal, in Revelation Chapter 6, John further prophesies that the earth movement will be accompanied by catastrophes in the sky: "Lo, there was a great earthquake, and the sun became black, and the moon turned red, and the stars of the heaven fell to the earth, and the sky split apart like an unrolled scroll." Other Bible prophecies describe the same events too, and indicate that the earth will be momentarily shifted on its axis: "Immediately after the sufferings of those days the sun will be darkened and the moon will not give her light and the stars will be moved out of place, and the power of the heavens will be shaken," Matthew 24:29; "And there will be signs in the sun, the moon and the stars, and on earth distress of the nations and confusion because of the displacement of the sea," Luke 21:25; "The earth is utterly broken down, the earth is utterly moved, the earth is staggering exceedingly. The earth shall reel to and fro like a drunkard and shall be shaken like a hut, and its transgressions shall be heavy upon it, and it shall fall and not rise again," Isaiah 24:19 and 20.

Nostradamus, in his "Epistle to Henri II," depicted the axis tilt this way: "There will be a solar eclipse more dark and gloomy than any since the creation of the world, except that after the death and passion of Christ. And it shall be in the month of October that a great movement of the globe will happen, and it will be such that it will be thought by many that the world will be plunged into the abyss and perpetual blackness of space. There will be portents and signs in the spring, extreme changes, nations overthrown, and mighty earthquakes."

As a result of the earth's shift, near the end of the present century, Nostradamus foresaw that the globe will be tilted at a new angle, so that the sun and moon will appear to move in different orbits in the sky:

You will see great transformation at the turn of a century,
Extreme horror, a judgement upon the guilty wicked,
The moon inclined at another angle,
The sun will appear higher in its circle. I, 56.

This calamity will mark the end of the Present Age, and the advent of the New Age, one that shall be of a very different nature:

After there is a great trouble among mankind, a greater change prepared,
The Great Mover of the Universe will renew Time,
Rain, blood, thirst, famine, steel weapons and disease,
In the heavens a fire seen, lengthening into shooting sparks. II, 46

Fathers and mothers will die of many sorrows,
Women mourning their husbands, because of a diseased female monster (the One World Church),
The great ones (world leaders) to be no more, all the world will end,
Then after great war, all shall live under peace and rest. Presage 82.

Between world leaders will hatred spring up,
Dissension and war to begin,
The tumult will grow, then comes the Great Change,
The age of the spiritual people will begin. Presage 95.

The greatest disaster in the history of man--the Armageddon experience--will pass quickly away, the cleansing process shall be over, and mankind will enter a new time, a New Age, to begin again, only this time to his nobler development....

59. IS A METEOR OR COMET GOING TO STRIKE THE EARTH?

One of the first among modern prophets to sound the warning bell that the earth is about to be jolted by an intruder from space was Washington seeress Jeane Dixon. A few years ago she made the startling prediction that some time within this century something she termed "literally earth-shattering" will occur: A natural catastrophe, an instrument of "Divine intervention" in the form of a meteor which will cause great shifting of water on the surface of the earth. Mrs. Dixon later enlarged on this prophecy by stating that a celestial object--which she now identified as a comet-- will smash into our planet about 1985. The collision will touch off large earth tremors and tidal waves, and the prophetess warned that the impact for the comet would be in one of the world's oceans--the name of which she says she knows, but does not wish to divulge.

The Californian seer, Criswell, has not been so reticent in disclosing the details of where the uninvited visitor will strike, predicting that the target area will be in the center of the Indian Ocean. The impact, Criswell foresees, will cause tremendous tidal waves which will sweep across east Africa, parts of Arabia, India, southeast Asia, the East Indies and the western half of Australia. The effects will also be world-wide. Criswell predicts a major earthquake to destroy southern California only days within the time of the meteor's tragic arrival.

Four hundred years ago, the French seer Nostradamus prophesied:

A great spherical mountain of seven stades,
At a time when peace will give way to war, famine and flooding,
It will roll end over end, sinking great nations,
Many of ancient origin, of great age. I, 69.

In line 1, the seer gives us the description of a "great spherical mountain." Its size will be "of seven stades"--in ancient Greek measurement, approximately one mile in diameter. In the third line is the clue that the so-called "mountain" is not of earthly origin: "It will *roll*" (in the original French, "roulera"--"end over end"), and in its revolving motion, it will "sink great nations." The last line identifies the specific nations to be severely affected: "Many of ancient origin, of great age." History reveals that the civilizations of greatest antiquity centered on the Nile in Egypt, in the Mesopotamian river valley of present-day Iraq and Syria, at Mohenjo-Daro and Harappa in India, in southeast Asia, and in China on the Hwang-Ho. Looking at a map of the world, we may note that each of these borders on or is in close proximity to the waters of the Indian Ocean.

The "spherical mountain" or meteor, according to the French prophet, will also be linked with a time when "after peace there will be war"--in other words, its fateful plunge will take place when war in the world will again be imminent. It will happen, too, when there is "famine" and "flood." In several other poems, Nosrtadamus alluded to most unusual conditions which appear to be directly associated with the coming meteor impact. First, he predicted *famine* caused by a tremendous "heat" from above, so severe in places that it will cause "fish to be cooked" in boiling lakes. Closely following the great heat wave, the opposite condition will prevail——massive rains and *flooding*. Nostradamus devoted a number of his poetic prophecies to a description of the future overflowing of all major European rivers and the extensive destruction it will cause. While the waters are still rising, the temperatures are to suddenly lower and, according to the French seer, great storms will plague his native country and other nations, while stretches of the North Atlantic--from the North Sea to the Bay of Biscay off western France--will be covered briefly with ice. Eventually conditions will return to normal.

Nostradamus' prophecies concerning a coming severe fluctuation in the world's weather finds an interesting parallel in another prediction made by California's Criswell. According to him, in the not too distant future rain will inexplicably cease to fall all over the world for ten months. Rivers and lakes will dry up, and great droughts will paralyze various nations, drastically cutting down the global supply of drinking water, and water for industry and electrical generation. Death resulting from thirst, starvation and disease will number in the hundreds of thousands. Criswell alludes to the fact that a war will be in progress at this time, an escalating international conflict that will temporarily cease as conditions for battle, and the maintenance of armies, worsen. Finally, at the end of ten months, the first rains will fall. But as the world returns to normal, the downpours will continue until suddenly, where there was once drought there will be widespread flooding. Criswell pinpoints the Mediterranean and European nations to be the hardest hit by the reversed developments: Spain will be cut in half by a wall of water, sections of Holland and Belgium will be submerged, and communications with Moscow will cease for several weeks, the city and hundreds of square miles of the surrounding country left completely inundated. The United States will suffer also. Much of the east coast including Washington will be flooded, as will be New Orleans, Florida and sections of California. Floods will also ravage the Midwest. The Far East will in no way be excluded, but will receive its share of water too, with Hong Kong inundated, parts of lowland China swamped, and sections of Japan will slide into the sea.

Once the flooding and rain finally appear to be abating, however, a new condition will prevail: According to Criswell, the earth will experience a world-wide freeze, accompanied by great ice and snow falls, and violent winds. It would seem that the clouds that will bring rain to the world will temporarily shut out the sun's light reaching the surface, causing the temperatures to drop. Once the clouds have dispersed, however, the freeze will pass, temperatures will approach normal again, and the world will begin to recover. It is significant that Criswell places these unusual climatic alterations in the exact same period in which he predicts the great meteor will be expected to visit our skies.

The description of a meteor or comet to plunge into the earth, and the short but disastrous climatic reversals to accompany it, are also portrayed in very similar terms in the first four of the Seven Last Trumpets, in the apostle John's Revelation, Chapter 8:

First Trumpet: "The first angel sounded, and there followed hail and fire mingled with blood, and they were cast upon the earth: and a third part of the trees was burnt up, and all the green grass was burnt up."

We have here the effects of a great *heat*.

Second Trumpet: "And the second angel sounded, and as it were a great mountain burning with fire was cast into the sea: and a third part of the sea became blood; and a third part of the creatures which were in the sea and had life, died; and a third part of the ships was destroyed."

The "great mountain burning with fire" which is "cast into the sea" sounds very much iike Nostradamus' "great round mountain" that "rolls end over end," to some day "sink great nations"--the fiery meteor or comet predicted to plunge into the Indian Ocean.

Third Trumpet: "And the third angel sounded, and there fell a great star from heaven, burning as it were a lamp, and it fell upon the third part of the rivers, and upon the fountains of waters; and the name of the star is called Wormwood: and a third part of the waters became wormwood; and many men died of the waters, because they were made bitter."

The "great star" burning like a "lamp" might be another figurative description of the "burning mountain" of the Second Trumpet. It is interesting that in some of his predictions, Nostradamus repeatedly made mention of a "bearded star" or "flaming torch" in the sky. Many interpreters have thought this to be a reference to Halley's comet, which is scheduled to return to the orbit of the earth in 1986. Could it be possible that the famous comet is what the prophets have been hinting at as the object to collide with our planet? According to the Revelation description, the "great star" will cause the waters of the world to be polluted with a bitter substance. Nostradamus, in another of his poems, described a great "celestial stone" the "fires" of which will one day "make the sea gritty."

Fourth Trumpet: "And the fourth angel sounded, and the third part of the sun was smitten, and the third part of the moon, and the third part of the stars; so as the third part of them was darkened, and the day shone not for a third part of it, and the night likewise."

198

The diminishing of light by a third of all the heavenly bodies, as well as the light of day and night, sounds very much like the great cloud layer that will form to produce the flood-causing rains. These, we noted, could conceivably block off the sunlight and other celestial light reaching the earths surface sufficiently enough to cause world temperatures to briefly drop below freezing over the globe.

As with the prophetic descriptions given by the other prophets, Revelation's chain of climatic disasters ends here also.

Do all these forecasts really portend the coming of a cosmic catastrophe? Only time--and the heavens--will tell.

60. STAR-CHILDREN OF THE AQUARIAN AGE

The movements of the heavenly planets not only influence the affairs of mankind from day to day, but they also lay down the patterns that will direct men through their lives. At birth, according to the astrologers, the imprint of planetary forces, as they exist at that precise moment, is placed upon the child, and by interpreting the natal positions of the orbs, one can determine something of the paths and destinies that are in store for the child as he grows and prospers. It is the outer planets in particular--Uranus, Neptune and Pluto-- that predict the future intellectual, emotional and spiritual states of mind. This is significant, for as we look forward toward things to come, it is possible to espy the future by seeing what kind of *people* will inhabit the future. And this we can do by examining where the outer planets fall in the birth charts of today's children, and their children, in the generations to come.

The planet Uranus was in Leo until 1962, and many children born at that time will become important leaders, aiding mankind through world-wide crisis, prophesied for just before and after 1990. Those born during the massive conjunctions of the planets in Aquarius in February of 1962 will play highly significant roles--some for good, others for evil. In 1965 and 1966, the conjunction of

Uranus and Pluto in Virgo also portend that babies born in such an intense period are going to generate tremendous personal power in the 1990's, and toward the beginning of the 21st century. These, in turn, will bring forth offspring during auspicious times: A conjunction between Saturn and Uranus--a configuration of strong karmic influence--will take place three times in Sagittarius in 1988, a time that is predicted to see momentous religious and social upheaval around the world, and particularly in the United States. These Saturn—Uranus conjunctions will occur also very close to the point where the center of the Galaxy is reflected upon the tropical zodiac, and several astrologers believe that those born at that time will receive a special inpouring of energy of cosmic origins--energy that will manifest itself spiritually when the children reach maturity in the 21st century.

With the dawning of the New Age, the Uranus influence will continue to produce in the newborn population many important characteristics for the period of rebuilding. When Uranus enters Sagittarius early in the next century, its children will be pioneers of religious reformation and educational methods. A key in their activity will be the synthesis of both scientific and metaphysical principles together into a new pattern of living, as well as the acceptance and homogenization of diverse beliefs and practices. They will travel the world over, their curiosity absorbing and reinterpreting everything they see into a holistic experience.

Later, toward the middle of the century, Uranus will pass into Capricorn, and children born then will be the instruments in formulating new global organizations of mankind into a true brotherhood. And beyond, when Uranus enters Aquarius, babies shall possess unusual insights into spiritual and metaphysical matters, and will lead the way in bringing about an understanding of principles of a Higher Order of Being. The Aquarian Age will come to its fruitation.

The next planet out, Neptune, will during these same periods be exercising influences of its own. From 1970 to 1984, Neptune will be in Sagittarius, and those coming into the world in this era will find their potentials in organizational matters, and at the beginning of the 21st century will have the opportunity of proving themselves as architects of new forms of society. These will also be the children who shall cast off the concepts of competition and factionalism that will bring about the near total ruin of the world, and who shall teach men in the ways of cooperation and acceptance of all disparate elements.

After 1988, Saturn and Uranus will conjoin with Neptune, and with Mars for a short while, in Capricorn. In 1990 Jupiter will oppose this grouping, and Venus and Mercury will add their influences to the Capricorn amassment in January-February. These highly significant conjunctions and oppositions are omens of great disturbances, both in tne forms of unheard-of geologic cataclysms, and political revolution and upheaval. The latter, according to the astrologers, will take the form of a forced attempt at establishing a global state, and the spread of an authoritarian and ruthless world religion. These will be experiences long etched into the memories of those generations who will live through them, and in particular those who will be born during them. Man's disharmony with the earth and the earth's revolt against its mistreatment at his hands, as well as the treachery and hypocricy of a false religion, will help to serve as negative examples for those who will later teach humanity to live at peace with the soil, and experience true spiritual love and truth.

With Neptune in Aquarius after the year 2000, babies born will have highly refined clairvoyant and psychic abilities--the powers of a truly Aquarian Age mind. In years after, Neptune shall go into Pisces and then Aries, guaranteeing for the children of the 21st century their role in establishing permanent peace; creating new forms of music, art, healing and scientific invention; and founding a true global unity of mankind.

From 1971 to 1984, the powerful planet of Pluto will be in Libra, and today's very young will in the next twenty years be involved in bringing sweeping changes, throwing out traditional values and experimenting almost to the point of obsession with untried modes of living--even to the detriment of society as a whole. There is a general downward path indicated here, accentuated when Pluto flies into Scorpio after 1984--portending a period of great global upheaval. Yet the children born during this calamitous era will learn the need for love and community among mankind--a need they will later help fulfill with the coming of the New Age, after 2000. One particular child born during this period will be very special indeed--he will become the Avatar or Savior, to grow to become the Man of Peace promised for untold ages.

When Pluto enters Sagittarius, its sons and daughters will not only be born physically but reborn spiritually. They will have a penetrating intellect and spiritual awareness--much that will have been acquired in past lives as disciples and holy ones. They will be instrumental in searching out the spiritual essence of all religions--and demonstrating that this essence is but expressions of the same eternal truths.

Beyond, Pluto's influence through Capricorn promises the conception of children one day knowledgeable in organizing a new "government" for the world. But unlike the governments of the Present Age, the new collective will be based on giving each and every individual the freedom to find and develop his own potential, based on ability and self-discipline. The last vestiges of old political and religious structures shall be laid bare, and a new era in human friendship and community will begin. With Pluto in Pisces, the links with the past on a subconscious level will be broken, and finally, when Pluto will be in Aries in the 22nd century, its children will see the order and perfection of the New Age come to its full maturity.

On a higher level of planetary perspective, we stand today in the great Procession of the Equinoxes at the transition point of two Ages. The Piscean Age, which has had its influences dominant for the past two millenia, is now ending, and we are at the doorstep of the next, or Age of Aquarius. This influence on such a higher dimension will also have its profound effects upon the youth of today and tomorrow. In such a period of transition, all values are questioned: The children born today will witness the destruction of all forms of established political and religious external authorities--a necessity so that self-discipline may be kindled within them, and they are free to discover and respond to the ideal authority, which is the spiritual. Then and only then can they build a truly lasting civilization--a new civilization, of the New Age.

As the Aquarius cycle begins, mankind and its children will see the manifestations of Aquarian influence in the world: It is the sign of reform in the area of human thought; it generates self-interest rather than a need for possessions which lead to competition and war; it is sympathetic and curious about different forms of belief and creates desire to learn from them all; it aids in the discovery and invention of unique forms of science and technology, and promotes their humanitarian use, not their utilization in self-destruction; and it brings about greater intuition, higher psychic powers for the perception of new spiritual dimensions. Above all, the Aquarian children will seek a purity of purpose, in no matter what they do. In religion especially, every symbol of the Divine will be banned. Everything of a material nature which blinded men to the personal realization of spiritual being--monetary possessions, temporal power, relics, images, vestments, etc.--will be cast off. Cathedrals, temples and altars will not be made of stone and glass--but in the very hearts of men. By so doing, the star-children being born today and hereafter, will finally fulfill and affirm the seeds of truth revealed by Christ, and Buddha, and Krishna, and Mohammed--seeds of truth which during the Piscean Age were sown and passed through dormancy, but which in the Age of Aquarius will sprout and bear their intended fruits. -

61. THE DAY ALL THE MACHINES WILL STOP

An Italian computer systems analyzer named Roberto Vacca, in a very revealing study entitled *The Coming Dark Age* (Doubleday, 1973), formulated an ominous prediction about the near future, based on his observations of present trends in modern technology. His thesis is that the world is far too dependent on the great "super-systems" of human organization by machine-- postal, telephone, telegraph, telecommunications, radio, television, computer, information retrieval, medical, pharmaceutical, railway, airline, shipping, highway, water, sewage, electrical, gas, nuclear power, petroleum production and distribution, industrial, military, defense, law enforcement, agricultural production and distribution systems. These, Vacca warns, are continuously being outstripped by demand, and that by increasing the overloading of usage, the systems are becoming unstable, and are breaking down. These breakdowns or stoppages we are experiencing today in the form of power blackouts and brownouts, utility outages and rising repair costs, food shortages, transportation strikes and slowdowns, energy crunches, and gasoline station closings. Vacca forecasts that these will grow in number, and could lead to the ultimate disaster: A major breakdown in one super-system precipitating a breakdown in all other overburdened systems. With no power or means of transportation, the monumental repair work would be very slow, if not perhaps impossible. The terrible result will be that our great urban centers, which are so dependent upon super-systems for their survival, are going to be totally paralyzed. Vacca envisions that a general crisis lasting for several days or weeks would transform the most modern cities into pandemonium: Without electricity or gas, many will suffer from extreme heat and cold; with most metropolises having only a few days' reserve of staple goods on their store shelves, food will quickly grow scarce, and starving mobs will take to the streets in desperate search; with law enforcement being made impossible without gasoline for patrol cars or helicopters, robbing and looting will be rampant and uncontrollable; and with no easy access to hospitals or doctors, coupled with no sewage or sanitation services, diseases could flourish and grow into epidemics. Vacca noted further that the higher income folk, whose homes are filled with mechanical and electric gadgetry for their everyday living, will be left completely helpless. Instead, it will be the slum dwellers and the poor, who--having learned to live most of the time without utilities--will find the crisis situation not so bad, even tolerable. They will survive--but hundreds of thousands of others will certainly not.

A general breakdown of the super-systems, and the chaos in the cities, will undoubtedly lead to an economic collapse of major proportions. Vacca is skeptical that a totally mechanized society such as in the United States, Japan, the Soviet Union and most European nations, could ever fully recuperate from such a disaster, and goes so far as to predict that, as one super-system breakdown could trigger the breakdown of all systems, so the collapse of one industrial nation by such means could begin a "domino effect" among the other nations, leading to a collapse of Western civilization. At the very least, we could be sure that such a global breakdown might activate a rapid series of dramatic economic and political crises that will end in a world war. It is interesting that there is today a new movement of people out of urban areas, people who are also leaving behind the conveniences of technology and are experimenting with building their own shelter, growing their own food, and producing their own energy needs with solar power and other alternative sources. These few have seen the near future as Vacca has--and they will be living in self-sufficient comfort long after the cities have disappeared....

62. NOSTRADAMUS ON THE NEW AGE AND BEYOND

The seer Nostradamus has sometimes been called a "prophet of doom and gloom," because so many of his predictions deal with disasters and catastrophes--especially those to occur in the next two decades. But Nostradamus also made several forecasts of a positive nature, and of hope--forecasts about the New Age to come. It is only when we read these verses for the 21st century and beyond, that we gain a true prospective on the "gloomy" prophecies: They are meant to show us what must be cleansed and swept away, before we can learn to appreciate the establishment of the Age of Peace to come after. Here are the prophet's words:

Mars and the sceptre (Jupiter) conjoined,
In Cancer, calamitous war ended,
And a new King will be anointed,
Who will bring Peace to the earth for a great time. VI, 24.

After the disaster of Armageddon, the New Age will be inaugurated with the coming of a true Savior or Avatar, who will guide the world in Peace for the millenium. The conjunction in line one will occur in June, 2002.

He will be born in times of trouble and darkness,
To rule the realm in Goodness,
An incarnate, teacher of ancient wisdom,
He will bring a return to the Golden Age. V, 41.

The Spiritual Leader of the New Age will be born during a time when the world will go through its darkest period. He will grow to manhood in the 21st century and help restore the earth and its peoples to a more perfect harmony and balance. He will be a reincarnate of holy Avatars and Messiahs of the past, who were sent into the world at critical times, and revealed the ancient wisdom of the Spirit.

206

A new Peace, places built without defense,
Uninhabitable regions settled once again,
Abandoned acreage, houses, fields, towns occupied at will,
After a long age of famine, disease and war, the land
returns to cultivation. II, 19.

During the New Age, the earth, scarred by the
destruction and pollution of the Present Age, will be
healed. Old cities, fallen into decay during the chaos of
revolution and war, will be rebuilt, structures will be
renovated, and crops will grow again. A period of erratic
weather and starvation will also be over, and food will
become plentiful once more. No where will resources be
wasted on weapons for defense, for there will no longer be
the need for war.

There will be Peace, a Union, and changes,
Estates, offices of power done away with,
For the first generation, painful readjustments,
Wars will cease, conflicts settled by civil processes and
debates. IX, 66.

The New Age to dawn in the 21st century will see a
great alteration in the concept of government. All existing
political structures and ideologies will be brushed aside.
The world's people will learn to live in true Brotherhood,
with settlements made with words of understanding, not
with arms. For those who will survive the holocaust of the
Present Age as adults, the transition will be difficult, for
they must leave behind all ideas of political power and
authority, of man dominating over other men. In the New
Age, all mankind will become One with the Spirit of God.

The soul touched by divine spirit shall prophesy,
Trouble to come: famine--then disease and war will follow,
Flood and droughts--then land and sea stained with blood,
But eventually comes the true Peace, political leaders
dead, spiritual leaders will take their place. Presage 1.

Nostradamus sums up in this verse what mankind will face between our present day, and the dawning of the New Age in the 21st century: There will be floods, droughts and famine, followed by the terror of World War III, religious persecution, and the climactic War of Armageddon. Our hope, however, is that beyond will come the "true Peace," a world in which there will be none of the present governments and politics--only Spiritual teachers who will guide mankind into greater levels of Being.

The revolution of the great seventh number (the Millenium) come,
At its inception, great slaughter,
But then the advent of the Great Millenial Age (of Peace),
When many who were dead will return to life. X, 74.

Nostradamus believed that our Present Age began in about 4000 B.C. The start of the "Seventh Millenium," the Millenium or Thousand Years of Peace, will occur in A.D. 2000--the beginning of the 21st century. After the "slaughter" of Armageddon, then many Spiritual Leaders will be reincarnated, including many of those who died for their Spirit-centered faith during the times of mass persecution.

The Prince of great understanding and compassion,
Bringing Peace into the world and to its people,
He will reveal the true nature of death and life,
When realms will rebuild amid security. VII, 17.

When the New Age peoples begin to revive the earth, and the Avatar teaches mankind in the ways of Spiritual Brotherhood, the true nature of death and reincarnation will be revealed. Man's relation to God and man in time and space will become the New Age teaching.

The body without soul no longer denied,
The day of death celebrated as the birthday to a new life,
Believing the divine Spirit will guide the soul to greater happiness
And seeing existence as never-ending. II, 13.

The prophet summarizes here the central theme of the New Age teaching: The immortal soul of each individual passes through many lifetimes and each death is only a doorway into another existence, in a new material body. Life after life, the Spirit guides the soul to higher levels of Awareness and Being, to greater self-fulfillment, until the soul no longer needs the mortal body as a vehicle, and becomes total Spirit.

Spirit forms, immortal and without end, made visible to the eye,
Where before they were obscured,
The invisible forms seen through the head, through the forehead,
And sacred prayers are silent. IV, 25.

During the New Age, the psychic consciousness of mankind will be raised, and every one will be able to "see" the invisible entities of the spirit realm, who are the more evolved souls. No longer will it be necessary to speak to them in prayers, for we shall "see" and "speak" to them telepathically face-to-face, through the psychic powers of the Third Eye, in the center of our foreheads.

The grand twentieth year (century) ends, also the position of the Moon,
It will hold a different monarchy in the sky for another 7,000 years
Then the sun too will be tired of its place,
And at that time will my prophecies for the world be finished and ended. I, 48.

The New Age will begin, according to Nostradamus, soon after the earth's axis shifts, resulting in changes in the heavenly orbits of the sun and moon, to take place in 2000. This will mark the evolution of man to a new Spiritual level. The seer predicts the next great earth upheaval will occur 7,000 years later, in about A.D. 9,000. This time, the earth will be completely destroyed, and Nostradamus foresees nothing for this planet beyond. This last upheaval will mark yet another step in the evolution of man, for by that far distant time mankind will

209

finally leave behind the material body, to become total spirit. It is significant that the year 9000 will fall near the beginning of the Age of Scorpio--the sign of death and regeneration. The earth will be destroyed because its purpose will be fulfilled, its material sphere no longer needed to support the needs of the soul. Only the Man-Spirit will remain--immortal and pure, on its ever-continuing journey back to union with the Divine--to drift through new Universes and Dimensions, forever experiencing, forever learning, forever growing....

Epilogue

The Seven Thunders are still, their prophesyings ended.

In Heaven there is a great Silence. All that remains is one Hour, a single Hour to reflect upon the Thunders' words. Time grows short; the angels wait with sealed scrolls, trumpets and vials of plagues. Shall they be called upon?

"The decision is not ours," answers the mighty angel. "The final decision of how the Age will end, rests solely in the hands of man."

Last Words

A wise soothsayer once said that a prophecy that is completely fulfilled is a prophecy that has *failed.* It is a failure because the true revelation of the future (as we noted in the Introduction) is to both warn *and to instruct.*

The pattern of things to come as foretold by the prophets and seers of the world reveals that we shall eventually enter into what many call a "New Age"-- a time when the dreams of peace and brotherhood and spiritual understanding will finally be realized. This is the inevitable outcome toward which mankind is heading; the ultimate goal toward which history is moving. But between now and then must come a Transition, a metamorphosis from how we exist now, to how we shall be. For this Transition period, the prophets have predicted dramatic, often tragic and cataclysmic events. That the Transition is necessary, there is no doubt--but the *degree* to which changes will take place is what can be altered, if we so choose. The dire prophecies concerning famine, war, earth upheavals, religious persecution, chaos and other world disasters do *not* have to take place with the severity foreseen--in fact, *they do not have to take place at all.*

In reality, all prophecies of doom and gloom are conditional; that is, they will take place only if the participants to whom the prophecy is given remain on the course they are on now. *But,* if there is a change of heart, if the participants take positive action to move into another, higher avenue of consciousness, then the prophecy need not come about--and thus its purpose, to generate change in men's minds, will be accomplished.

As an example from the past, most everyone is familiar with the Bible story of Jonah and the whale, so often repeated in Sunday school. But most people forget or do not know the background to that story. Jonah, as a seer, was commissioned by the Divine to prophesy to the citizens of Nineveh, concerning the imminent destruction of their city. At first Jonah refused to take the job, and tried to escape his responsibility by sailing away aboard ship in a direction away from Nineveh. The Divine had other plans, however: Jonah fell overboard, a whale swallowed him--and three days later it spat the prophet out onto the seashore back near Nineveh. After this experience, Jonah decided to fulfill his appointed work, and soon he began preaching to the Ninevites--telling them to change their ways, their minds and their habits for the better, or in forty days their great metropolis would succumb to sudden catastrophe.Day in and day out, Jonah continued to make his forecast to everyone who would listen. Finally, after the appointed forty days were up, however, nothing happened: The sky refused to open up, the lightning would not fall, and Nineveh remained unconsumed. Jonah, perplexed and somewhat angry that his prophesyings had not come about, left the city and sat under a tree to sulk. After a while, the Divine came to him, and showed him the real result of his labor: The people had listened to Jonah's predictions, had decided to transform themselves, to live in a more positive way and productive way, and so there was no need for the prophesied destruction. The prophecy had failed in its fulfillment, but had won in *getting men to change themselves*, rather than let *events around them force them to change.*

The world today is a modern Nineveh, and the prophets of the world are the Jonahs walking up and down the streets, warning of coming upheaval and disorder. But whether the world at large will listen, like the Ninevites, and in so doing avert the forecasts--or the world will continue on its present pathway and suffer the full measure of tragic events outlined by the prophecies--that is the real and most pertinent question today.

Once our awareness reveals to us that a .change is necessary, then the next step is to decide what is the better route that we should be taking. We know that the purpose of the coming Transition is to prepare us for the New Age beyond--therefore, it follows that the better route involves learning about this New Age now, and in effect *beginning to live our daily lives as if we are already in the New Age.*

The learning process can start with studying those prophecies about the coming New Age--that is their purpose, to reveal to us the new life, the new philosophy, the new way of thinking on a higher plane. Once the prophecies have been studied and understood, then look around you. Are there people you know who seem to be already living the New Age ideals? If so, then learn from them--for these are the first "teachers" who will help bring the New Age about. Finally, your studying must be accompanied by *doing*, by applying the lessons to your life. In this way, for you, the Transition will be of a personal nature--you will experience your own metamorphosis, your own inner transformation and new growth. And the result will be you yourself becoming a "teacher" of the New Age, becoming an example to others of what the future will be.

The real goal, of course, is to multiply that personal Transition several billion times--so that each and every inhabitant of planet Earth has undergone it. If such a world-wide Transition by the action of self-will and self-realization took place, there would be no need for the prophesied Transition by destruction and upheaval. The world will have *become* the New Age on its own, rather than having to be nudged into it.

But the time to start this change to happen, to begin the Re-Creation of the world, is *now*, because the prophesies warn our clock is running out, when "higher forces" may deem it necessary to begin the Transition process by other means. Like Nineveh, our forty allotted days are almost up. What form the Transition will take,

213

then--whether by our personal choice and change, or by drastic global alterations beyond our control--is always, ultimately, our decision alone to make.

With Knowing comes Responsibility.
With Responsibility comes Choice.
With Choice comes the Future.

Bibliography

Agee, Doris *Edgar Cayce on ESP* New York: Paperback Library, 1969.

Allen, Don Cameron *The Star-Cross Renaissance* Durham, N.C.: Duke University Press, 1941.

Allen, Hugh *Window in Provence* Boston: Bruce Humphries, 1943

Allen, Philip J., ed. *A. Sorokin in Review* Durham, N.C.: Duke University Press, 1963.

Anderson, Wing *Seven Years That Changed the World; 1941 to 1948* Los Angeles: The Kosmon Press, 1940.

Archer, Fred *Exploring the Psychic World* New York: William Morrow, 1967.

Ballou, Robert O. *The Bible of the World* New York: Viking Press, 1939.

Beard, Charles and others *History of Civilization: Our Own Age* Boston: Gunn and Company, 1945.

Berdyaev, Nicholas *The End of Our Time* London: Sheed and Ward, 1933.

Berdyaev, Nicholas *The Fate of Man in the Modern World* Ann Arbo, Mich.: The University of Michigan Press, 1963.

Bevan, Edwyn *Sibyls and Seers* London: George Allen and Unwin, 1928.

Binder, Otto *Unsolved Mysteries of the Past* New York: Tower Publications, 1970.

Bjornstad, James *Twentieth Century Prophecy:Jeane Dixon and Edgar Cayce* New York: Pyramid Publications, 1970.

Boehm, George A.W. "Futurism" *Think* July-August, 1970, 22-23.

Boswell, Rolfe *Nostradamus Speaks* New York: Thomas Y. Crowell, 1941.

Bowman, Frank *The Coming World Helper* San Francisco: Readers Service, 1944.

Bradley, Dorothy B. and Robert A. Bradley *Psychic Phenomena: Revelation and Experience* West Nyack, N.Y.: Parker Publishing, 1967.

Brinsmead, Robert C. *Revelation* Bryn Maur, Ca.: Prophetic Research International, 1963.

Brown, Florence V. *Nostradamus: The Truth About Tomorrow* New York: Tower Publications, 1970.

Brown, Vinson *Voices of Earth and Sky* Harrisburg, Pa.: Stackpole Books, 1974.

Brusher, Joseph S. *Popes Through the Ages* New York: D. Van Nostrand, 1965.

Canham, Erwin D. *Man's Great Future* New York: Longmans, Green and Co., 1959.

Carter, Mary Ellen *Edgar Cayce on Prophecy* New York: Paperback Library, 1968.

Cayce, Edgar Evans *Edgar Cayce on Atlantis* New York: Paperback Library, 1968.

Cayce, Hugh Lynn *Venture Inward* New York: Harper and Row. 1964.

Cerminara, Gina *Many Mansions* New York: The American Library, 1967.

Chaij, Fernando *Preparation for the Final Crisis* Mountainview, Ca.: Pacific Press Publishing Assoc., 1966.

Cheetham, Erika *The Prophecies of Nostradamus* G.P. Putnam's Sons, 1975.

Chen, Philip S. *A New Look at God* South Lancaster, Mass.: Chemical Elements Publishing Co., 1962.

Christopher, Milbourne *ESP, Seers and Psychics* New York: Thomas Y. Crowell, 1970.

Clancy, John G. *Apostle for Our Time: Pope Paul VI* New York: J.P. Kenedy and Sons, 1963.

Clarke, A.C. *Man and Space* New York: Time, Inc., 1964.

Clarke, Arthur C. *Profiles of the Future* New York: Bantam Books, 1968.

Clarke, Gerald "Putting the Prophets in Their Place" *Time* February 15, 1971, 38-39.

Cleveland, Harlan *The Promise of World Tensions* New York: The Macmillan Co., 1961.

Cohen, Daniel *Myths of the Space Age* New York: Dodd, Mead and Co., 1967.

Cottrell, Leonard *Lost Worlds* New York: Dell Publishing, 1964.

Coulson, John, ed. *The Saints* New York: Guild Press, 1957.

Cournos, John, ed. *A Book of Prophecy* New York: Charles Scribner's Sons, 1942.

Criswell *Criswell Predicts from Now to the Year 2000* Anderson, S.C.: Drake House, 1968.

Criswell *Your Next Ten Years* Anderson, S.C.: Drake House, 1969.

Croly, George *The Apocalypse of St. John* London:C. and J. Rivingtons, 1828.

Crummere, Maria E. *The Age of Aquarius* New York: Golden Press, 1970.

Culleton, R. Gerald *The Prophets and Our Times* St. Benedict, Ore.: St. Benedict Press, 1941.

Cumont, Franz *Astrology and Religion Among the Greeks and Romans* New York: Putnam's Sons, 1912.

Dagobert, D. Runes *Despotism: A Pictorial History of Tyranny* New York: Philosophical Library, 1963.

Davydd, L. *The Signpost* London: The Covenant Publishing Co., n.d.

Delcourt, Marie *L'Oracle de Delphes* Paris: Bibliotheques Historique, 1955.

Drucker, Peter F. *Landmarks of Tomorrow* New York: Harper and Brothers, 1959.

Dupont, Yves *Catholic Prophecy* Rockford, Ill.: Tan Books and Publishers, 1973.

Dusterdeick, Friedrich *Critical Exegetical Handbook to the Revelation of John* New York: Funk and Wagnells, 1887.

Ebon, Martin *Doomsday* New York: Signet Books, 1977.

Ebon, Martin *Reincarnation in the Twentieth Century* New York: New American Library, 1970.

Edmonds, I.G. *Second Sight: People Who Read the Future* Nashville: Thomas Nelson, Inc., 1977.

Ehrlich, Paul R. *The Population Bomb* New York: Ballantine Books, 1970.

Faber, George S. *The Sacred Calendar of Prophecy* London: W.E. Painter, 1844.

Fletcher, Adele W. "The Lady Behind the Crystal Ball" *Family Weekly* January 15, 1967.

Forman, Henry J. *The Story of Prophecy* New York: Tudor Publishing, 1940.

Frazer, J.T. *The Voices of Time* London: The Penguin Press, 1968.

Freeman, Hobart H. *An Introduction to the Old Testament Prophets* Chicago: Moody Press, 1968.

Freud, Sigmund *Civilization and Its Discontents* New York: W.W. Norton and Co., 1962.

Fritchey, Clayton "Gullibility in Washington" *Harper's* June, 1967.

Gabor, Eileen J. *The Sense and Nonsense of Prophecy* New York: Berkley Publishing, 1968.

Geffcken, John *Die Oracula Sibyllina* Leipzig: J.C. Hinrich'ssche Buchandlung, 1902.

Gilbert, F.C. *Divine Predictions Fulfilled* Lancaster, Mass.: Good Tidings Press, 1969.

Glass, Justine *They Foresaw the Future* New York: G.P. Putnam's Sons, 1969.

Goodavage, Joseph F. *Astrology: The Space Age Science* West Nyack, N.Y.: Parker Publishing, 1966.

Goodavage, Joseph *Our Threatened Planet* New York: Prentice-Hall, 1978.

219

Goodman, Jeffrey *We Are the Earthquake Generation* New York: Seaview Books, 1978.

Greenhouse, Herbert B. *Premonitions: A Leap into the Future* New York: Warner Paperback Library, 1971.

Halley, Henry H. *Pocket Bible Handbook* Chicago: Henry H. Halley, 1948.

Halliday, W.R. *Greek Divination* London: Macmillan and Co., 1913.

Harnack, Adolf *What is Christianity?* New York: G.P. Putnam's Sons, 1903.

Haskell, Stephen K. *The Story of the Seer of Patmos* Washington: Review and Herald, 1908.

Hassel, Max *Prophets Without Honor* New York: Ace Books, 1971.

Helfrich, Harold W., Jr. *The Environmental Crisis* New Haven: Yale University Press, 1970.

Hengstenberg, E.W. *Dissertations on the Genuineness of Daniel and the Integrity of Zechariah* Edinburgh: Published for the Continental Translation Society, 1847.

Heuer, Kenneth *The End of the World* New York: Rinehart and Co., 1947.

Hindley, Charles, ed. *The Old Book Collector's Miscellany* vol. V London: Reeves and Turner, 1873.

Hindus, Maurice *The Kremlin's Human Dilemma* Garden City, N.Y.: Doubleday and Co., 1967.

Hix, Elsie *Strange As It Seems #3* New York: Bantam Books, 1962.

Holzer, Hans *Prediction: Fact or Fallacy?* Greenwich, Conn.: Fawcett Publications, 1969.

Holzer, Hans *The Prophets Speak* New York: Bobbs-Merrill, 1971.

Hurwood, Bernhardt J. *Strange Talents* New.York: Ace Books, 1967.

Impact Team *The Weather Conspiracy* New York: Ballantine Books, 1977.

James, Paul *California Superquake* Hickville, N.Y.: Exposition Press, 1974.

Jaspers, Karl *The Future of the World* Chicago: University of Chicago Press, 1961.

John, Eric, ed. *The Popes: A Concise Biographical History* London: Burns and Oates, Publishers to the Holy See, 1964.

Kahn, Herman and Anthony J. Wiener *The Year 2000* New York: The Macmillan Co., 1967.

Kaplan, S.A. *Can Persecution Arise in America?* Washington: Review and Herald, 1966.

Keith, Alexander *Evidence of Prophecy* Edinburgh: William White and Co., 1841.

Keller, Werner *The Bible as History* New York: William Morrow and Co., 1956.

Kent, Carolo *Corona Catholica* London: C. Kegan Paul and Society, 1880.

King-Hele, Desmond *The End of the Twentieth Century?* New york: Saint Martin's Press, 1970.

Lamont, Andri *Nostradamus Sees All* Philadelphia: W. Foulsham Co., 1944.

Laver, James *Nostradamus* London: Penguin Press, 1952.

Lemesurier, Paul *The Pyramid Decoded* New York: Seaview Books, 1978.

Leoni, Edgar *Nostradamus: Life and Literature* New York: Exposition Press, 1961.

Lewinsohn, Richard *Science, Prophecy and Prediction* New York: Harper and Brothers, 1961.

Lewis, H. Spencer *The Symbolic Prophecy of the Great Pyramid* San Jose, Ca.: Supreme Grand Lodge of AMORC Printing and Publishing Department, 1936.

Lewis, Richard *The Protestant Dilemma* Mountainview, Ca.: Pacific Press Publishing Assoc., 1961.

Lobeck, R. *Geomorphology* New York: McGraw-Hill, 1939.

Logan, Daniel *The Reluctant Prophet* New York: Avon Books, 1969.

Lorenzen, Coral E. *The Shadows of the Unknown* New York: New American Library, 1970.

Luddy, Ailbe J. *Life of Saint Malachy* Dublin: M.H. Gill and Son, 1950.

Lumby, J. Rawson, ed. *Bernardus de cura rei familiaris* London: Trubner and Co., 1880.

Lusson Twins *The Beginning or the End: Where Are We Going?* Virginia Beach, Va.: The Donning Company/Publishers, 1975.

McCann, Lee *Nostradamus: The Man Who Saw Through Time* New York: Creative Age Press, 1941.

McMaster, R.E. *Cycles of War* Kalispell, Mont.: War Cycles Institute, 1978.

MacNiece, Louis *Astrology* Garden City, N.Y.: Doubleday and Co., 1964.

Mackenzie, Donald A. *Teutonic Myth and Legend* New York: William H. Wise and Co., 1934.

Marchi, John de *The True Story of Fatima* St. Paul, Minn.: Catechetical Guild Educational Society, 1956.

Matt, Leonard von *The Popes* Zurich: NZN Buchverlag, 1963.

Maxwell, Arther S. *This is the End* Mountainview, Ca.: Pacific Press Publishing Assoc., 1967.

Millard, Joseph *Edgar Cayce: Mystery Man of Miracles* Greenwich, Conn.: Fawcett Publications, 1967.

Montgomery, Ruth *A Gift of Prophecy* New York: Bantam Books, 1966.

Morfill, W.R. and R.H. Charles *The Books of the Secrets of Enoch* Oxford: Clarendon Press, 1896.

Mukerjee, Radhakamel *The Destiny of Civilization* New York: Asia Publishing House, 1964.

Noorbergen, Rene *Jeane Dixon: My Life and Prophecies* New York: William Morrow and Co., 1970.

O'Brien, M.J. *An Historical and Critical Account of the Prophecy of Saint Malachy Regarding the Succession of the Popes* Dublin: Privately Published, 1880.

O'Kearney, Nicholas *The Prophecies of Saint Columbkille* New York: P.J. Kenedy, Excelsior Catholic Publishing House, 1901

Over, Raymond van *ESP and Clairvoyants* New York: Exposition Press, 1970.
223

Paddock, William and Paul *Famine, 1975* New York: Little, Brown, 1967.

Parke, H.W. *A History of the Delphic Oracle* Oxford: Kemp Hall Press, 1939.

Plagemann, Stephen H. and John R. Gribbin *The Jupiter Effect* New York: Vintage Press, 1974.

Platt, Rutherford H., Jr. *The Forgotten Books of Eden* New York: Alpha House, 1927.

Playfair, Guy L. and Scott Hill *The Cycles of Heaven* New York: St. Martin's Press, 1978.

Price, George M. *The Time of the End* Nashville: Southern Publishing Assoc., 1967.

Prideaux, Humphrey *The Old and New Testament Connected in the History of the Jews* New York: Harper and Brothers, 1842.

Prieditis, Arther *The Fate of the Nations* St. Paul, Minn.: Llewellyn Publications, 1957.

Quasten, Johannes and Joseph C. Plumpe, eds. *Ancient Christian Writers* Westminster, Md.: Newman Press, 1948.

Read, Anne *Edgar Cayce on Jesus and His Church* New York: Paperback Library, 1970.

Robb, Stewart *Nostradamus on Napoleon* New York: Oracle Press, 1961.

Robb, Stewart *Nostradamus on Napoleon, Hitler and the Present Crisis* New York: Charles Scribner's Sons, 1941.

Robb, Stewart *Prophecies on World Events by Nostradamus* New York: Liveright Publishing, 1961.

Robb, Stewart *Strange Prophecies That Came True* New York: Ace Books, Inc., 1967.

Roberts, Henry C. *The Complete Prophecies of Nostradamus* New York: Nostradamus, Inc., 1949.

Robinson, Lytle W. "In Slumber Deep" *American Mercury* August, 1959.

Rothschild, J.H. *Tomorrow's Weapons* New York: McGraw-Hill, 1964.

Rudhyar, Dane *The Sun is Also a Star* New York: E.P. Dutton. 1975.

Seasons of Changes, Ways of Response Virginia Beach, Va.: Heritage Publications/Associations of the Light Morning, 1974.

Seligman, Kurt *The History of Magic* New York: Pantheon Books, 1948.

Smith, Uriah *The Prophecies of Daniel and Revelation* rev. ed. Washington: Review and Herald, 1944.

Smith, Wilbur M. *Israeli-Arab Conflict and the Bible* Glendale, Ca.: G/L Publications, 1967.

Smith, William *Smith's Bible Dictionary* New York: Pyramid Publications, 1967.

Smythe, Charles P. *Life and Work at the Great Pyramid*, vol.3 Edinburgh: Edmont and Douglas, 1867.

Solomon, Paul *The Paul Solomon Tapes* Virginia Beach, Va.: Fellowship of the Inner Light, 1974.

Sorokin, P.A. *Fluctuations of Social Relationship, War and Revolution* (vol. 3 of *Social and Cultural Dynamics*) New York: American Books, 1937.

Sparkes, Rev. Samuel *A Historical Commentary on the Eleventh Chapter of Daniel* Binghamton: Adams and Lawyer, Printers, 1858.

Spellman, Francis Cardinal "The Day the Sun Danced" *Saturday Review* January 7, 1967.

Spengler, Oswald *The Decline of the West* New York: Alfred A. Knopf, 1926.

Spraggett, Allen *The Unexplained* New York: The New American Library, 1967.

Stearn, Jess *The Door to the Future* Garden City, N.Y.: Doubleday and Co., 1963.

Stearn, Jess *Edgar Cayce: The Sleeping Prophet* Garden City, N.Y.: Doubleday and Co., 1967.

Steele, Joel and Esther *Barnes Brief General History* New York: American Book Co., 1899.

Steiger, Brad *Know The Future Today* New York: Paperback Library, 1970.

Steiger, Brad and Warren Smith *What the Seers Predict for 1971* New York: Lancer Books, 1970.

Stewart, Basil *The Great Pyramid: Its Construction, Symbolism and Chronology* London: The Covenant Publishing Co., 1933.

Sugrue, Thomas *There is a River: the Story of Edgar Cayce* New York: Dell Publishing, 1968.

Talbot, Louis T. *The Great Prophecies of Daniel in the Light of Past, Present and Future Events* Beverly Hills, Ca.: Radio station KMPC, 1934.

Taylor, Gordon R. *The Biological Time Bomb* New York: New American Library, 1969.

Tenney, Merrill C. *Proclaiming the New Testament: The Book of Revelation* Grand Rapids, Mich.: William B. Eerdmans Publishing, 1957.

Terry, Milton S. *The Sybylline Oracles* New York: Macmillan and Co., 1890.

Thiele, Edwin R. *Outline Studies in Revelation* Berrien Springs, Mich.: Emmanuel Missionary College, 1959.

Timbs, John *Predictions Realized in Modern Times* London: Lockwood and Co., 1880.

Titus, Harold T. *Living Issues in Philosophy*, 4th ed. New York: American Books, 1964.

Toynbee, Arnold J. *Civilization on Trial* New York: Oxford University Press, 1948.

Tuberville, Rev. Henry *An Abridgement of Christian Doctrine* New York: Kenedy, 1833.

Tyso, Joseph *An Elucidation of the Prophecies* London: Jackson and Walford, 1838.

Vaughan, Alan *Patterns of Prophecy* New York: Hawthorne Books, 1973.

Velikovsky, Immanuel *Earth in Upheaval* Garden City, N.Y.:Doubleday and Co., 1955.

Voldben, A. *After Nostradamus* Secaucus, N.J.: The Citadel Press, 1973.

Von Dollinger, John *Prophecies and the Prophetic Spirit in the Christian Era* London: Rivingtons, 1873.

Wallace, Robert "February 3--Once Again the World Ends" *Life* February 9, 1962.

Waters, Frank *The Book of the Hopi* New York: Ballantine Books, 1963.

Ward, Charles A. *Oracles of Nostradamus* New York: Charles Scribner's Sons, 1940.

Welles, Samuel, ed. *The World's Greatest Religions* New York: Time Inc., 1957.

Wells, H.G. *The Shape of Things to Come* New York: The Macmillan Co., 1934.

White, John and Stanley Krippner *Future Science* Garden City, N.Y.: Doubleday and Co., 1977.

Willoya, John and Vinson Brown *Warriors of the Rainbow* Healdsburg, Ca.: Naturegraph Co., 1962.

Wollner, Christian *Das mysterium des Nostradamus* Leipzig, 1926.

Zumberge, James H. *Elements of Geology* New York: John Wiley and Sons, 1958.

Abernathy, Rev. Donald; 72

Abraham; 117

Adventist, Seventh-Day; 142

Aegean Sea; 48, 49

Africa, Africans; 24, 45, 48, 51, 77, 89, 95, 98, 121, 122, 126, 131, 133, 141, 142, 150, 195

Age of Aquarius; 52, 134, 135, 158, 167, 199, 200, 201, 202-203

Alabama; 46, 92, 163

Alaska, Alaskans; 33, 46, 47, 90, 152, 153

Aleutian Islands; 90

Algeria; 77, 78

"Almen"; 52

Amarillo; 92

America (North), Americans; 22, 24, 26, 29, 33, 34, 36, 41, 42, 44, 47, 51, 54, 66, 67, 71, 75, 76, 78, 79, 80, 86, 91, 99, 100, 107, 108, 114, 121, 122, 129, 137, 147, 149, 151, 160, 168, 186

American Indians; 11, 86, 113, 114

American Revolution; 24

Amida; 82

Ammon; 141

Amphipolos; 63

Anderson, R.C. "Doc"; 69

Angola; 107

Ankara; 45

Antarctic, Antarctica; 36, 37, 51

Anthony; 63, 64, 65

Antichrist; 52-56, 59, 76, 77, 101, 151, 189

Antony, Marc; 99

Apennine mountains; 131

Aquarius; 47, 54, 130, 131, 135, 188, 189, 199, 200, 201

"Aquilon"; 128, 130, 133, 149, 150, 186

Arabia, Arabs; 22, 23, 46, 60, 61, 77, 89, 95, 126, 127, 128, 131, 141, 142, 189, 195

Arctic; 37, 51, 67, 129, 130, 171, 172

Aries; 49, 188, 201, 202

Arizona; 181

Armageddon; 77, 185-193, 206, 208

Armenia; 130, 131

Asia, Asians; 24, 29, 45, 48, 49, 50, 51, 82, 100, 121, 122, 129, 133, 147, 150, 154, 195, 196

Associations of the Light Morning; 21, 22

Association for Research and Enlightenment; 32

Atlantic Ocean; 24, 26, 35, 36, 43, 51, 76, 77, 92, 99, 161, 196

Atlantis; 116

Augustus, Octavius; 99

Australia; 45, 46, 47, 51, 70, 113, 195

Auxentius; 78

Avatar; 52, 80-88, 202, 206, 208

Aztecs; 39, 86, 87

Babylon; 23, 24, 56, 133, 165, 166, 186

Baffin Island; 45

Bahamas; 36, 51

Balder the Peaceful; 105

Balkans; 63

Baltimore; 26

Bay of Biscay; 196

Belgium; 140, 197

Benares; 85

Beneath the Moon and Under the Sun; 87

Benedictines (Olivetans); 28, 58

Berdyaev, Nicholas; 174, 175

Bering Straits; 90

Berlin; 58

Bhagavad Gita; 83, 149

Biafra; 122

Bible; 11, 43, 55, 149, 158, 167, 192, 212

Big Bear mountain; 181

Billiante, Countess Francesca de; 46

Black Elk; 87

Black Sea; 91, 131, 180

Blavatsky, Helena; 84, 160

Blue Star; 112, 113

Bodhisattvas; 82

Bolshevik Revolution; 30

Borneo; 153

Bosco, Don; 96

Bonston; 26

Boulder Dam; 180

Bowman, Frank; 85

Brahan Seer; 62

Brandt, Joe; 178-181

Brazil; 107

Britain, British (English); 23, 32, 37, 46, 47, 51, 56, 62, 70, 91, 92, 100, 116, 153, 159-161, 181

Buddha, Buddhism, Buddhists; 52, 80, 82, 147, 149, 203
Bufalo, St. Gaspere de; 140
Caesar, Julius; 99, 176
Calambria; 124
California, Californians; 22, 25, 34, 35, 46, 51, 67, 70, 71, 72, 74, 84, 90, 91, 92, 140, 144, 153, 180, 181, 195, 196, 197
Canada, Canadians; 36, 45, 51, 90, 114, 122, 144, 153, 172
Cancer; 206
Capricorn; 109, 134, 135, 156, 200, 201, 202
Caracalla, Emperor; 79
Cardinals; 93, 95, 96, 97, 98, 100, 126, 187
Caribbean; 34, 36, 51, 91
Carlsen, Daniel; 72
Carolinas; 34, 69, 92, 153
Cayce, Edgar; 15, 26, 29, 30, 32, 33, 34, 35, 36, 37, 45, 56, 75, 76, 85, 121, 122, 152, 154, 159, 163, 164
Central America; 37, 46, 86, 107, 189
Central Intelligence Agency; 123
Central Premonitions Directory; 29
Cleft Rock, John of the; 96
Charles I; 15
Charleston, S.C.; 35
Chesapeake Bay; 51
Chicago; 35, 47, 94
China (Red), Chinese; 22, 29, 45, 46, 47, 80, 87, 89, 92, 107, 131, 157, 172, 196, 197
"China syndrome"; 63
Christ, Christians, Christianity; 16, 43, 52, 54, 55, 76, 77, 80, 83, 84, 85, 88, 101, 107, 117, 118, 125, 132, 146, 147, 149, 154, 164, 173, 174, 189, 191, 192, 203
Colombia; 180
Colorado; 36, 70, 181
Colorado River; 90
Communism; 29, 30, 156, 157, 158, 164
Congress; 79, 137
Connecticut; 26, 35, 76
Consumer Economic Index Forecast Update; 44
Copenhagen; 92
Coptic Fellowship/Coptic Order of Egypt; 84
Corinth; 48, 49
Cortéz, Hernán; 86

Cosmic Awareness Communications; 44
Crassus; 99
Crater Lake; 90
Criswell; 15, 25, 46, 56, 140, 141, 195, 196, 197
Crucified Jesus, Sister Marie of
Cyclades; 63
Dakotas; 36
Daniel; 15, 16, 55, 56, 141-142
Dardenelles; 91
Davis Straits; 45
Dead Sea; 142
Deganawida; 88, 114
Denmark; 92
Depression; 41, 45, 122
Dimanne, Thomas; 164
Dixon, Jeane; 15, 45, 53, 54, 56, 94, 195
Djojobojo; 86
Dnieper River; 156
Dow Jones Industrials; 44
Drake Passage; 36
Dutch; 86
East, East coast; 33, 35, 51, 70, 72, 76, 90, 121, 142, 179, 197
East river; 144
Eastern Orthodox Church; 147
Edom; 141
Egypt, Egyptians; 22, 45, 46, 55, 60, 61, 87, 117, 141, 142, 196
El Paso, Tx.; 92
Elysian Fields; 99
Emmerick, Anna-Katerina; 96
Enoch; 167-168
Ephesus; 48, 49
Eskimo; 87
Ethiopia, Ethiopians; 107, 141
Etna, mount; 22, 33, 180
Euphrates river; 61, 88, 190
Eureka, Ca.; 72, 90
Europe, Europeans; 24, 27, 37, 47, 48, 62, 63, 76, 89, 91, 92, 107, 127, 128, 129, 131, 132, 133, 134, 142, 149, 171, 172, 174, 175, 182, 196, 197, 205
European Common Market; 61
"Evergreens"; 44
Exodus; 117
Far East, East; 45, 66, 80, 88, 89, 100, 114, 129, 130, 133, 147, 164, 191, 197

Fatima, Portugal; 30, 94
Faudais, Marie de la; 139
Fellowship of the Inner Light; 75
Fez; 77, 131
Fiesole, mount; 48, 49, 50
Fimbul Winter; 104
Finland; 92
Fiore, de Giaocchino; 124-125
Florida; 46, 51, 70, 76, 92, 152, 197
Fluh, Nicholas of; 96
Formosa; 107
Four Horsemen of the Apocalypse;
124, 158-159
Fort Knox; 43
France, French; 31, 91, 100, 101,
107, 123, 131, 133, 149, 196
Fresno, Ca.; 178
Future Foundation; 69
Gairloch House; 62
Galilee, Sea of; 142
Ganges river; 133
Gavin, Jim; 25
Gemini; 49, 50
Geological Survey; 25
Georgia; 34, 51, 69, 76, 92, 153
Germany, Germans; 15, 37, 58, 76,
146, 147, 181
Gibraltar; 91
Giza; 116
Goodman, Jeffrey; 89, 151
Grand Canyon; 70, 180
"Great Initiate"; 117
"Great Judge"; 28
Great Lakes; 22, 36, 51, 76, 90, 92,
153
Great Pyramid; 116-119
Greece, Greeks; 16, 33, 43, 48, 49,
50, 63, 64, 65, 91, 99, 121, 129, 164,
195
Greenland; 37, 45, 47
Gregory XII; 27
Gribbin, John; 121
Gulf of Mexico; 35, 46, 51, 70, 71
Hades; 159
Halley's Comet; 66, 95, 109, 131, 198
Hamid Bey; 84
Harappa; 196
Harrell, Rev. C.F.; 71
Harrison, William H.; 155
Hassan II; 77
Hati-Managarm; 104
Hawaii; 92, 180

"Henri II, Epistle to"; 101, 133, 149,
186, 189, 192
Henry, Danny; 70, 71
Hermes; 129
Hesperia, Hesperians; 43, 100
Hildegarde, St.; 66, 67
Hindus, Hinduism; 52, 83, 87, 147
Hitler, Adolph; 15, 59
Hobbs, William H.; 25
Hollywood, Ca.; 72
Hollywood Blvd.; 178, 179, 180
Holy Grail; 77
Holy Land; 23
Holzer, Hans; 29, 47
Hopi Indians; 87, 110, 113, 114
Hudson River; 144
Hughes, Irene; 47, 94
Huns; 80
Idaho; 90
Ikhnaton; 53
Illinois; 35, 36
"Immaculate Heart"; 30
Imperial Valley, Ca.; 69, 90
India; 22, 46, 47, 82, 85, 87, 91, 92,
107, 122, 133, 195, 196
Indian Ocean; 195, 196, 198
Indiana; 36
Indonesia; 46, 86, 92
Iolcus; 49
Ionian Sea; 49
Iran; 46, 61, 84, 107
Iraq; 22, 24, 60, 61, 91, 190, 196
Ireland, Irish; 26, 62, 75, 91, 153, 181
Iroquois Indians; 88, 114
Israel (Palestine); 22, 23, 24, 59, 60,
91, 141, 142, 190
Istanbul; 180
Italy, Italian; 22, 33, 49, 50, 76, 91,
95, 100, 107, 124, 131, 153, 182, 203
James, Paul; 34, 35
Japan, Japanese; 22, 36, 46, 51, 76,
86, 91, 92, 153, 180, 197, 205
Jason; 48, 49
Javada; 83
Jensen, J.L.; 45
Jerusalem; 23, 24, 43, 54, 55, 142
Jews, Jewish; 52, 55, 83, 117, 150,
167
Jochmans, J.R.; 11-12
John, St.; 15, 16, 55, 58, 88, 124, 125,
139, 158, 159, 185, 186, 190, 191, 197
John XXIII; 26, 94

John Paul I; 27
John Paul II; 27
John "Peniel"; 76, 77, 85
Jonah; 212
Jones, Jim; 135
Jordan river; 132
Jupiter; 45, 108, 109, 131, 156, 186,
188, 201, 206
Jupiter Effect; 121
Kaliyuga; 84
Kalki; 52, 83
Kansas; 36, 92
Kansas City; 44
Kate-Zahl; 37, 39, 40
Kaye, Doris; 27
Kennedy, John F.; 15, 155
Kentucky; 163
King, Martin Luther; 15
Koran; 149
Korea, Koreans; 46, 80, 107, 158
Kremlin; 157
Krishna; 83, 203
Kurii Trench; 37
Kurthy, Zolton; 72
Lake Michigan; 35
Larissa; 63
Latin; 97, 171, 188, 189
League of Nations; 174
Lemesurier, Peter; 116, 118
Leo; 61, 130, 188, 189, 199
Lepidus; 99
Libra: 47, 100, 130, 132, 135, 156, 201
Libya, Libyans; 45, 95, 131, 142
Lifthraser and Lif; 105
Lisbon; 51
Livingston, Montana; 36
Liturgy; 77, 78
Loire river; 132
London; 92, 160, 161
Long Island; 25, 76
Los Angeles; 33, 34, 69, 70, 71, 72,
74, 90, 153, 178, 180
Louis XVI; 15, 101
Louisiana; 153
Lucia; 94
Lusson Sisters; 50-52
Luther, Martin; 117, 147
Lycia; 129
Macedon, Macedonia; 63
Magnesia; 49, 50
Maine; 26
Maitreya; 52, 82, 83

Malachy, St.; 26-29
Malaya; 46
Malta; 131
Manhattan; 25, 26, 91, 143, 1?
Mars; 47, 48, 49, 61, 109, 130,
132, 133, 134, 186, 187, 188, 189
201, 206
Martinique; 34
Mas, Balthassar; 160
Massachusetts; 76, 92
McLeod, Diane; 69
Mediterranean: 33, 46, 61, 70, 7?
126, 142, 197
Medusa, Medusine; 99
Memphis, Tenn.; 91
Mercury; 48, 49, 108, 109, 131
201
Merlin; 124
Mesopotamia; 60, 88, 117, 196
Mexico; 22, 46, 51, 71, 86
Meyers, Ethel J.; 29
Michigan; 163
Middle East; 45, 46, 47, 53, 5
59, 60, 61, 76, 77, 83, 87, 89, 107
127, 129, 133, 134, 141, 147, ?
Midgard; 104, 105
Midwest; 22, 35, 36, 91, 121,
Miles, David; 70
Millenium; 56, 119, 208
Mississippi river, valley; 22, 3
70, 76, 92, 153
Mississippi (state); 153
Moab; 141
Modin, D.; 47
Mohammed, Mohammedan (
lem); 23, 52, 83, 126, 147, 149
Mohenjo-Daro: 196
Mongolia, Mongols; 46, 89, 131
Montana; 36
Moctezuma; 86, 87
Moon; 48, 49, 59, 109, 193, 2?
More, Sir Thomas; 156
Mormons; 168-169
Morocco; 77-78
Morse, Louise; 44
Moscow; 157, 197
Mu; 34
Muntazar; 52, 83
Mysia; 129
Naples; 182
Napoleon; 15, 101
National Guard; 79

232

Nazis; 59, 150
Nebraska; 36, 92, 163
Nerfertiti; 53
Neptune; 47, 109, 134, 135, 199, 200, 201
Nero; 150
Nevada; 153, 181
New Age; 12, 52, 53, 102, 118, 134, 135, 137, 145, 165, 175, 193, 200, 202, 203, 206, 207, 208, 209, 211, 213
"New City"; 143, 144, 145
New England; 144
New Guinea; 46
New Hebrides; 33
New Jerusalem; 58
New Jersey; 145
New Madrid, Mo.; 35
New Orleans; 35, 197
New Testament; 55, 83, 187
New World; 66, 100, 129, 160
New York City; 22, 25-26, 29, 34, 35, 47, 51, 90, 91, 142-145, 163, 169, 181
New York (state); 26, 35, 76, 145, 163
New York Stock Exchange; 43
New Zealand; 152
Nicopolis; 63
Nineveh, Ninevites; 212, 213
Nixon, Richard; 50
Noah; 125
Norfolk; 163
North Platte, Neb.; 92
North Pole; 46, 129, 130, 171
North Sea; 196
Norway; 92
Nostradamus, Michele de; 15, 23, 30, 31, 41, 42, 43, 44, 48, 56, 60, 63, 64, 77, 94, 97, 99, 100, 101, 102, 120, 121, 122, 123, 124, 126, 128, 133, 137, 138, 139, 143, 144, 145, 147, 148, 150, 156, 157, 160, 161, 169, 171, 172, 186, 187, 189, 190, 191, 195, 196, 198, 206, 208, 209
Nova Scotia; 22
Odin; 102, 104
"Ogmios"; 149
Ohio; 36
Old Testament; 55, 167, 187
Olympus, mount; 48, 49, 50
Ontario; 88
Oregon; 90, 153
Orient, Orientals; 46, 47, 59, 89, 128, 129, 131, 132, 133, 142, 157, 190, 191

Orwell, George; 44, 164
Ozanne, C.G.; 56
Pacific Ocean; 24, 33, 36, 51, 67, 69, 76, 90, 92, 163
Pahana; 110, 111, 112, 113
Pakistan; 107
Palestine Liberation Organization; 126
Palmer Peninsula; 36
Pamphilia; 129
"Papal Prophecies"; 26
Paris; 107
Paul, St.; 55, 58, 84
Paul VI; 27
Peking; 46, 92, 107, 132
Pelee, mount; 34, 91
Peloponnesus; 63
Pendragon, John; 26, 46, 160
Pennsylvania; 145
Pentagon; 143, 144
Perinthus; 63
Persia, Persian Gulf; 16, 45
Peter, St.; 27, 60, 93, 94, 96, 100, 125, 147
Peterson, Ross; 152-154
Petit, Bertha; 140
Philadelphia; 26, 90
Philippines; 51
Phoenix, Az.; 71, 92
Pierce, Jasper; 69, 70
Pisces; 158, 188, 201, 202
Pittsburg; 26
Pius IX; 96
Pius X; 97
Plagues; 139, 186, 190, 192, 211
Pluto; 109, 132, 134, 135, 137, 199, 200, 201, 202
Poland, Polish; 27, 181
Pompey; 99
Portugal; 107, 153, 182
Praetorian Guard; 79
Pratt, Orson; 169
President, Presidential; 78, 79, 137, 155-156, 179
"Prophecy of Fatima"; 93, 94
"Prophecy of Premol"; 96
Protestants; 146, 147, 165
Ragnarok; 102
Rampa, T. Lobsang; 82
Read, Michael B.; 44
Reformation; 117
Reno, Nev.; 180

233

Revelations; 18-19, 55, 58, 88, 89, 124, 158, 185, 186, 190, 191, 197, 198, 199
Rhone river; 133, 171
Richter scale; 33, 69, 91
Ritter, Betty; 29
Robb, Stewart; 32
Rocky Mountains; 70
Roerich, Nicholas; 82
Roman Catholic Church (Catholicism); 27, 28, 30, 52, 59, 61, 93, 95, 96, 97, 98, 99, 100, 101, 102, 117, 125, 126, 127, 134, 139, 146, 147, 150, 154, 173, 174, 187, 189
Rome, Romans; 16, 28, 43, 59, 78-80, 94, 95, 96, 97, 98, 99, 100, 101, 131, 132, 146, 173, 174, 184, 186, 187, 188, 189
"Rose," the; 98, 100, 101
Russia, Russians; 29, 30, 37, 45, 46, 47, 80, 92, 121, 130, 131, 132, 142, 149, 154, 157, 186
Rycempel, Nicol; 58
Sabato, Mario de; 62, 107-108
Sacramento; 69, 70
Sagittarius; 109, 128, 131, 134, 135, 137, 200, 202
St. Helens, mount; 90
St. Hiliare, Josephine; 82
St. Lawrence seaway, river; 35, 36, 91, 153
St. Louis; 35, 91
St. Matthew's Cathedral; 93
Saint-Remy; 171
"Samarobryn"; 171
Samos; 48
San Andreas fault; 67, 69, 71, 72
San Angelo castle; 95
San Bernardino; 71, 90, 180
San Diego; 70, 90, 92
San Francisco; 33, 34, 67, 69, 70, 71, 90
San Gorgino, mount; 70
San Joaquin Valley; 72, 153
Santa Barbara; 34, 70, 72
Santa Monica; 72
Saoshyant; 84
Sardina; 95
Saturn; 45, 108, 109, 128, 129, 130, 131, 132, 134, 156, 188, 200, 201
Satyayuga; 84
Scandinavia; 22, 91, 102

Schuetz, Egon; 71
Scorpio; 128, 129, 134, 202.
Scotland, Scottish; 62, 116, 1[181
Seattle; 92
Seneca; 184
Septentroinale; 100
Shasta, mount; 84
Shearer, Tony; 87
Sheridan, Wyo.; 92
Shockley, Paul; 44
Siberia; 46, 90
Sibylline oracles; 124, 184-1[
Sicily; 33, 180, 182
Sioux Indians; 87
Skoll; 104
Skylab; 113, 172
Smith, Uriah; 89
Smythe, Charles O.; 116
Solomon, Rev. Paul; 75-77
South America; 22, 36, 46, 51, 107, 121, 122, 180, 189
Soviet Union, Soviets; 29, [128, 156, 157, 164, 169, 172]
Spain, Spanish; 39, 51, 77, 107, 132, 153, 182, 189, 197[
Sparta; 63
Stalin; 29
Staten Island; 25
Sun; 47, 61, 109, 131, 147, 1[
Sun Bear; 114
Supreme Court; 137-138
Surtur; 102
Sweden; 92
Syria; 22, 24, 45, 60, 61, 141,
Tagus river; 132
Taigi, Anna Marie; 140
Taos, N.M.; 110
Taurus; 139, 156
Taylor, John; 116
Teotihuacán; 39
Thailand; 46
Thames river; 160, 161
Thanksgiving; 129
Thessalonians, Second; 55
Thessaly; 63
Third Eye; 209
Thrace; 63
Thrasibulus; 186
Three Mile Island; 62
Thunders, the Seven; 18-19
Tiber river; 95
Tibet; 82

Tierra del Fuego; 36
Toltecs; 37, 39
Toronto; 44
Toynbee, Arnold J.; 173, 174, 175, 176
Transjordan; 141
Treasury bonds; 44
Triumvir; 99
True White Brother; 87
Trumpets; 88-89, 197, 198, 211
Tula; 37, 39
Tunis, Tunisia; 77, 78, 98
Turkey, Turks; 48, 49, 61, 89, 91, 107, 129, 130, 131
Ukraine; 37, 91, 156
United Nations; 129, 174
United States; 24, 29, 33, 36, 44, 45, 46, 47, 48, 66, 67, 78, 85, 87, 89, 107, 113, 114, 121, 122, 128, 137, 138, 142, 144, 153, 156, 169, 172, 197, 200, 205
U.S. Treasury; 43
Uranus; 45, 108, 109, 134, 135, 199, 200
Utah; 168, 181
Vacca, Roberto; 203-205
Valley Forge; 24
Vancouver; 71, 90, 92
Vatican; 26, 95, 96, 127
Vatiguero, John de; 96
Venezuela; 180
Venice; 25, 27, 131
Venus; 61, 109, 131, 147, 201
Vermont; 46, 144
Vesuvius, mount; 22, 33, 34, 91
Vidar the Silent; 104
Vietnam; 80, 107, 158
Virgin Islands; 51
Virgin Mary; 30, 93, 94
Virginia; 21, 32, 36, 75, 163
Virginia Beach; 32, 36, 163
Virgo; 47, 156, 200
Vishnu; 83
Vishnu Purana; 83
Wallraf, Helen; 96
Washington, D.C.; 43, 53, 90, 93, 195, 197
Washington, George; 24
Washington (state); 70, 90, 153
Watergate; 50, 137
West, West coast; 33, 34, 35, 36, 47, 76, 85, 90, 121
Westminster Abbey; 161
"White Burkhan"; 82

White, Ellen G.; 142, 143
White Feather; 110, 111, 112, 113
White House; 137
World War I; 31, 117, 158, 174, 182
World War II; 31, 158, 174, 182
World War (III); 32, 45-48, 128-134, 166, 174, 182, 189, 208
Wormwood; 198
Wyoming; 36
Ygdrasil; 104
Yom Kippur; 50
Young, Brigham; 168
Young, David; 110, 111, 112, 113
Yuma, Az.; 92
Zarathustra; 84
Zoastrian Vestas; 84

After 1975; 84
after 1977; 24
1978 to 1998; 33
1980's; 25, 45, 46, 47, 48, 51, 128, 144
Early 1980's; 47, 53, 172
Beginning 1980; 44, 45
Beginning 1980 or 1981; 76
1980; 59, 155, 156
End of 1980; 54
Christmas, 1980 to March, 1981; 109
Between 1980 and 1985; 46, 90
Before 1981; 69
Beginning 1981; 83
1981; 54,59
Winter 1981-1982; 108
By the end 1981; 78, 109
By 1982; 51, 134
early 1982; 132
1982; 56, 59
December, 1982 to November, 1985; 129
1982 to 1983; 44
1982 to 1984; 121
1983; 59
April-May, 1983; 49
July-August, 1983; 130
1983 to 1985; 134
1983 to 1990; 134
By 1984; 135, 200, 201
1984; 44, 59, 75, 84, 202
February and August, 1984; 134
1984 to 1985; 134
Between 1984 and 1987; 153
1984 to 2000; 135, 137
1985; 45, 59, 83, 195

235

June, 1985; 49
November 30, 1985; 118
1985 to 1990; 91
Mid-1980's; 65, 75
Late 1980's; 45
Beginning 1986; 51
1986; 59, 109, 182, 198
February, 1986; 131
1986 to 1987; 66
1987; 59
August 21, 1987; 61
1988; 59, 109, 182, 200, 201
1989; 56, 59
1989 or 1990; 153
1990's; 91, 145, 200
1990; 199, 201
1990 to 1997; 134
1991; 59
1991 or 1992; 54
1992; 56, 59
1993; 52, 59, 107, 109
February, 1993; 47
1994; 59
1995; 59
1996; 59, 182
1997; 59
1997 to 1998; 135
1998; 22, 32, 60, 85
February and March, 1998; 188
April, 1998; 188
1998 or 1999; 154
1999; 54, 56, 60
February 21, 1999; 118
July, 1999; 191
August 18, 1999; 141
2000; 52, 58, 60, 76, 84, 92, 135, 137,
151, 158, 182, 201, 202, 209

May 5, 2000; 75
Beginning 21st century; 52, 85, 1
200, 201, 206, 207
By 2001; 206
June, 2002; 206
Between 2003 and 2031; 107
2004 to 2025; 118
2005; 83
By 2006; 153
By 2019;
By 2030; 152, 153
October 31, 2034; 118
October 21, 2039; 118
About 2076; 118
2100; 163
22nd century; 202
March 28, 2116; 118
About 2132/3; 118
2238; 118
2264; 118
2279; 118
2368; 118
2394; 118
2422 to 2477; 118
2499; 119
February 21, 2499; 119
2547 to 2737; 107
2569; 119
2800; 108
July 2, 2989; 119
3279; 119
June 30, 3989; 119
6225; 119
7276; 119
8276; 119
84th century; 119
9000; 209

J. R. JOCHMANS

Author's Biography

Joey R. Jochmans was born in Chicago, Illinois, on August 18, 1950. He presently lives in the central part of The U.S., writing , studying, and lecturing about the mysteries of the past and future. He has traveled widely, and lived abroad in Europe, and done research for 18 years in London, Paris, Roma, Amsterdam, Brussels, Montreal, New York, Chicago, and Washington D.C. He did the research for, and ghost co-authored, the book "Secrets of the Lost Races," with Rene Noorbergen, recently published by Bobbs-Merrill of New York. He is presently director of the Forgotten Ages Research Society, and editor of their journal: Time Spirals.

Mr. Jochmans has had articles published in the Bible-Science Newsletter, Specula, The New Atlantean Journal, and Journal of Borderland Science. Other areas of research include Biblical and ancient prophecy, psychic phenomena, and the life and prophetic works of Nostradamus.

He attended Andrews University in Berrien Springs, Michigan; Eastern Illinois University in Charleston, Ill.; and Union College in Lincoln, Nebraska, majoring in history and religion. In 1975 Mr. Jochmans received an Honorary Doctorate of Literature from Northgate College, a member of the American Association of Specialized Colleges, and a center for Biblical research. The degree was awarded for pioneering contributions in the study of "Antediluvian" civilizations and technology, and their influences upon the know ancient cultures.

Other Books

There is another book called "Rolling Thunder." It is about an Indian Medicine Man and teaches the Indian way of life...and survival. By Doug Boyd, 273 pages, Dell Books.

Also recomended is "The Dynamic Laws of Prosperity" by Cathrine Ponder, 253 pages, Reward Books.

OTHER SUN BOOKS TITLES
which you may find of interest:

THE LIGHT OF EGYPT (2 Vol. Set) **by Thomas H. Burgoyne**
Contains the Realms of Spirit and Matter, The Mysteries of Sex, Incarnation and Re-Incarnation, Karma, Mediumship, Soul Knowledge, Immortality, Influence of Stars, Alchemical Nature of Man, The Zodiac, Astro-Theology, Symbolism and Alchemy, The Planetary Rulers, The Secret of the Soul, etc.

MEDITATION FOR HEALING by Justin F. Stone
Contains What is Meditation, Different Modes of Meditation, Circulating the Chi, Working with the Breath, Mantra and Breath Counting, Fixation, Visualization, Chanting, Mind Control, Zen Instruction, Moving Meditation, etc.

FROM POVERTY TO POWER by James Allen (Author of "As a Man Thinketh")
Contains the Silent Power of Thought, Controlling and Directing One's Forces, The Secret of Health, Success, and Power, The Lesson of Evil, Secret of Happiness, etc.

BENEATH THE MOON AND UNDER THE SUN by Tony Shearer
A Dramatic Re-Appraisal of the Sacred Calendar and the Prophecies of Ancient Mexico.

MAN, MINERALS,AND MASTERS by Charles W. Littlefield, M.D.
Contains School of the Magi, Three Masters, The Cubes, First Initiation: Tibet, Second Initiation: Hindustan, Third Initiation: Egypt, History Prophecy by Personal Numerology, Human Physical Perfection, etc.

FOR A FREE LIST of other Sun Books titles write to: . Book List, Sun Publishing Company, P.O. Box 4383, Albuquerque, N.M. 87196 U.S.A.

OTHER SUN BOOKS TITLES
you may find of interest:

AMERICAN INDIANS

BENEATH THE MOON AND UNDER THE SUN by Tony Shearer
The Sacred Twins, Tezcatlipoca-The Dark Lord, The Symbolic
Glyphs, The 13 Sacred Numbers, The Dark House, Quetzalcoatl,
The Prophecies Unfold, The Ceremony.

ASTRAL PROJECTION

THE PHENOMENA OF ASTRAL PROJECTION by Sylvan Muldoon and Hereward Carrington. Man's Spiritual Body, Multiple
Bodies, Drugs and Anaesthetics, Accidents and Illness, Projections at the Time of Death, Experimental and Hypnotic Projections.

ASTROLOGY

**ALAN LEO'S DICTIONARY OF ASTROLOGY by Alan Leo and
Vivian E. Robson.** Aaron's Rod, Casting the Horoscope, Disposition, Ecliptic, Equinoxes, Period of Sun, Objects Governed by
the Planets, Mean Time.

ASTROLOGY: HOW TO MAKE AND READ YOUR OWN HOROSCOPE by Sepharial The Alphabet of the Heavens, The Construction of a Horoscope, How to Real the Horoscope, The Stars in
Their Courses.

**THE DIVINE LANGUAGE OF CELESTIAL CORRESPONDENCES
by Coulson Turnbull** Esoteric Symbolism of the Planets, Mystical Interpretation of the Zodiac, Kabalistical Interpretation of the
12 Houses, Evolution and Involution of Soul, Character of the
Planets, Hermetic Books, Nature of Signs, etc.

HEBREW ASTROLOGY by Sepharial Chaldean Astronomy, Time
and it's Measures, The Great Year, The Signs of the Zodiac, How
to Set a Horoscope, The Seven Times, Modern Predictions.

THE INFLUENCE OF THE ZODIAC UPON HUMAN LIFE by Eleanor Kirk. The Quickening Spirit, Questions and Answers, Disease, Development, A Warning, Marriage, The Fire, Air, Earth,
and Water Triplicities, Etc. (This is an excellent book!)

**THE LIGHT OF EGYPT or THE SCIENCE OF THE SOUL AND
THE STARS by Thomas H. Burgoyne.** Vol. I: Realms of Spirit
and Matter, Mysteries of Sex, Incarnation and Re-Incarnation,
Karma, Mediumship, Soul Knowledge, Mortality and Immortality,
Basic Principles of Celestial Science, Stellar Influence on Humanity, Alchemical Nature of Man, Union of Soul and Stars. Vol.II:
The Zodiac and the Constellations, Spiritual Interpretation of the
Zodiac, Astro-Theology and Astro-Mythology, Symbolism and
Alchemy, Talismans and Ceremonial Magic, Tablets of AEth Including: The Twelve Mansions, The Ten Planetary Rulers, The
Ten Great Powers of the Universe, and Penetralia--The Secret of
the Soul.

MANUAL OF ASTROLOGY by Sepharial. Language of the
Heavens, Divisions of the Zodiac, Planets, Houses, Aspects, Calculation of the Horoscope, Reading of a Horoscope, Measure of
Time, Law of Sex, Hindu Astrology, Progressive Horoscope, Etc.

1

STARS OF DESTINY--THE ANCIENT SCIENCE OF ASTROLOGY AND HOW TO MAKE USE OF IT TODAY by Katherine Taylor Craig. History and Description of the Science, The Sun From Two Standpoints, The Moon and the Planets, Astrological Predictions That Have Been Verified, Practical Directions for Casting a Horoscope, Sample of General Prediciton for a Year.

A STUDENTS' TEXT-BOOK OF ASTROLOGY by Vivian E. Robson Fundamental Principles of Astrology, Casting the Horoscope, Character and Mind, Occupation and Position, Parents, Relatives and Home, Love and Marriage, Esoteric Astrology, Adoption of the New Style Calendar.

WHAT IS ASTROLOGY? by Colin Bennet:. How an Astrologer Works, Sign Meanings, How Aspects Affect a Horoscope, Numerology as an Astrological Aid, Psychology in Relation to Astrology, Etc.

ATLANTIS/LEMURIA

ATLANTIS IN AMERICA by Lewis Spence. Atlantis and Antillia, Cro-Magnons of America, Quetzalcoatl the Atlantean, Atlantis in American Tradition and Religion, Ethnological Evidence, Art and Architecture, Folk-Memories of an Atlantic Continent, Analogy of Lemuria, Chronological Table,. Etc.

WISDOM FROM ATLANTIS by Ruth B. Drown. Being, Divine Selfishness, Service, Nobility of Self Reliance, Harmony Divine Love, Principles of Life and Living, Man's Divine Nature, Faith, True Thinking.

AUTOSUGGESTION/HYPNOTISM

THE PRACTICE OF AUTOSUGGESTION BY THE METHOD OF EMILE COUÉ by C. Harry Brooks. The Clinic of Emile Coué, A Few of Coué's Cures, Thought is a Force, Thought and the Will, The General Formula, How to Deal With Pain, Autosuggestion and the Child, Particular Suggestions, Etc.

SELF MASTERY THROUGH CONSCIOUS AUTOSUGGESTION by Emile Coué. Self Mastery Through Autosuggestion, Thoughts and Precepts, What Autosuggestion Can Do, Education as it Ought to Be, A Survey of the "Seances", the Miracle Within, Everything for Everyone, Etc.

CONSPIRACY

THE ILLUMINOIDS--SECRET SOCIETIES AND POLITICAL PARANOIA by Neal Wilgus. Detailed picture of Weishaupt's Order of the Illuminati as well as other secret societies thruout history. Ties various far-reaching areas together Including important information relating to the J.F. Kennedy assasination. "The best single reference on the Illuminati in fact and legendry"--Robert Anton Wilson in Cosmic Trigger.

GENERAL OCCULT

BYGONE BELIEFS--AN EXCURSION INTO THE OCCULT AND ALCHEMICAL NATURE OF MAN by H. Stanley Redgrove. Some Characteristics of Mediaeval Thought, Pythagoras and his Philosophy, Medicine and Magic, Belief In Talismans, Ceremonial Magic in Theory and Practice, Architectural Symbolism, Philosopher's Stone, The Phallic Element In Alchemical Doctrine, Roger Bacon, Etc. (Many Illustrations).

2

THE COILED SERPENT by C.J. van Vliet. A Philosophy of Conservation and Transmutation of Reproductive Energy. Deadlock in Human Evolution, Spirit Versus Matter, Sex Principle and Purpose of Sex, Pleasure Principle, Unfolding of Spirit, Marriage and Soul-Mates, Love Versus Sex, Erotic Dreams, Perversion and Normalcy, Virility, Health, and Disease, Freemasonry, Rosicrucians, Alchemy, Astrology, Theosophy, Magic, Yoga, Occultism, Path of Perfection, Uncoiling the Serpent, The Future, Supermen, Immortality, Etc.

COSMIC SYMBOLISM by Sepharial. Meaning and Purpose of Occultism, Cosmic Symbology, Reading the Symbols, Law of Cycles, Time Factor in Kabalism, Involution and Evolution, Planetary Numbers, Sounds, Hours, Celestial Magnetic Polarities, Law of Vibrations, Lunar and Solar Influences, Astrology and the Law of Sex, Character and Environment, Etc.

THE INNER GOVERNMENT OF THE WORLD by Annie Besant. Ishvara, The Builders of a Cosmos, The Hierarchy of our World, The Rulers, Teachers, Forces, Method of Evolution, Races and Sub-Races, The Divine Plan, Religions and Civilizations, Etc.

MAN, MINERALS, AND MASTERS by Charles W. Littlefield, M.D. School of the Magi, Three Masters, The Cubes, Initiation in Tibet, Hindustan, and Egypt, History Prophecy, Numerology, Perfection. 172p. 5x8 Paperback.

MEANING OF THE NEW MEXICO MYSTERY STONE by Dixie L. Perkins. Early Sea Travel, Ancient Writing, Sea Travelers and Writers, A Traveler's New Home, The Settler's Story, The Translation.

THE OCCULT ARTS by J. W. Frings. Alchemy, Astrology, Psychometry, Telepathy, Clairvoyance, Spiritism, Hypnotism, Geomancy Palmistry, Omens and Oracles.

OCCULTISTS & MYSTICS OF ALL AGES by Ralph Shirley. Apollonius of Tyana, Plotinus, Michael Scot, Paracelsus, Emanuel Swedenborg, Count Cagliostro, Anna Kingsford.

WHAT IS OCCULTISM? by Papus. Occultism Defined, Occult Philosophical Point of View, Ethics of Occultism, Aesthetics of Occultism, Theodicy--Sociology, Practice of Occultism, The Traditions of Magic, Occultism and Philosophy.

HEALING

DIVINE REMEDIES--A TEXTBOOK ON CHRISTIAN HEALING by Theodosia DeWitt Schobert. Fuller Understanding of Spiritual Healing, Healing of Blood Troubles and Skin Diseases, Freedom from Sense Appetite, Healing of Insanity, Healing of Insomnia, Healing of Poisoning of Any Kind, General Upbuilding and Healing of the Body Temple.

THE FINER FORCES OF NATURE IN DIAGNOSIS AND THERAPY by George Starr White, M.D. The Magnetic Meridian, Vital and Unseen Forces, Polarity, Cause of Un-Health, Colors, Magnetic Energy, Sympathetic-Vagal Reflex, Actions of Finer Forces of Nature, The Human Aura, Moon-Light, Light and Sound, Treatment with Light and Color, Etc.

MEDITATION FOR HEALING by Justin F. Stone. Many Medita-
tions--Many Effects, What is Meditation?, Different Modes of
Meditation, Circulating the Chi, Breath, Way of Mindfulness.
Chih-K'uan, Visualization, Tibetan Dumo Heat, Chanting Zen,
Mind Control, Moving Meditation, Spiritual Side of Meditation.
Etc.

**THE PHILOSOPHY OF MENTAL HEALING--A PRACTICAL EXPO-
SITION OF NATURAL RESTORATIVE POWER by Leander Ed-
mund Whipple.** Metaphysical Healing, Metaphysics Versus Hypnotism, The Potency of Metaphysics in Surgery, The Progress of
the Age, Intelligence and Sensation, Mental Action, The Physical
Reflection of Thought.

**THE PRINICPLES OF OCCULT HEALING Edited by Mary Weeks
Burnett, M.D.** Occult Healing and Occultism, Healing and the
Healing Intelligence, The Indestructible Self, Latent Powers of
Matter, The Auras and the Ethers, Polarization, Music, Healing
by Prayer, Angel or Deva Helpers, Thought Forms and Color in
Healing, Magnetism--Mesmerism, Healing Miracles of the Christ,
Etc.

HERBS

**THE COMPLETE HERBALIST or THE PEOPLE THEIR OWN
PHYSICIANS by Dr. O. Phelps Brown.** By the use of Nature's
Remedies great curative properties found in the Herbal Kingdom
are described. A New and Plain System of Hygienic Principles
Together with Comprehensive Essays on Sexual Philosophy.
Marriage, Divorce, Etc.

HOLLOW EARTH

ETIDORHPA or THE END OF EARTH by John Url Lloyd. Journey
toward the center of the Earth thru mighty mushroom forests and
across huge underground oceans with an entire series of fantastic experiences. A true occult classic! "Etidorhpa, the End of
Earth, is in all respects the worthiest presentation of occult
teachings under the attractive guise of fiction that has yet been
written." --New York World.

INSPIRATION/POSITIVE THINKING

FROM PASSION TO PEACE by James Allen. Passion, Aspira-
tion, Temptation, Transmutation, Transcendence, Beatitude.
Peace.

FROM POVERTY TO POWER by James Allen. (Author of "As a
Man Thinketh") Two books in one: The Path to Prosperity includ-
ing World a Reflex of Mental States, The Way Out of Undesirable
Conditions, Silent Power of Thought, Controlling and Directing
One's Forces, The Secret of Health, Success, and Power, Etc
and The Way of Peace including Power of Meditation, The Two
Masters, Self and Truth, The Acquirement of Spiritual Power,
Realization of Selfless Love, Entering into the Infinite, Perfect
Peace, Etc.

HEALTH AND WEALTH FROM WITHIN by William E. Towne
Health From Within, Awakening of the Soul, Will, Love and
Work, The Voice of Life, Non-Attachment, The Woman--The Man,
The Supreme Truth, Power of Imagination and Faith, Practical
Self-Helaing, The Way to Gain Results, Lengthen and Brighten
Life, Etc.

4

THE SUCCESS PROCESS by Brown Landone. Five Factors Which Guarantee Success, The Process of Vivid Thinking, Tones Used In Persuading, Use of Action, Overcoming Hiderances, Developing Capacities, Securing Justice, Augmenting Your Success by Leadership, Etc.

LIGHT

PHILOSOPHY OF LIGHT--AN INTRODUCTORY TREATISE by Floyd Irving Lorbeer. The Ocean of Light, Sight and Light, Light and Perception, Some Cosmic Considerations, Light and Health, Electrical Hypothesis, Temperament, Beauty, and Love and Light, The Problem of Space and Time, Unity and Diversity, Deity, Soul, and Immortality, Light and the New Era, Etc.

MEDITATION

CONCENTRATION AND MEDITATION by Christmas Humphreys The Importance of Right Motive, Power of Thought, Dangers and Safeguards, Particular Exercises, Time, Place, Posture, Relaxation, Breathing, Thoughts, Counting the Breaths, Visualization and Color, Stillness, Motive, Self Analogy, Higher Meditation, The Voice of Mysticism, Jhanas, Zen, Satori, Koan, Ceremonial Magic, Taoism, Occultism, Mysticism, Theosophy, Yoga, The Noble Eightfold Path, Etc.

THE JOYS OF MEDITATION by Justin F. Stone. Our all-time best selling title includes chapters on What Is Meditation?, Great Circle Meditation, Three Modes of Japa, Zen Meditation, Satipattana, Secret Nei Kung, Two Tibetan Meditations, How and Why Does Meditation Work?, Glossary, Etc.

MEDITATION FOR HEALING (See Healing above)

NEW AGE

THE MESSAGE OF AQUARIA by Curtiss. The Mystic Life, The Sign Aquarius, Are These the Last Days?, Comets and Eclipses, Law of Growth, Birth of the New Age, Mastery and the Masters of Wisdom, Mother Earth and the Four Winds, The Spiral of Life and Life Waves, The Message of the Sphinx, Day of Judgement and Law of Sacrifice, The Spiritual Birth, The True Priesthood, Etc.

NUMEROLOGY

NAMES, DATES, AND NUMBERS---A SYSTEM OF NUMEROLOGY by Roy Page Walton. The Law of Numbers, The Character and Influence of the Numbers, Application and Use of Numbers, Strong and Weak Names, The Number that Governs the Life, How Each Single Name Effects the Life, The Importance of Varying the Signatue, How the Name Discloses the Future, Choosing a Suitable Name for a Child, Names Suitable for Marriage, How to Find Lucky Days and Months, Points to Bear in Mind.

ORIENTAL

THE BUDDHA'S GOLDEN PATH by Dwight Goddard. Prince Siddhartha Gautama, Right Ideas, Speech, Behaviour, Right Vocation, Words, Conduct, Mindfulness, Concentration, Resolution, Environment, Intuition, Vows, Radiation, Spiritual Behaviour, Spirit, Etc.

**FUSANG or THE DISCOVERY OF AMERICA BY CHINESE BUD-
DHIST PRIESTS IN THE FIFTH CENTURY by Charles G. Leland.**
Chinese Knowledge of Lands and Nations, The Road to America,
The Kingdom of Fusang or Mexico, Of Writing and Civil Regu-
lations in Fusang, Laws and Customs of the Aztecs, The Future
of Eastern Asia, Travels of Other Buddhist Priests, Affinities of
American and Asiatic Languages, Images of Buddha, Etc.

THE HISTORY OF BUDDHIST THOUGHT by Edward J. Thomas.
The Ascetic Ideal, Early Doctrine: Yoga, Brahminism and the
Upanishads, Karma, Release and Nirvana, Buddha, Popular Bod-
hisattva Doctrine, Buddhism and Modern Thought, Etc.

SACRED BOOKS OF THE EAST by Epiphanius Wilson. Vedic
Hymns, The Zend-Avesta, The Dhammapada, The Upanishads,
Selections from the Koran, Life of Buddha, Etc.

**WAY OF THE SAMURAI Translated from the classic Hagakure by
Minoru Tanaka.** This unique translation of a most important
Japanese classic offers an explanation of the central and upright
character of the Japanese people, and their indomitable inner
strength. "The Way of the Samurai" is essential for business-
men, lawyers, students, or anyone who would understand the
Jampanese psyche.

THE WISDOM OF THE HINDUS by Brian Brown. Brahmanic
Wisdom, Maha-Bharata, The Ramayana, Wisdom of the Upanishads, Vivekananda and Ramakrishna on Yoga Philosophy, Wisdom of Tuka-Ram, Paramananda, Vivekananda, Abbedananda,
Etc.

PHILOSOPHY

**GOETHE--WITH SPECIAL CONSIDERATION OF HIS PHILOSO-
PHY by Paul Carus.** The Life of Goethe, His Relation to Women,
Goethe's Personality, The Religion of Goethe, Goethe's Philosophy, Literature and Citicism, The Significance of "Faust", Miscellaneous Epigrams and Poems. (Heavily Illustrated).

PROPHECY

CHEIRO'S WORLD PREDICTIONS by Cheiro Fate of Nations,
British Empire in its World Aspect, Destiny of the United States,
Future of the Jews, Coming War of Wars, Coming Aquarian Age,
Precession of the Equinoxes.

**THE COMING STAR-SHIFT AND MANY PROPHECIES OF BIBLE
AND PYRAMID FULFILLED by O. Gordon Pickett** God Corrects
His Clock in the Stars, English Alphabet as Related to Numerics,
Joseph Builder of the Great Pyramid, Numerical Harmony, Pro-
phecy, World Wars, Star-Shifts, The Flood, Astronomy, The
Great Pyramids, etc.

COMING WORLD CHANGES by Curtiss The Prophecies, Geological Considerations, The Philosophy of Planetary Changes, The
King of the World, The Heart of the World, The Battle of Armageddon, The Remedy

ORACLES OF NOSTRADAMUS by Charles A. Ward. Life of Nostradamus, Preface to Prophecies, Epistle to Henry II, Magic, His-
toric Fragments, Etc.

6

ROLLING THUNDER: THE COMING EARTH CHANGES by J. R. Jochmans. The Coming Famine and Earth Movements, The Destruction of California and New York, Future War, Nostradamus, Bible, Edgar Cayce, Coming Avatars, Pyramid Prophecy, Weather, Coming False Religion and the Antichrist, and much, much, more! This book is currently our best selling title.

THE STORY OF PROPHECY by Henry James Forman. What is Prophecy?, Oracles, The Great Pyramid Speaks, The End of the Age: Biblical Prophecy, Medieval Prophecy, Astrologers and Saints, Prophecies Concerning the Popes, Nostradamus, America in Prophecy, The Prophetic Future.

PSYCHIC ARTS

PSYCHIC GROWTH--DANGERS AND ECSTASIES by Kenneth Naysmith. Spirit of Mother Earth, Immortal Flame: Sex and Yoga, Some Psychic Dangers, Marriage, Duality, and Humility, Fall of a Titan, Splintering Souls, Possessiveness: The Beginnings of "Possession", Etc.

REINCARNATION

THE NEW REVELATION by Sir Arthur Conan Doyle. The Search, The Revelation, The Coming Life, Problems and Limitations, The Next Phase of Life, Automatic Writing, The Cheriton Dugout.

REINCARNATION by George B. Brownell. He Knew Who He Was, Memories of Past Lives, A Remarkable Proof, Lived Many Lives, An Arabian Incarnation, Dreamed of Past Life, Great Minds and Reincarnation, The Bible and Reincarnation, Karma, Atlantis Reborn, Thought is Destiny, The Celestial Body, The Hereafter, Etc.

REINCARNATION by Katherine Tingley. What Reincarnation Is, Arguments for Reincarnation, Supposed Objections to Reincarnation, Reincarnation and Heredity, Reincarnation in Antiquity, Reincarnation the Master-Key to Modern Problems, Reincarnation in Modern Literature.

THE RING OF RETURN by Eva Martin. Pre-Christian Era, Early Christian and Other Writings of the First Five Centuries A.D., Miscellaneous Sources Before A.D. 1700, A.D. 1700-1900, The Twentieth Century. In this book, Miss Eva Martin has brought together a most complete and scholarly collection of references to past, present, and future life.

SPIRITUAL

NATURAL LAW IN THE SPIRITUAL WORLD by Henry Drummond. Biogenesis, Degeneration, Growth, Death, Mortification, Eternal Life, Environment, Conformity to Type, Semi-Parasitism, Parasitism, Classification.

TAROT

THE ILLUSTRATED KEY TO THE TAROT--THE VEIL OF DIVINATION by L. W. de Laurence. The Veil and Its Symbols, The Tarot In History, The Doctrine Behind the Veil, The Outer Method of the Oracles, The Four Suits of Tarot Cards, The Art of Tarot Divination, An Ancient Celtic Method of Divination.

THE KEY OF DESTINY by Curtiss. The Initiate, Twelve-fold Division of the Zodiac, Reincarnation and Transmutation, The Solar System, The Letters of the Tarot, The Numbers 11 thru 22, Twelve Tribes and Twelve Disciples, The Great Work, The Labors of Hercules, Necromancy, Great Deep, Temperance, Man the Creator vs. the Devil, Celestial Hierarchies, The New Jerusalem, Etc.

THE KEY TO THE UNIVERSE by Curtiss. Origin of the Numerical Systems, Symbol of the "O" and the Serpent, The "O" as the Egg and the Cat, The "O" as the Aura and the Ring Pass Not, Symbol of the ☉, Letters of the Tarot, The Numbers 1 thru 10, The 7 Principles of Man, The 7 Pleiades and the 7 Rishis, Joy of Completion.

WESTERN MYSTICISM

BROTHERHOOD OF MT. SHASTA by Eugene E. Thomas. From Clouds to Sunshine, Finding the Brotherhood, The Lake of Gold, The Initiation, Memories of the Past, In Advance of the Future, Prodigy, Trial, and Visitor, The Annihilation and the King, The Lost Lemuria.

MYRIAM AND THE MYSTIC BROTHERHOOD by Maude Lesseuer Howard. A novel in the western mystic tradition.

THE WAY OF ATTAINMENT by Sydney T. Klein. The Invisible is the Real, The Power of Prayer, Spiritual Regeneration, Dogma of the Virgin Birth, Finding the Kingdom of Heaven "Within", Realizing Oneness with God, Nature of the Ascent, Reaching the Summit.

THE WAY OF MYSTICISM by Joseph James. God Turns Towards Man, The Unexpected, The Still Small Voice, His Exceeding Brightness, Man Turns Towards God, The Obstructive 'Me', Where East and West Unite, Beside the Still Waters, Love's Meeting Place, Work--A Prayer, Every Pilgrim's Progress, Love's Fulfillment.

For a **FREE LIST** of other Sun Books titles write: **Book List,**
Sun Publishing Company
P.O. Box 5588
Santa Fe, New Mexico 87502-5588 U.S.A